CHINA'S
LEADERSHIP
IN THE
21ST CENTURY

CHINA'S LEADERSHIP
IN THE
21ST CENTURY

The Rise of the Fourth Generation

David M. Finkelstein and Maryanne Kivlehan
Editors

AN EAST GATE BOOK

M.E. Sharpe
Armonk, New York
London, England

An East Gate Book

Library of Congress Cataloging-in-Publication Data

China's leadership in the twenty-first century : the rise of the fourth generation / edited
by David M. Finkelstein and Maryanne Kivlehan.
    p. cm.
"An East gate book."
Includes bibliographical references and index.
ISBN 0-7656-1115-5 (cloth: alk. paper) — ISBN 0-7656-1116-3 (pbk.: alk. paper)
    1. China—Politics and government—1976– 2. Political leadership—China. I
Finkelstein, David Michael. II. Kivlehan, Maryanne.

JQ1516.C4527 2002
320.951—dc21   2002029410

Printed in the United States of America

The paper used in this publication meets the minimum requirements of
American National Standard for Information Sciences
Permanence of Paper for Printed Library Materials,
ANSI Z 39.48-1984.

BM (c) 10   9   8   7   6   5   4   3   2   1
BM (p) 10   9   8   7   6   5   4   3   2   1

Contents

List of Tables and Figures

Tables

Figures

Acknowledgments

The editors of this volume would like to thank each of the contributing authors for their excellent scholarship, cooperation, and bonhomie throughout the course of this project. A special debt of gratitude is extended to Ms. Patty Loo of M.E. Sharpe for her invaluable efforts to make the vision a reality.

I

Introduction

1

The Rise of the
Fourth Generation

Overview and Implications

David M. Finkelstein and Maryanne Kivlehan

A Significant Leadership Transition Is Now Underway

As this book goes to press, China is in the process of a wide-ranging and very significant changeover in national leadership. Begun in the fall of 2002, it will continue through the spring of 2003.

The Sixteenth Congress of the Chinese Communist Party (CCP), scheduled to take place in the fall of 2002, will result in a new national political elite ascending to the most critical positions of authority in the Party, including, potentially, a new general secretary of the CCP. The subsequent convocation of the Tenth National People's Congress (NPC)—the state's legislative body, most likely in March 2003—will complete the process of leadership change "at the center." At this next NPC, a new group of leaders will be elevated to the topmost State positions.

By the time these two events are concluded, there will be a substantial number of leadership changes across the board in China—changes that cut across the Party, State, and military bureaucracies at the national level, in many secondary and tertiary positions and portfolios, and, eventually, beyond Beijing's ring roads and into the provinces.

Party congresses and leadership changes in China are always subjects of great interest. However, this particular leadership succession is being watched and followed with more than the usual intensity for three reasons: the nature of the process itself, the rise to power of a new generation of leaders, and the daunting challenges these new leaders will face.

The Succession Process

The Party Congress, and the subsequent convocation of the NPC, represents an historic moment in Chinese succession politics. This will be the first time since the founding the People's Republic of China (PRC) in 1949 that the topmost positions in the Party and State have been open for changeover without the presence of a "paramount leader," such as a Mao Zedong or Deng Xiaoping, to broker, guide, or subvert the process. Consequently, students of Chinese elite politics will be carefully watching to see whether the process of leadership selection is smooth or contentious, with an eye toward drawing implications from either scenario. Second, should Jiang Zemin relinquish his formal party and state positions—an assumption held by many over the past few years—it will represent the first time that an institutionalized transfer of power has taken place in post-1949 China. Moreover, the implications of a "partial succession" (Jiang retaining some formal position) will be equally intriguing for what it tells us about the state of political play in Beijing.

A Generational Shift

Aside from the nature of the process itself, the second reason that this political succession will be of more than usual interest is that it will initiate a turnover of national leadership from one generation to another. Mao Zedong dominated the "First Generation" leadership of the PRC. The era of Deng Xiaoping and his cohorts defined the "Second Generation" of leadership. Should Jiang Zemin relinquish power, other "Third Generation" leaders will likely step aside, presumably at least formally, and pass the baton of rule to a rising group of politicians, the "Fourth Generation," epitomized by Hu Jintao.

The accession to power of the "Fourth Generation" leadership—and the "Fifth Generation" officials who will rise to positions of influence in the bureaucracies on their coattails—will have profound implications for China itself, for nations in the region, and certainly for the national interests of the United States. The abilities and policy predilections of this new Fourth Generation of leadership will have a profound impact on the future course of this large and ever-evolving nation.

Facing Great Challenges

A third reason that the upcoming rotation of political elites will be watched with such attention is the timing of this event. The challenges these leaders will face at home and abroad are daunting. They come to power at a moment when China's domestic milieu is undergoing tremendous change and at a time when all of the easy, less painful solutions to social, economic, and political problems have already been instituted. These are the men and women who will have to grapple with the increasingly difficult task of pushing forward economic and structural reforms while at the same time managing the increasingly apparent social, economic, and political dislocations attendant to those reforms. They will have to manage the continuing challenge of developing the nation's western regions and closing China's east-west prosperity gap. They will have to deal with the looming economic, social, and political fallout, as yet unknown, of China's accession to the World Trade Organization (WTO)—especially as it applies to the moribund state sector enterprises. (The labor unrest of the spring of 2002 may be just the beginning.)

These new leaders will have to find solutions to the problems plaguing the agricultural sector, problems that affect the majority of China's 1.3 billion people. Indeed, the economic and social problems in the countryside are weighing as heavily on the minds of the central leadership as are challenges in the cities. China's leaders realize that solutions to the "Three Rural Problems" (*san nong wenti*—agriculture, *nongye*; peasants, *nongmin*; and villages, *nongcun*) will not wait indefinitely. Moreover, the new Chinese leadership will have to deal with the issue of internal reform of the Party itself, as the CCP races to stay relevant in a country that is changing faster and in more ways than Zhongnanhai—the seat of power in Beijing—may be able to control.

Beyond its own shores this new leadership will also have to develop foreign policies and strategies to cope with a changing international security environment that Chinese statements often describe as complex, and, at times, foreboding. The new leadership will have to decide what type of role China will choose to play in the international community of nations. Will China step forward as a leader in international affairs in a manner that comports with the status and respect it demands as a nation of consequence, or will it sit on the sidelines, when convenient, and merely claim to be the world's largest developing nation? How will the new leadership deal with the United States? What policies will they craft to reconcile their own analyses that, on the one hand, good relations with Washington are critical to further reform at home while, on the other hand, assessing that the "true intentions" of the United States are, ultimately, to "Westernize China" (*xihua Zhongguo*) and "split China" (*fenhua Zhongguo*)? And, of course, the issue of Taiwan and the objective of reunification will present increasing challenges to China's new leaders as political developments on the island become more complex and political solutions become more difficult to envision, even as Beijing and Taipei become more economically entwined.

What do we know about the Fourth Generation leaders? What worldviews will they bring to office with them? What solutions might they have in mind for China's domestic and international challenges? It is a remarkable statement on the still relatively opaque nature of the Chinese political process that, after almost twenty-five years of "reform and opening up," many basic questions about how Chinese leaders are chosen, with whom they are aligned, and what policies they favor is still subject to debate, conjecture, and a good deal of uncertainty.

Given the profound importance of the subject, and the relative lack of understanding at hand, The CNA Corporation's "Project Asia" convened a major conference in December 2001 in an attempt to enhance our understanding and identify the most important questions surrounding the ongoing succession. For two days some of the most renowned international scholars of Chinese politics from the United States, Canada, Hong Kong, the Republic of Korea, and elsewhere gathered at our institute in Alexandria, Virginia, to present papers and engage in discussions about China's future leadership—at "the center," in the provinces, in the military, and beyond.

This volume presents the results of the conference. Collectively, the chapters herein provide a tremendous amount of insight surrounding the upcoming succession and its implications. It is the hope of the editors that interested readers—specialists and nonspecialists alike—will find this book a useful guide in navigating the arcanum of contemporary Chinese politics as well as deriving an appreciation of just how complex the task of ruling China is becoming and will continue to be.

The volume is divided into five major sections addressing many of the key questions and issues surrounding the upcoming leadership transition: (1) the introduction and overview; (2) the individuals who comprise the core of the Fourth Generation; (3) the institutions—formal and informal—that drive and inform policy; (4) the challenges to governance and reform that China's new leaders will face; and (5) the role of the "generation after next"—the "Fifth Generation"—including future prospects for the Chinese Communist Party itself. The remainder of this chapter provides an overview of the chapters and key points made by the authors.

China's New Leaders: The Core of the Fourth Generation

This section presents three studies that focus on the identities and backgrounds of China's Fourth Generation of leaders. In the first chapter in this section, Cheng Li offers an overview of the upcoming leadership transition and the Fourth Generation leaders. He makes the case that the upcoming succession is not just a matter of a changing of the guard. Rather, he submits, it represents a significant benchmark in China's quest to regularize its political processes and strengthen the institutional basis of rule in China. Li identifies and discusses the strengths and weaknesses of four rising stars, who, he argues, will serve as the core of China's Fourth Generation: Hu Jintao, Wen Jiabao, Zeng Qinghong, and Li Changchun. Li then looks at the role of cohorts and networks in the upcoming political transition. He observes that, despite Hu Jintao's wide network of associates, Hu is less disposed to utilizing traditional patron-client ties with his protégés than has been the usual case with Chinese political elite. Li predicts that Zeng Qinghong will inherit Jiang Zemin's "Shanghai Gang" but that this group's ability to influence policy will be limited.

Finally, Li discusses the post–Party Congress fate of Jiang Zemin. He offers that there will be mounting pressure on Jiang to relinquish at least his formal positions, noting four reasons. First, Li argues that Jiang is not, and never was, a Deng Xiaoping. In other words, China is moving away from a system of governance by single all-powerful leaders both by choice and due to the reality that fewer and fewer political elite have the types of cross-institutional bases of power possessed by previous generations of leaders. Second, Li argues, there is increasing momentum within the CCP to institutionalize the basis of governance, making Jiang's departure from the posts of president of the PRC and general secretary of the Party a virtual certainty. Third, Li makes the intriguing argument—possibly heterodox argument in some circles of Sinology—that although Jiang might retain his post as chairman of the Central Military Commission, the importance and relevance of this post at this point in time, when not buttressed with other positions of institutionalized power, is increasingly uncertain. Overall, Li asserts, in the events leading up to and immediately following the Party Congress, Jiang will be distracted by concerns over his political legacy. His attention will be focused on attempting to canonize the achievements of his tenure and brokering the terms of his post-retirement status as a Party elder.

In chapter 3, Murray Scot Tanner focuses the reader squarely on Hu Jintao, discussing his rise to power and his relationship with Jiang Zemin, and assessing Hu's capacity to build support and to address the challenges China will face in coming years. Tanner begins by discussing what he feels will be Hu's greatest challenge, which he describes as the "successor's dilemma." Tanner argues that, during the lead-up to the Party Congress, in order to ensure his position as successor, Hu will have to maintain the trust of Jiang while building his own independent power base. At the same time, however, any effort by Hu to build an independent power base will make Jiang feel insecure and more likely to attempt to undermine Hu. Tanner uses the logic of the successor's dilemma to lay out criteria by which one can evaluate Hu Jintao's progress and prospects: (1) his capacity to build the support and trust of current leaders and patrons; (2) his simultaneous capacity to build independent power sources; and (3) his ability to use issues to strengthen his capacity to survive if the bases of power shift in the course of reform.

On the question of Hu's capacity to build support among other Fourth Generation leaders, Tanner acknowledges the wealth of analysis supporting the view that Zeng Qinghong, not Hu Jintao, is Jiang Zemin's primary Fourth Generation protégé. He then suggests that a number of points in Jiang's and Hu's relationship are equally compatible with two very different interpretations of Jiang Zemin's predilections toward Hu: that Jiang trusts and respects Hu enough to support his promotion, or simply that whatever Jiang's reservations and preferences are, he lacks the power to dislodge Hu as designated successor and build sufficient support to allow for an alternative candidate to take Hu's place.

On the question of Hu's progress in building independent bases of power within the Party, Tanner concludes that based on the numbers of current officials with identifiable ties to Hu Jintao, Hu still has a good deal of work to do in order to build his support base in the Party's central organs, the State Ministries, and the provinces. However, Tanner argues, Hu has made good use of his Communist Youth League connections and his position as president of the Central Party School and other potential bases of support. In addition, Tanner states, Hu reportedly headed personnel arrangements for the Fifteenth Central Committee selected in 1997, and is reportedly in charge of similar arrangements for the Sixteenth Congress. During the upcoming Party Congress, a very large proportion of the current Central Committee members selected in 1997 are expected to step down in 2002, and a large percentage of those who are likely to be reelected for a second term are those whom Hu Jintao helped promote in 1997. For these reasons, Tanner argues, when the new Central Committee is selected, Hu Jintao is likely to have significant numbers of clients on the Central Committee—perhaps more than Jiang or Zeng.

Beyond the requisite support he will need within the Party organization, Hu has already demonstrated a capacity to accrue some degree of popular support as an additional base of legitimacy. Tanner assesses that Hu will likely support tough crackdowns on crime and political corruption, and possibly flirt with nationalist appeals if this serves his ends. (We recall that it was Hu Jintao who went on Chinese television in May 1999 to address the nation after the errant bombing by the United States of the PRC Embassy in Belgrade.) Both of these tactics would likely play well to populist sentiments. While these moves might enhance Hu's personal stature among the citizenry, Professor Tanner leaves open whether or not Hu would be able to translate his personal popularity into support for the Party as an institution.

Zhiyue Bo offers an extremely informative chapter that looks beyond the selection of China's top-level central leaders. He shifts the reader's attention onto the career paths and grooming processes for civilian leadership in China and the increasingly important role experience in the provinces plays in this process. According to Bo, under the leadership of Deng Xiaoping, the CCP began to take a systematic approach toward grooming civilian leaders. Placing rising stars in provincial posts for seasoning and experience has by now become an integral part of this process. Bo states that provincial leaders have several types of opportunities to maintain ties with the center during their time away from Beijing, such as attending plenary sessions of the CCP Central Committee, attending meetings of the National People's Congress, and meeting central leaders during inspection tours of their provinces and during training courses in Beijing.

Bo then applies this information to the upcoming leadership transition. He predicts that members of the following groups are most likely to be promoted prior to and directly after the Sixteenth Party Congress: provincial party secretaries and current Politburo members such as Huang Ju and Li Changchun; "Chinese prefects" (provincial leaders who started their careers in the central government) such as Wang Xudong, Xu Youfang, and Song Defu; provincial party secretaries from western areas such as Li Jiangguo of Shaanxi; and governors such as Li Keqiang of Henan and Bo Xilai of Liaoning. Bo also predicts that provincial party secretaries at or nearing the retirement age of 65 could also be called back to Beijing to serve either in the NPC or the Chinese People's Political Consultative Conference (CPPCC). His list of leaders to watch includes: Zhang Lichang of Tianjin, Jiang Zhuping of Hubei, Mao Rubai of Ningxia, and Xu Guangdi, former mayor of Shanghai.

Formal and Informal Institutions

The third section of this volume examines several of the institutions that drive and inform policy in China. The first contribution is by Taeho Kim, whose chapter explores the roles of "Leading Small Groups," *lingdao xiaozu*, in the Chinese policy formulation process. Leading Small Groups (LSGs) are the CCP's central-level nonstanding bodies of policy deliberation and coordination. According to Kim, the makeup of these groups and how they interact with the leaders of China's Fourth Generation are key unknowns that will have far-reaching repercussions. Kim explains that the basic role of LSG is to act as a bridge between the top leadership and China's major bureaucracies. He then discusses several of the major LSGs such as the Foreign Affairs Leading Small Group, the Taiwan Affairs Leading Small Group, the Financial and Economic Leading Small Group, and the Political and Legal Affairs Committee, and examines how their composition and mandates might change with the rise of the Fourth Generation. He concludes that the transfer of power to the new generation will inevitably necessitate a significant membership turnover in the major LSGs, but that in cases where LSGs are currently headed by the members of the "Fourth Generation," continuity will likely be the norm rather than an exception.

Significantly, Kim asserts that establishing control over the key LSGs will be a crucial first step for new leaders in securing their position and status. Kim further suggests that depending on the relationships that emerge, Third Generation elders may find positioning protégés in the LSGs to be a safer and more effective means of prolonging their influence (or policy preferences) as opposed to attempting to push favorite protégés into more high profile Party and State positions. He also points out that while membership in these long-established groups will remain critical for the accrual of political power and influence, it is possible that the next generation of leaders may find it necessary to establish new LSGs to more effectively cope with the growing complexities of China's domestic and international challenges.

Next, James C. Mulvenon and Michael S. Chase explore the role of the *mishu*—or personal secretary—in Chinese policymaking. Their chapter examines the scope of current *mishu* duties and the changes we can expect to see in coming years. Mulvenon and Chase assert that the role of the *mishu* is organizationally ubiquitous—*mishu*s are a presence in nearly all political and economic units throughout China. Moreover, spanning a wide array of vocations, their duties include serving as advisers, acting as ghostwriters for principals, serving as personal representatives and policy coordinators, as well as serving as office administrators, personal managers, bodyguards, and even as servants. The authors describe *mishu*s as "intellectual entrepreneurs" and explain the critical role they often play in consensus building within the complex structure of China's "fragmented authoritarianism." Mulvenon and Chase describe the placement of *mishu*s in the bureaucratic landscape, their roles in the document drafting process and "secrecy work," and then look at how these roles might change with the coming generation of leaders.

Mulvenon and Chase write that many *mishu*s to Fourth Generation leaders will need an enlarged skill set in order to successfully fulfill the new roles they may be asked to play. Expertise in today's leaders is less broad than it was in leaders of previous generations. Unlike Mao or Deng, Fourth Generation leaders will not be able to claim experience that spans the military, economic, and political arenas. For this reason, write Mulvenon and Chase, leaders will look to *mishu*s for expertise on a broader range of issues than they did in previous times. Today's *mishu*s need more than proficiency in history, politics, and ideology. Mulvenon and Chase conclude by discussing these new skills. They write that, as the *mishu* begins to take on the role of technical adviser and leaders begin to experiment with limited pluralism, they will need to be familiar with a wide range of subjects such as geography, economics, finance, education, medicine, and mathematics. Moreover, they must become increasingly skilled at digesting new types of information, particularly when attempting to provide input on understanding public opinion. Placing individuals to serve in these positions will be a critical first step for the next generation of leadership.

In the final chapter in this section, Joseph Fewsmith discusses the changing role of intellectuals and think tanks in Chinese policymaking. He begins by clarifying the role of intellectual advisers. He observes that it is difficult to predict which individuals or groups truly do have the capacity to sway decision making or policy formation in China because the groups and individuals offering ideas and advice to China's top leaders are many and change over time. Often the influence of a given group or individual is more a function of informal relations than structural or institutionalized arrangements.

Fewsmith goes on to discuss the ways in which the relationship between the Chinese leadership and intellectuals has changed over the past decade. On the one hand, expertise has never been more in demand. As leaders have become better educated and more comfortable discussing and debating issues and ideas, intellectual input in policy formation has gained increasing legitimacy. Moreover, as the basic policy choices confronting top leaders now revolve around how to reform—not whether to reform—there is an increasing need for more technical and detail-oriented expertise. On the other hand, Fewsmith points out that think tanks and universities may no longer have a monopoly on expertise. He points to the increasing prevalence of experts within the government's ranks. Finally, the community of experts in China—which was collectively known as the "intellectual class" in more ideologically orthodox times—has itself become more fragmented, with some entering government and becoming technocrats, some joining the commercial economy, and some remaining in—or retreating to—the universities.

Fewsmith describes the current wide array of think tanks on the scene in today's China—the independent think tanks, semi-independent think tanks, and government-run think tanks. Finally, he comments on the current ferment at Hu Jintao's organization, the Central Party School, which is considered by some Sinologists to be the epicenter of the CCP's thinking about political reform. Fewsmith highlights the role of the Central Party School in the formulation of Jiang Zemin's recent attempt to make a theoretical contribution to Chinese communist ideology—the "Three Represents"—and the Central Party School's prospects for promoting political reform. Fewsmith argues that the Central Party School is doing interesting and significant research on political reform, including international outreach activities (such as participating in discussions with the Social Democrats in Germany) but that the tradition of the CCP has been to approach political reform cautiously, always attempting to temper change by maintaining continuities with the past. He concludes by cautioning readers against premature speculation about the potential for significant political reform under the leadership of the Fourth Generation.

Challenges to Governance and Reform

The four chapters in the fourth section of the book describe changing circumstances in China and the host of challenges the upcoming generation of leaders will face in coming years. Collectively, these chapters assess the current efforts of the Chinese government to maintain social order and look at the ways in which social changes will affect, and be affected by, the polices formulated by the core of the Fourth Generation.

On July 1, 2001, at a ceremony commemorating the eightieth anniversary of the Chinese Communist Party, Party General Secretary Jiang Zemin delivered a controversial speech stating that private entrepreneurs should be encouraged to become Party members. Although it was criticized as a heterodoxy by the left (the CCP is supposed to be the vanguard of the working class), this speech is widely viewed as a high-water mark in Jiang's efforts to revitalize the Party's ideology and to redefine the nature of the Chinese Communist Party. The framework Jiang proposed for revitalization and redefinition is called the "Three Represents" (*Sange Daibiao*). It suggests that the CCP must strive to represent: (1) the requirements of China's advanced productive forces; (2) the orientation of the development of the country's advanced culture; and (3) the fundamental interests of the overwhelming majority of the Chinese people. This third point is arguably at odds with the Party's tradition of defining itself exclusively as the political representative of the three working classes (peasants, workers, and soldiers). It is commonly argued among *savants* that the "July 1 Speech" and the "Three Represents" formulation is also a final attempt by Jiang Zemin to leave an ideological legacy before he steps down from office by having his ideas raised at least to the status of "Theory" (*lilun*) and adopted into the Party Constitution. In so doing "Jiang Zemin Theory" would reside on a par with the theoretical contributions of Deng Xiaoping, and right below the exalted status of "Mao Zedong Thought" (*sixiang*).

While these ideological machinations are seemingly arcane to outside observers, they underscore the continued role that ideology plays in China as a justification for major policy decisions. In his excellent chapter, Guoguang Wu addresses these issues and draws out the implications that the adoption of the "Three Represents" might have for Fourth Generation leaders.

Wu offers three levels of explanation for the issuance of the "July 1 Speech." First, it can be viewed as a response by the CCP to some of the harsher effects of globalization and China's entry into the WTO. Next, it can be viewed as a program to reconnect the CCP with the new social groups that have grown in number and importance during the socioeconomic transitions China has undergone in the past two decades. Finally, it can be viewed as a part of Jiang Zemin's personal political strategy to maintain influence during and after the period of leadership transition. Wu discusses each of these in detail, and indicates how, regardless of the outcome of many of the questions surrounding the Sixteenth Party Congress, each of these factors will constitute important challenges for the leaders of China's Fourth Generation.

Next, Bruce J. Dickson focuses on the decision to allow entrepreneurs into the Party, and looks at what role these entrepreneurs might play in enacting future political reform. He highlights and examines this critical question: Are entrepreneurs likely to be partners with the Party, promoting regime goals of economic growth and political stability, or will they ultimately contribute to the undermining of China's remaining communist institutions?

According to Dickson, the CCP's objective is to bring the entrepreneurs into the tent. In pursuit of this objective, it has adopted a two-pronged strategy for controlling private entrepreneurs; first by co-opting entrepreneurs through membership in the Party, and second, by linking the private entrepreneurs to the Party through the use of business associations. These unique organizations are designed to represent the interests of its entrepreneurial members while, at the same time, serving as a mechanism to provide Party leadership over the private sector. Overall, the approach Dickson lays out is reminiscent of the CCP's time-honored "united front tactics."

In an effort to assess the CCP's success in these approaches, Dickson conducted a survey and interview project targeting owners and operators of large and medium-scale private companies and the local government officials with whom they interact. He found that the vast majority of businessmen in his survey believed the business associations do in fact represent their interests as well as the government's position, and that the entrepreneurs have enough confidence in these groups to look to their business associations for assistance in resolving their business problems. However, Dickson also found indications of conflicting perceptions between entrepreneurs and local government officials. While a majority of businessmen believe that they possess the capability to influence policy implementation, the majority of government officials surveyed stated that the entrepreneurs, in fact, are unable to influence policy or how it is implemented. In the future, this case of mismatched perceptions, or, more important, of mismatched expectations, could create a situation in which entrepreneurs are increasingly frustrated by their inability to affect CCP economic policy. At the same time, Dickson finds that, rather than seeking autonomy to enhance their power and wield influence over the state, entrepreneurs in his survey sample tended to seek closer integration with the political system as it exists.

Dickson concludes that, although China's "red capitalists" may be potential kingmakers, for the present, they seem more interested in good governance rather than the promotion of democracy. This is a significant statement. If they are valid beyond his sample, then Dickson's findings raise questions about the argument, often advanced in the West, that the expansion of free enterprise in China will eventually lead to political democratization.

Carol Lee Hamrin looks at the problems of governance and the prospects for reform by examining China's budding civil society—specifically, nongovernmental organizations and social groups, which she refers to as the "Third Sector." Hamrin looks at the CCP's traditional mechanisms for co-opting and controlling social groups and nongovernmental organizations (NGOs). She describes a dual track control mechanism through government registration and functional affiliation. Under this system, groups or organizations are required to obtain general legal approval from the Ministry of Civil Affairs and maintain an official affiliation with a party organization, government agency, or official monopoly. Among other duties, the NGOs affiliated with government organizations are responsible for supervising the group's registration, political and ideological work, finance and accounting, personnel management, and external relations.

Despite the rhetoric of extensive formal control over China's "Third Sector," Hamrin contends that the CCP is facing a new reality in which its capacity to realize its espoused control is increasingly limited. She explains that in the mid- to late 1990s, Third Generation leaders allowed an expansion of social organizations and actually discussed implementing a host of more liberal policies, but that enthusiasm for this type of reform quickly waned, and top leaders turned to a more authoritarian option. They focused instead on rebuilding the Party's capacity to control social organizations. This took the form of a nationwide crackdown on "evil cults" or "illegal" religious organizations, a freeze on the registration of social organizations, and new attempts to reinstitute Party controls and co-opt social groups.

Hamrin argues that, ultimately, these strict control policies will be ineffective because they fail to address the underlying social needs that have prompted the development of China's "Third Sector." She maintains that social polarization may indeed be the greatest challenge faced by China's next generation of leaders and that although these leaders may prefer to adopt a conservative, go-slow approach, events could come together at any time to prompt a fundamental questioning of national identity and political authority.

The challenge of seeking creative ways to exercise control over nonstate entities in China extends beyond the realm of social and religious groups. In her chapter, Anne Stevenson-Yang addresses this question with regard to China's media. Stevenson-Yang describes current regulatory practices in fascinating detail and offers a brief history of media regulation. She recounts a period of rapid growth and more lax regulation of media outlets, followed by a move by the government to reassert authority. She states that what may appear externally to be a cyclical policy of laxness followed by paranoiac crackdown actually traces a time-honored Chinese regulatory strategy: relaxation of control in order to encourage growth, co-option of a portion of that growth for the benefit of the central government, and further regulation to keep any particular nongovernment organization from growing large enough to wield threatening political and economic power.

Stevenson-Yang states that reform of media regulation does appear to fit into the long-term plan of China's leaders, but explains that in the run-up to the Sixteenth Party Congress, we can expect to see more stringent control of the media in an effort to maintain a stable environment. She reports that a press law and various regulatory measures to allow a gradual opening of the media have been stalled in pre–Party Congress gridlock, as have the issuance of permits to foreign-invested companies that would legalize their publication of information on the Internet, and the promulgation of an official policy establishing an "experimental area" for foreign participation in broadcasting in Guangdong Province.

Stevenson-Yang describes the evolving role of the media in Chinese society, indicating that media exposure has become an increasingly common tool in regulating both official behavior and the marketplace. She writes that China's leadership, along with the rest of Chinese society, has discovered how potent exposure in the press can be for pressuring corrupt officials, vendors of substandard products, autocratic employers, and other oppressors small and large. She concludes by looking at the CCP's record of permitting, both actively and passively, the advent of new and contentious voices in the media while maintaining ultimate authority to close down media outlets and generally to use the media to form public opinion. She compares this practice to riding a tiger and raises the question of how long China's central government will be able to continue this practice without being thrown from the beast.

The Generation After Next and Future Prospects for the Party

In the final section of this volume, Willy Wo-Lap Lam and David Shambaugh look to the future. They offer their thoughts and observations about the Fifth Generation leaders—the "generation after next"—that will succeed those who take the helm after the Sixteenth Party Congress in 2002. They also examine the challenges the Chinese Communist Party will face as it strives to remain relevant, modernize China, and adapt itself to a rapidly changing domestic and international environment.

Lam assesses that the tenure of the Fourth Generation of leadership can be expected to stretch from the Sixteenth Party Congress (Fall 2002) to the Eighteenth Party Congress (to be held, most likely, in 2012). After this, they will probably move out of the spotlight and be replaced by a fifth generation of top political elite. According to Lam, the Fourth Generation leaders will spend their tenures in office focused on completing the reforms of the Deng-Jiang eras and managing the aftershocks of WTO entry. Consequently, the Fourth Generation will be preoccupied with the agenda set by its predecessors and be unlikely to walk down any new and bold paths in the realm of political reforms.

As for the "generation after next," Lam constructs an intriguing mosaic. Lam points out that, as a generational cohort, Fifth Generation leaders are likely to be individuals who have benefited greatly from the policy of "reform and opening up." But he cautions that although this generation of leadership will have had more exposure to Western values than any of their predecessors, it is unrealistic to expect that this will necessarily translate into an inclination toward faster political reform. He suggests that we will likely see a continuation of the strategy of broadening the base of the CCP's elites.

At the same time, Lam predicts that one of the greatest foreign policy challenges Fifth Generation leaders will face likely will be relations with the United States. Although these individuals will have had a good deal of exposure to the United States (and other Western nations), Lam believes they will be subject to the twin pressures of nationalism and anti-Americanism from within the Party and among the general populace. Resisting these forces may prove to be extremely difficult regardless of the personal views Fifth Generation elite may have of America. Indeed, Lam predicts that during the tenure of the Fifth Generation, leftism and nationalism will serve as focal points for cohort or group formation alongside other factional groupings such as the Communist Youth League, the Shanghai Faction, the Zhu Rongji Faction, and the "Gang of Princelings"—holdovers from the eras of Deng Xiaoping and especially of Jiang Zemin.

Finally, in assessing the challenges of elite political dynamics for both the Fourth and Fifth Generations, Lam concludes that power sharing in the future will require Chinese leaders to acquire a "win-win mentality." Only through such a change, writes Lam, will the CCP be able to make the transition from an unstable, angst-ridden, and (says Lam) ultimately doomed one-party dictatorship to a pluralistic system where a liberalized CCP may have the chance of running a stable China. Openness and equal competition in the internal political process will be necessary. Lam states that whether such a leap forward in worldview can be achieved could be the biggest question surrounding the emergence of the Fifth Generation.

In the last chapter in this volume, David Shambaugh looks at the challenges the CCP will face over the coming decades as it struggles both to maintain control and to remain relevant in Chinese society. He lists a host of daunting issues that leaders of the Fourth Generation will face. Among them are increased social stratification, rising corruption, and growing pressures for an enfranchised civil society. He questions the ability of the rising political elite to surmount many of those challenges. For Shambaugh, the Fourth Generation will be characterized by people with educational backgrounds as engineers (technocrats), an increasingly narrow set of work experience, and, significantly, minimal exposure to the outside world. These experience sets, he argues, will be ill-suited to finding comprehensive solutions to interrelated problems that will require creativity, flexibility, and a keen appreciation for the global context of China's situation.

Professor Shambaugh also takes a hard look at the prospects for the viability of the Chinese Communist Party itself by making some comparisons with the fates of other (now defunct) communist parties. He argues that it is unlikely that the CCP is going to follow the same path to reform or transformation as communist parties in the former Soviet Union, identifying several factors present in China today to make his case. Shambaugh also addresses the Party's ability to manage the changes taking place in Chinese society, examining the evidence of adaptation and decay from several levels—including a macroscopic look at the CCP's relations with the government and military, Party membership and organization, and the Party's role vis-à-vis society. He concludes that the evidence is mixed and the prognosis for the CCP's future is still open to question.

However, Shambaugh notes that the greatest evidence of gradual decay in the CCP is apparent when looking at the Party's role vis-à-vis society. He argues that the greatest challenge the Party will face may be that of rising expectations on the part of the Chinese people. He posits that, as the populace reaches a threshold where essential material needs are satisfied and lifestyles have diversified and improved (to the point that they have today in many, but not all, parts of China), they will place increasing demands for improvements and reforms in other areas of life, such as spiritual life. In other words, people will expect their demands to be addressed, and they will expect adequate channels to articulate those demands. Like Willy Lam, Shambaugh argues that the Party leadership's zero-sum view of political power-sharing and resistance to the enfranchisement of civil society will continue to hinder its ability to be responsive to the demands of a changing polity.

For Shambaugh, the ultimate challenge facing the CCP is its ability to remain relevant, and its key shortcoming is its lack of an original vision of where it seeks to lead the nation. He argues that a Marxist-Leninist future seems out of the question (even, perhaps to the leaders of the CCP), but what has replaced it—in his view, a desire to attain wealth and power, enhance nationalism and international dignity, preserve unity and prevent chaos—is no different than the vision of many of the leaders of the past. (Indeed, the editors would argue, this is the same vision that every post-imperial regime has had for China, even the Kuomintang.)

In sum, Shambaugh suggests that, if managed carefully, the CCP can adapt and respond effectively to the rising demands placed upon it by society. However, offering a convincing vision for the future of the nation will require more than just a simple set of reactive policies. In addressing the challenges it will face, a proactive party-state that has a sound sense of its own institutional identity will be needed to inspire the country and lead it in new directions.

The Challenges Ahead

As one digests the chapters within this volume, it will be difficult not to be struck by the magnitude of the challenges facing the political elites of China's Fourth Generation. Regardless of which personalities emerge from the Sixteenth Party Congress, the new leadership will have to cope with a host of domestic and international pressures that will test their abilities almost immediately. At home, the list of issues is indeed daunting: social polarization, regional economic disparities, "WTO shock," the potential for social unrest, the challenges of military modernization, and reform of the CCP, to name just a few. The challenges from abroad will be equally weighty. China's leaders will have to grapple with the collateral impact of the globalization of the world economy and culture, with the information revolution, and with a post–Cold War international security environment that is still evolving.

It is clear that these challenges will be beyond the capacity of any single leader in Beijing to solve. As the authors in this volume underscore, the days of the omnipotent paramount Chinese leader is likely over in any event. It may also be the case, as some herein have suggested, that the solutions to China's multifaceted challenges will increasingly be beyond the ability of the government alone to address.

How this new generation of leaders chooses to deal with the issues at hand, their ability to find solutions to China's most pressing internal problems, and the path they will take as an international actor will all have an impact far beyond their own shores. For this reason, it is our hope that this volume will provide interested readers with an informed context against which to consider the implications of China's continuing transformation.

II

China's New Leaders

— 2 —

Poised to Take the Helm

Rising Stars and the Transition to the Fourth Generation

Cheng Li

Each generation has distinctive characteristics fostered by the sociopolitical environment during formative years. Consequently, generational cohorts often share collective behavioral attributes.[1] In the People's Republic of China (PRC), the concept of generations—or, more precisely, political elite generations—has also been based on the distinctive historical experiences of elites.[2] The first three elite generations in the PRC are identified as the "Long March generation," the "Anti–Japanese War generation," and the "Socialist Transformation generation," represented by Mao Zedong, Deng Xiaoping, and Jiang Zemin, respectively.

The upcoming Sixteenth Congress of the Chinese Communist Party (CCP) and the Tenth National People's Congress (NPC) will mark the shift to the so-called Fourth Generation of leaders. Now in their 50s to early 60s, the Fourth Generation leaders all had their formative experiences during the Cultural Revolution. They were either in school (elementary school, middle school, or college) or had just begun work when the Cultural Revolution took place in 1966. This "unparalleled revolution in the history of mankind" (borrowing Mao's words) had an everlasting impact on them because their loyalty was betrayed, their dreams were shattered, their education was lost, and their careers were interrupted. Some Fourth Generation leaders have attributed their political advancement today specifically to the lessons learned, the hardships endured, and the wisdom derived during the Cultural Revolution.[3]

It is critically important to study both the generational attributes and idiosyncratic characteristics of new leaders. The upcoming succession, however, is not just a changing of the guard. Its ramifications go beyond that of generational change. This political succession constitutes a severe test of whether

China can take a major step toward a peaceful and more institutionalized power transition. To a certain extent, the power transition from Deng Xiaoping to Jiang Zemin was peaceful. The difference between the preceding succession and this upcoming one is that, for many years, Jiang's legitimacy was based on the support of Deng and other elders; but top contenders of the new generation can stand on their own, even now. This is precisely the reason why China-watchers are paying so much attention to this power transition and to the characteristics of the Fourth Generation leaders.

An analysis of the career patterns and political behaviors of Fourth Generation leaders reveals a paradox. Nepotism in various forms (e.g., school ties, blood ties, regional affiliations, or patron-client ties) has played a very important role in the selection of new leaders. But, at the same time, some institutional mechanisms (e.g., age limits for retirement, term limits, intra-Party elections, and regional representation) have been adopted as part of the Chinese political system in order to curtail favoritism. The front-runners of the Fourth Generation—Hu Jintao, Wen Jiabao, Zeng Qinghong, and Li Changchun—have all expedited their political careers through *guanxi* (connections), yet they are now far more interested in seeking legitimacy through institutional channels than their predecessors were. The unfolding of these paradoxical developments will not only determine who will rule China for most of this decade and beyond, but, even more important, how this most populous country in the world will be governed.

Hu's on First? Four Top Contenders to Watch

It has been widely believed that current Vice President Hu Jintao, Vice Premier Wen Jiabao, Head of the CCP Organization Department Zeng Qinghong, and Guangdong Party Secretary Li Changchun are four front-runners in the new generation of leadership (see Table 2.1). They are in their late 50s or early 60s. All of them were trained as engineers in China's elite engineering schools, but had political careers as Party functionaries or industrial managers. They all joined the Party during their college years, but acquired their first major political experience during the Cultural Revolution. None of them was a radical activist during the Cultural Revolution, yet their political and professional careers were all interrupted.[4] Hu and Wen were sent to Gansu, a poor inland province, where both worked for over a decade. Zeng was also sent first to a military base in Guangdong, and then to a collective farm in Hunan where he worked as a manual laborer. Li was not sent to a distant place; instead he worked for many years as an electric welder in Shenyang. Enormous physical hardship and an ever-changing political environment nurtured within all of

Table 2.1

Four Top Contenders in the Fourth Generation Leadership

Name	Brief biography	Current post	Network	Strengths	Weaknesses
Hu Jintao	Born in 1942; Anhui; engineer by training; CCP functionary; head of Communist Youth League; Party chief in Guizhou and Tibet	Vice President; Politburo Standing Committee Member; Vice Chair, Central Military Commission	(1) "Qinghua clique"; (2) Chinese Communist (3) Central Party School	(1) designated successor to Jiang; (2) solid power base; (3) low-profile; (4) known for nationalist appeal, especially to young people; (5) popular among the public; (6) acceptable to both left and right	(1) no connection with the military; (2) no concrete achievements; (3) no experience in economic and foreign policy

Table 2.1 *(continued)*

Name	Brief biography	Current post	Network	Strengths	Weaknesses
Wen Jiabao	Born in 1942; Tianjin; engineer by training; CCP functionary; chief of staff, general office in CCP	Vice Premier; Politburo Member	(1) close association with Zhu Rongji	(1) work experience as chief of staff for three bosses of the CCP; (2) broad leadership experiences in various sectors, especially agriculture and finance/banking; (3) no factional background; (4) popular among the public	(1) no power base; (2) no connection with the military; (3) political courage is yet to be tested
Zeng Qinghong	Born in 1939; Jiangxi; engineer by training; CCP functionary; Jiang Zemin's chief of staff	Head, CCP Organization Department; Politburo Alternate	(1) close association with Jiang Zemin; (2) "Shanghai Gang"; (3) princeling	(1) a visionary leader; (2) a well-rounded tactician; (3) currently in charge of personnel affairs	(1) too close to Jiang Zemin; (2) princeling background; (3) no experience in economic and foreign policy

| Li Changchun | Born in 1944; Liaoning; engineer by training; industrial manager; mayor of Shenyang; governor of Liaoning; Party Secretary in Henan and Guangdong | Party Secretary of Guangdong Province; Politburo Member | (1) close association with Jiang Zemin; (2) close association with many provincial leaders | (1) a courageous leader who often handles tough jobs; (2) relatively young; (3) broad provincial experience in three major provinces: Liaoning, Henan, and Guangdon | (1) some of his associates were involved in corruption scandals; (2) often seen as a protégé of Jiang Zemin |

them some valuable traits such as adaptability, endurance, and grass-roots consciousness.

Hu Jintao: A Recognized Successor

Among these four contenders, Hu Jintao is undoubtedly the first poised to take the helm. If he survives the next year without a major blunder, he will replace Jiang as Party chief and president of the state. All signs thus far suggest that this is the most likely scenario. Since his appointment as vice president of the PRC in 1998, Hu has widely been recognized as the successor to Jiang. This became even clearer when Hu was also appointed as vice chair of the Central Military Commission (CMC) in 1999. These two appointments made it clear that there is an unambiguous pecking order in the political succession. Hu Jintao was not a protégé of Jiang. He was promoted by Deng and was later appointed by Jiang. This places Hu in a very advantageous position; he has Jiang's endorsement, but his rise to the top leadership will not be seen as a result of nepotism.

What makes Hu a favorite in the upcoming succession is not only the current positions that he holds but also the broad political associations that he has established throughout his career. Hu is a prominent member of the so-called Qinghua University Clique; he headed the Chinese Communist Youth League (CCYL) in the early 1980s; and he has served as president of the Central Party School since 1993.[5] All three of these institutions have now become the main sources of elite recruitment.

In addition, Hu has been known for his low-profile personality. This is the main reason that foreign observers have often characterized Hu as a "mystery," although he recently had his widely publicized "coming-out-party" by traveling to Western Europe, Russia, and the United States. Hu has to be politically cautious because he knows too well that in the history of the PRC many appointed heirs (e.g., Liu Shaoqi, Lin Biao, and Wang Hongwen under Mao; Hu Yaobang and Zhao Ziyang under Deng) fell suddenly from favor. It would be unwise for Hu to be too much in the spotlight or to express his opinions too openly while his boss, Jiang Zemin, is still in charge.

Another advantage that Hu has is his leadership experience in youth affairs and his nationalistic appeal to young people in the country. He recently stated that the future of the CCP would largely depend on whether the new leadership could win over public support, especially among the country's younger generations.[6] Hu's widely publicized television speech in response to the Chinese Embassy bombing in Belgrade was another example that showed his nationalistic appeal during a time of crisis. Chinese nationalism is on the rise. In sharp contrast to the Tiananmen movement in 1989, a large number of public intellectuals and college students are calling for a strong state and a powerful national leadership. Chinese national consciousness (*minzhu yishi*) has ree-merged and become an effective glue.

Because he has an image of being both open-minded and effective in ex-pressing patriotic sentiment, Hu is acceptable to both the liberal and conser-vative wings of the CCP. Furthermore, Hu will likely benefit from the "age effect." A relatively young leader such as Hu Jintao can sometimes convey a sense of competence and confidence that can lead to popularity among the general population.

While all these factors suggest that Hu's chance of succeeding Jiang is secure, he has three main shortcomings: (1) he has little connection with the military, (2) he achieved very little as a provincial chief either in Guizhou or in Tibet, and has also accomplished little at the national level, and (3) he has yet to demonstrate his competence in economic and foreign affairs.

Wen Jiabao: A Leading Candidate for Premier

Wen Jiabao is the most likely candidate to replace Zhu Rongji as premier in 2003. Wen is one of the most popular political leaders in the country; he is often seen as a Zhou Enlai–like figure. Wen's experience is remarkable; he worked as a chief of staff for three bosses (Hu Yaobang, Zhao Ziyang, and Jiang Zemin), two of whom were purged while he survived. Wen has gained broad administrative experience over the past decade—handling political crises such as the 1989 Tiananmen incident, coordinating power transitions, and com-manding the anti-flood campaign in 1998 (which gave him as much popularity in China as Mayor Giuliani received in New York City after the September 11 attack on the World Trade Center).

Furthermore, since the late 1990s, Wen has supervised the nation's agri-cultural affairs and has overseen the reform of the financial and banking sys-tems. While his boss in the State Council, Zhu Rongji, has seldom praised his junior colleagues, Wen Jiabao, a quick learner and a brilliant self-taught econ-omist, was an exception. Wen's caliber as a superb administrator and his role as a coalition-builder explain his legendary survival and success.

Wen not only has strong support from Zhu, but also is a leader who is acceptable to many, including Jiang and Hu. However, Wen has two main weaknesses: (1) unlike Hu, Wen does not possess a solid power base and (2) like Hu, Wen does not have much connection with the military. Wen's political courage also has to be tested as he moves to the "driver's seat" in the State Council. The negative impact upon the agricultural sector of China's entry into the World Trade Organization (WTO) and the far-reaching changes resulting from financial liberalization are two daunting challenges for the Chinese leadership. The political pressure on Wen is overwhelming.

Zeng Qinghong: Chief of Personnel Affairs

Zeng Qinghong's idiosyncratic personality and performance are even more remarkable. As both a *taizi* (princeling) and *mishu* (personal secretary), Zeng differs from most *taizi*s and *mishu*s in one important aspect—while many others rush for quick promotion and instant profits, Zeng is a well-rounded tactician with long-term vision and a great sense of timing. Many choices that he has made during his career demonstrate Zeng's unconventional wisdom. In the early 1980s, when a majority of princelings rushed to be part of the business sector, especially sectors involving foreign trade, Zeng quit his post as deputy director of the Foreign Liaison Department under the Ministry of the Petroleum Industry, one of the most lucrative jobs in the country. Even more surprising to many observers, Zeng did not join the military when his mentor, Yu Qiuli, was appointed director of the General Political Department of the People's Liberation Army (PLA), a top military post. Zeng would not allow any short-term material gain to jeopardize his great political ambition. Moreover, Zeng did not want to advance his political career through the military because he foresaw the declining role of the military in domestic affairs.

When he was head of the Organization Department in Shanghai in the early 1980s, Zeng selected five bright young college graduates in the city and sent them to the United States to study political science instead of the then-fashionable academic disciplines such as physics and engineering. Unlike many of his peers at that time, Zeng sensed the importance of political science and law to the future of China's reform. Unsurprisingly, it was Zeng who initiated the recent investigative report on official corruption and social unrest in the country, revealing the enormity of the sociopolitical problems that China faces.

Zeng has been patient about his own promotion and has been very cautious to avoid unnecessary conflicts with other political "heavyweights" who are of similar age. It was recently reported in the Western media that Zeng experienced a major setback because he did not get promoted from an alternate to a full member of the Politburo at the Sixth Plenum of the Central Committee held in September 2001. But this can be seen as another example of Zeng's great sense of timing and priority. As head of the CCP Organization Department, Zeng is in charge of personnel affairs. His priority at present is perhaps to promote his own people, first to top provincial and ministerial leadership posts and then to the next Central Committee. Zeng himself will almost certainly obtain a seat on the Politburo standing committee during the Sixteenth Party Congress. Right now a full seat on the Politburo is not important to him.

Zeng's main weakness, however, is that he has been too closely tied to Jiang. Zeng has often been seen as Jiang's "hand, ear, and brain," although he is not known to fawn upon his boss. Zeng has also intimidated many other leaders because of his formidable skills in political manipulation. It was widely reported that Zeng helped Jiang fight successfully against Jiang's rivals such as the "generals of the Yang family," the Deng children, Chen Xitong (former Party chief in Beijing), and Qiao Shi (former head of the NPC), during the past decade.

Now Zeng has two dilemmas. First, while he can take advantage of his power as head of the CCP Organization Department to appoint his own people to important positions, his favoritism will surely be in the political spotlight, thus creating more public resentment against him. Second, while Zeng needs strong endorsement from Jiang Zemin in the power transition, at the same time, he should begin to keep a distance from Jiang in order to fulfill his own political agenda and promote his vision for institutional change.

Li Changchun: A Top Contender Among Provincial Chiefs

Some future top leaders will be selected from today's provincial chiefs. The top leadership positions in China's provinces and major cities have often been steppingstones to national political offices in the PRC, and this has especially been the case during the post-Mao period. Jiang Zemin and Zhu Rongji both served as Party secretary and mayor in Shanghai for four years before moving on to the most important posts in the national leadership. In the current twenty-four-member Politburo, twenty (83 percent) have had administrative experience at the provincial level. Fourteen (58 percent) have served as provincial chiefs (either as Party secretary and governor or mayor in provincial-level administration).[7] This indicates that the criteria for selecting national leadership have shifted from revolutionary credentials (such as participation in the Long March) to administrative skills (such as both vertical and horizontal coordination in the policymaking process).

The provinces that these leaders have governed are large socioeconomic entities. It is often said that a province is to China what a country is to Europe. In fact, Chinese provinces are much bigger in terms of population than most of the countries in Western Europe. China's provincial chiefs, like top leaders of European nations, have constantly been concerned about regional economic development and have coped with daunting challenges such as unemployment, political instability, and social welfare needs in their jurisdictions. For China's future leaders, provincial administration provides an ideal training ground. In addition, China's provincial leadership is also a political force in its own right. Provincial leaders have carried much more weight in the decision-making process during the reform era than they did in the first three decades of the PRC.

Among provincial chiefs, Li Changchun has a good chance of obtaining a seat on the standing committee. Li is currently the youngest member of the Politburo; he also holds the record for being China's youngest-ever mayor of a capital city and also governor. His broad leadership experience in three large provinces has prepared him to deal with tough challenges. This is especially the case in his appointment as Party secretary of Guangdong, a province known for its cultural resistance to outsiders. Li effectively established authority over the autonomy-minded Cantonese officials soon after he took over the post of provincial Party secretary in 1998. However, recent corruption scandals in Liaoning, which have involved many of his protégés, may hurt his career advancement. He himself has also been seen as one of Jiang Zemin's protégés.

All four rising stars in the new generation are capable political tacticians. None of them is a "lightweight" figurehead. To put it a different way, none of them is powerful enough to knock down any of the other three potential rivals. Power sharing and consensus building are essential for all four. It is always possible that two or three heavyweights might form a coalition to get rid of one or two relatively weaker rivals. But if that kind of coalition occurs, the rules of the game in Chinese factional politics will have profoundly changed. In the new political climate, coalition building takes time, and it often involves political negotiation and compromise. It is unlikely that factional struggles will cause catastrophic social destruction, such as the disruption caused by the Cultural Revolution and the Tiananmen tragedy.

Limitations of Political Networking? Two Prominent Factions to Watch

Factional politics was, is, and will be a key part of the Chinese political process. Chinese leaders, like politicians in other countries, are "political animals" more than anything else. During power transitions, the political system has always been particularly factional and dynamic. Among the various factions, two deserve particular attention. One is Hu Jintao's network and the other is the "Shanghai Gang"—leaders who have been promoted from Shanghai by Jiang Zemin and Zeng Qinghong. The fate of the former will demonstrate Hu Jintao's ability to effectively consolidate his power base after he succeeds Jiang. The success of the latter will demonstrate the status and the potential of the "Shanghai Gang." If the "Shanghai Gang" occupies too many seats on the next Politburo and the central committee, it could cause strong resentment both among leaders in other regions and among the general public. The traits and changing nature of these two factions have profound implications for the legitimacy of the new leadership as a whole.

Hu Jintao's CCYL Associates

Unlike Jiang Zemin, who has been known for his nepotism, Hu Jintao has thus far not been seen as a leader who is obsessed with patron-client ties. Although Hu has been well connected with Qinghua University, the CCYL, and the Central Party School (CPS)—three main cradles of the Fourth Generation leaders, he does not have his own "Zeng Qinghong–like aide" in the national leadership. No one in the current Politburo has been seen as Hu's protégé. The Qinghua Clique, the CCYL, and the CPS are interconnected. For example, graduates and faculty members of Qinghua University have often occupied many important leadership positions in the secretariat of the CCYL and at the CPS. Yet, these three informal networks have also overlapped with other factions, including the "Shanghai Gang." Hu has cautiously avoided being seen as a political patron who has cultivated a web of personal ties dependent upon his connections.[8] Nonetheless, it is most likely that some of his friends and close associates will enter the Politburo during the Sixteenth Party Congress.

Table 2.2 shows a list of Hu Jintao's CCYL associates in the Fourth Generation leadership. Most of them have already occupied the posts of ministers and provincial chiefs. All except one are in the Fifteenth Central Committee of the CCP, either as a full member or as an alternate. They have served as national or provincial officials in the CCYL during the early 1980s—the period during which Hu Jintao headed the secretariat of the CCYL (1982–85). Like Hu, three of them, Minister of Public Security Jia Chunwang, Minister of Justice Zhang Fusen, and Executive Deputy Head of the CCP United Front Work Department Liu Yandong, attended Qinghua University. Shen Yueyue, Li Keqiang, and Li Yuanchao were all born in the 1950s. Their youth is an advantage for their future political careers.

Song Defu and Li Keqiang are likely candidates for the next Politburo. Song Defu served in the CCYL Secretariat between 1982 and 1993. He has had leadership experience in various sectors: in the military (as deputy director of the Organization Department under the PLA General Political Department), the Party (as deputy director of the CCP Organization Department), the State Council (as minister of personnel), and the provincial leadership (currently as Party secretary in Fujian). In 1982, at the age of 36, Song joined the Central Committee at the Twelfth Party Congress. In addition to his relative youth, his seniority as Central Committee member, and his broad leadership experience,

Table 2.2

Hu Jintao's Chinese Communist Youth League (CCYL) Associates in the Fourth Generation Leadership

Name	Current position	Fifteenth CC	Born	Native	Education	Major	Communist Youth League experience
Song Defu	Party secretary of Fujian	Member	1946	Hebei	2-year college		Member of the CCYL Secretariat 1982–93
Li Keqiang	Governor of Henan	Member	1955	Anhui	Beijing University (G)	Economics, Law	Member of the CCYL Secretariat 1983–98
Qian Yunlu	Party secretary of Guizhou	Member	1944	Hebei	Hubei University	Economics	Secretary of Hubei CCYL, 1979–83
Ji Yunshi	Governor of Jiangsu	Alternate	1945	Jiangsu	Shandong University	Physics	Deputy secretary and secretary of Jiangsu CCYL, 1982–84
Ma Qizhi	Governor of Ningxia	Alternate	1943	Ningxia	Central National University	Chinese	Deputy secretary of Ningxia CCYL, 1981–83
Du Qinglin	Minister of Agriculture	Member	1946	Jilin	Jilin University (G)	Economics, Law	Secretary of Jilin CCYL, 1979–84
Li Dezhu	Minister of Mirorities Affairs	Member	1943	Jilin	Yanbian University	Politics	Deputy secretary of Jilin CCYL 1980–85
Jia Chunwang	Minister of Public Security	Member	1938	Beijing	Qinghua University	Engineering	Standing member of the CCYL, 1982–87

Name	Position	Year	Province	University	Field	CCYL
Zhang Fusen	Minister of Justice	Member	1940	Beijing	Qinghua University	Engineering	Deputy secretary of Beijing CCYL, 1981–84
Sun Jiazheng	Minister of Culture	Member	1944	Jiangsu	Nanjing University	Chinese	Secretary of Jiangsu CCYL, 1979–83
Zhang Weiqing	Minister of Family Planning	Member	1944	Shaanxi	Beijing University	Philosophy	Secretary of Shanxi CCYL, 1982–83
Liu Yandong (f)	Executive deputy head, CCP United Front Work Dept.	Alternate	1945	Jiangsu	Qinghua University	Engineering	Member of the CCYL Secretariat, 1982–91
Shen Yueyue (f)	Deputy party secretary of Anhui	Alternate	1957	Zhejiang	Ningpo Normal College	Mathematics	Deputy secretary and secretary of Zhejiang CCYL, 1986–93
Sun Shuyi	Party secretary of Jinan	Alternate	1945	Shandong			Deputy secretary of Shandong CCYL, 1978–85
Li Yuanchao	Deputy party secretary of Jiangsu	—	1950	Jiangsu	Fudan University / Beijing University (G)	Mathematics / Economics	Member of the CCYL Secretariat, 1983–88

Notes: CC = Central Committee; f = female; G = Graduate Program.

all of which will help him further advance his political career, Song is also a confidant of Hu Jintao.

Li Keqiang has been in the spotlight in the country for many years. He was born in Anhui where he also worked as a "sent-down youth" in rural areas during the Cultural Revolution. In 1978, Li passed the national examination for college entrance and enrolled in the law department at Beijing University. He later obtained a Ph.D. in economics at the same school. His political career has been spent largely in the Chinese Communist Youth League (CCYL), where he held a leadership position for about fifteen years. In 1998, at the age of 43, Li became governor of Henan, China's most populous province. However, Li's political future has been clouded by two fires that caused about 400 deaths during his tenure in Henan. These two fires, though politically damaging to him, may not jeopardize Li's chance for promotion because many other regions such as Shanghai have also experienced major accidents in recent years.

Jiang and Zeng's "Shanghai Gang"

Table 2.3 shows the prominent members of the "Shanghai Gang" in the Fourth Generation. In comparison, members of the "Shanghai Gang" have closer personal ties with Jiang Zemin than do their counterparts in the CCYL with Hu Jintao. Quite often, Jiang Zemin has offered a direct hand in promoting them to their current positions. Jiang's "Shanghai Gang" originated when he was a mayor and Party chief in Shanghai during the 1980s. Since Jiang was promoted by Deng from Party secretary of Shanghai to general secretary of the CCP after the Tiananmen incident, he has promoted some of his friends from Shanghai to important national leadership positions. Jiang brought Zeng Qinghong (his chief of staff), You Xigui (his bodyguard), and Jia Tingan (his personal secretary) to Beijing with him in 1989. A few years later, two of Jiang's deputies in Shanghai, Wu Bangguo and Huang Ju, were promoted to Politburo members as part of Jiang's effort to consolidate his power in Beijing.

Jiang has also promoted his "Shanghai Gang" members to heads of the central government's main propaganda organs. Gong Xinhan and Zhou Ruijin were transferred from Shanghai to be deputy head of the Propaganda Department of the CCP and deputy editor-in-chief of the *People's Daily*, respectively. Xu Guangchun, former head of the Shanghai Branch of the Xinhua News Agency, was promoted first to editor-in-chief of *Guangming Daily*. He also served as a spokesperson for the Fifteenth CCP Congress and is now head of the State Administration of Radio, Film, and Television under the State Council and deputy head of the Propaganda Department of the CCP.[9]

In 2000, Jiang promoted Wang Huning, Cao Jianming, and Zhou Mingwei,

Table 2.3

Prominent Members of the "Shanghai Gang" in the Fourth Generation

Name	Current position	Fifteenth CC	Born	Native	Education	Principal experience in Shanghai
Zeng Qinghong	Head, CCP Organization Department	Alternate	1939	Jiangxi	Beijing Institute of Engineering	Head, Organization Dept., 1985–86; Deputy Party Secretary, 1986–89
Wu Bangguo	Vice premier	Member	1941	Anhui	Qinghua University	Deputy Party secretary, 1985–91; Party secretary, 1991–95
Huang Ju	Party secretary of Shanghai	Member	1938	Zhejiang	Qinghua University	Chief of staff, 1984–85; vice mayor, 1986–91; mayor 1991–95; Party secretary 1994–present
Zeng Peiyan	Minister of State Development Planning Commission	Member	1938	Zhejiang	Qinghua University	Director of the Research Institute under No. 1 Machine Industry, 1978–85
Chen Zhili (f)	Minister of Education	Member	1942	Fujian	Fudan University (G)	Head, Propaganda Dept., 1988–89; deputy Party secretary, 1989–97
Xu Kuangdi	Former mayor of Shanghai, president of Chinese Academy of Engineering	Member	1937	Zhenjiang	Beijing Institute of Steel Industry	Head of Education Bureau, 1989–91; vice mayor, 1992–95; mayor, 1995–present
Zhang Wenkang	Minister of Public Health	Member	1940	Shanghai	Shanghai No.1 Medicine School	Vice commandant, No. 2 PLA Medical Univ. in Shanghai, 1984–90

Table 2.3 *(continued)*

Name	Current position	Fifteenth CC	Born	Native	Education	Principal experience in Shanghai
Meng Jianzhu	Party secretary of Jiangxi	Alternate	1947	Jiangsu	Shanghai Institute of Engineering (G)	Deputy chief of staff, 1992–93; vice mayor 1993–97; deputy Party secretary, 1996–2001
Chen Liangyu	Executive vice mayor of Shanghai	Alternate	1946	Zhejiang	PLA Institute of Engineering	Deputy chief of staff, 1992–96; deputy secretary, 1997–present; executive vice mayor 1998–present
Zhao Qizheng	Head, Information Office, State Council	—	1940	Beijing	China's Univ. of Science and Technology	Head, Organization Dept., 1984–91; vice mayor 1991–97; head of Pudong District, 1992–97
Hua Jianmin	Director, General Office, Finance and Economics Leading Group	—	1942?		Qinghua University	Vice mayor, 1994–98
Wang Huning	Deputy Director Genera, Policy Research Center	—	1955	Shanghai	East China Normal Uni. Fudan University (G)	Dean of Law School at Fudan University, 1993–97
Cao Jianming	Vice president of Supreme People's Court	—	1955	Shanghai	Institute of East China Political Science and Law (G)	President, Institute of East China Political Science and Law, 1998–present

Name	Position		Birth	Province	Education	Other positions
Zhou Mingwei	Vice chair, Association for Relations across the Taiwan Strait	—	1956?	Shanghai	Fudan University, SUNY Albany (G)	Director, Foreign Affairs Office, 1997–99
Gong Xinhan	Deputy head, CCP Propaganda Department	—	1940	Zhejiang	Fudan University	Deputy Propaganda Department, 1986–93
Xu Guangchun	Head, State Radio, Film, and TV Administration	—	1944	Zhejiang	People's University	Director, Shanghai Bureau of Xinhua News Agency, 1985–91
Zhou Ruijin	Deputy editor, *People's Daily*	—	1939	Zhejiang	Fudan University	Deputy editor, *Jiefang Daily*, 1985–93
You Xigui	Deputy director, General Office of the Central Com.	Alternate	1939	Hebei	PLA Institute of Engineering	Commander, Military Garrison Command, 1985–89
Jia Tingan	Director, PRC President's Office	—	1950	Hebei	—	Jiang Zemin's personal secretary, 1985–89

Notes: CC = Central Committee; f = female; G = Graduate Program.

three well-educated Shanghai leaders in their early 40s, to the central government. Wang Huning, former dean and professor of the Law School at Fudan University, was promoted to deputy director general of the CCP Policy Research Center. Wang has also served as Jiang's personal assistant during Jiang's travels both at home and abroad. Cao Jianming, another professor of law and president of the Institute of East China Political Science and Law in Shanghai, now serves as vice president of the Supreme People's Court. Zhou Mingwei, a U.S.-educated specialist in international affairs and former director of the Office of Foreign Affairs in the Shanghai municipal government, was recently promoted to vice chair of the Association for Relations across the Taiwan Strait.

Chen Zhili, Jiang's deputy on the Shanghai Party Committee, now heads the Ministry of Education. Zeng Peiyan, Jiang's long-time associate, now serves as Minister of the State Development Planning Commission. In the upcoming Sixteenth Party Congress, Zeng Qinghong, Wu Bangguo, and Huang Ju will be among the candidates for seats on the Politburo's standing committee. Chen Zhili and Zeng Peiyan will be front-runners for new membership on the Politburo. Some of these Shanghai leaders may be transferred to other regions to serve as provincial chiefs, as has already happened to former Vice Mayor Meng Jianzhu who is now Party secretary of Jiangxi. Zhao Qizheng and Hua Jianmin, who also served as vice mayors in Shanghai, will likely hold important positions on the State Council. Wang Huning and Xu Guangchun will play even larger roles in propaganda affairs during and after the Sixteenth Party Congress.

It is important to point out that Zeng Qinghong has played a crucial role in the formation of the "Shanghai Gang." The promotion to national leadership of many Shanghai leaders—for example, Wang Huning, Cao Jianming, and Meng Jianzhu—should be attributed to both Jiang and Zeng. This is especially true at present as Zeng is in charge of personnel affairs. Beyond a doubt, Zeng will naturally "inherit" the "Shanghai Gang" after Jiang's retirement.

Not all leaders who originate from, or pass through, Shanghai belong to Jiang's "Shanghai Gang." Zhu Rongji, former mayor of Shanghai, has also promoted his associates in Shanghai to central government positions. But people from other regions are aware of the distinction between Jiang's "Shanghai Gang" and leaders promoted by Zhu, although there are some ambiguities. Most of the officials whom Zhu promoted are financial and economic experts. To a certain extent, Xu Kuangdi, former mayor of Shanghai, is often seen as a protégé of Zhu, not Jiang. Some tensions may exist between officials who are promoted primarily by Jiang and those promoted by Zhu.

When Zhu Rongji took over the governorship of the People's Bank of China in 1993, he immediately appointed two close colleagues from Shanghai as vice governors of the bank. They were Dai Xianglong, former governor of the Shanghai-based Bank of Communications, and Zhu Xiaohua, former vice governor of the Shanghai branch of the Bank of China.[10] Recently, Zhu's close associate during his years in Shanghai, Lou Jiwei (former vice chair of the Shanghai Economic Restructuring Commission and Zhu's personal secretary), was named executive vice minister of finance. In 2000, Wu Xiaoling and Jiang Jianqing, two officials who worked in the financial sector of Shanghai, were promoted to vice governor of the People's Bank and governor of the Industrial and Commercial Bank of China, respectively. Jiang, 47 years old, now runs the largest commercial bank in China.

The presence of the "Shanghai Gang" in the central leadership, however, has received growing opposition and criticism, not only from Chinese society, but also from deputies of both the Party Congress and the NPC, who have routinely blocked the election of nominees favored by Jiang. For example, in the preliminary election of the Fifteenth Party Congress, three men from Shanghai (including two vice mayors and You Xigui) had to be dropped from full to alternate membership as a result of not receiving enough votes.[11] That explains why many of the people listed in Table 2.3 are not members or alternates of the Fifteenth Central Committee.

In election to government positions in the Ninth NPC held in 1998, Jiang's "Shanghai Gang" again fared badly. Han Zhubin, nominee for procurator-general of the State and Jiang's long-time associate in Shanghai, was almost rejected by the NPC because about 35 percent of the deputies opposed the appointment.[12]

Since the mid-1990s, institutional arrangements have been made to curtail over-representation of certain regions in the central leadership. On the Fifteenth Central Committee, all but one of the thirty-one provincial-level administrations has two full members. These two seats are usually occupied by the party secretary and the governor of the province.[13] This further explains why, just a few days before the Fifteenth Party Congress, Jiang transferred his close friend, Chen Zhili, to Beijing where she became head of China's education commission. Thus, she was able to become a full member of the Central Committee.

It remains to be seen how many members of the "Shanghai Gang" will enter the next Politburo and Central Committee. While the members of the "Shanghai Gang" are often highly visible, the number of Shanghai leaders who have been promoted to the central government or transferred to the top leadership in other provinces is quite limited. If Jiang and Zeng have basic political antenna, they will certainly realize how unpopular they may become if they appoint too many members of the Shanghai Gang to the national leadership during the next Party Congress. The above analysis of Hu Jintao's CCYL associates and Jiang and Zeng's "Shanghai Gang"—arguably the two strongest factions in the Chinese leadership at present—reveals that even these two factions have severe limitations in terms of power and influence. While any factional leader wants to maximize his own power by appointing his protégés to important positions, the potential backlash is too strong to be ignored. That is why Hu and Zeng are both being cautious in expanding their factions at present.

Will Jiang Really Step Aside?

A frequently raised question is whether Jiang will continue to influence policy by holding on to his third position, chair of the Central Military Commission, after the Sixteenth Party Congress. In addition, Jiang can also play an important behind-the-scenes role as the paramount leader, much as Deng did previously. It has never happened before in PRC history that a top leader has really retired. Often, even if a top leader wants to hand over power to his successor, the leader's subordinates and family members will interfere, urging the leader to retain some grip on power and influence. While it is a bit early to assess Jiang's role during the post–Sixteenth Party Congress period, the most likely scenario is that Jiang's successors will push him aside for the following four reasons.

First, Jiang is no Deng Xiaoping. Jiang has never had the enormous power and influence that Deng wielded during the 1980s and early 1990s. As discussed earlier, Jiang was not even able to place some of his protégés on the central committee during the Fifteenth Party Congress. To a certain extent, Jiang has remained in power since 1989 largely through coalition building and political maneuvering. What is most evident in Chinese politics today is the broad shift from an all-powerful single leader, such as Mao or Deng, to greater collective leadership, as evidenced by the Jiang era. When Jiang's time is up, the collective leadership will not give him the chance to become another strongman.

Second, there is increasing pressure within the CCP establishment to make political institutionalization genuine. The term limit and the age limit for retirement are two important measures of political institutionalization in present-day China. According to the regulations issued by the Politburo in 1997, with the exception of extraordinary circumstances, all top leaders (including the members of the Politburo and the premier and vice premier of the State Council) must retire by the age of 70.[14] Jiang did make an exception in 1997 when, at the age of 71, he retained all of his positions in the Fifteenth Party Congress. According to the Hong Kong media, Jiang once said that there would be no more exceptions.[15] It is almost certain that Jiang will no longer hold the posts of president of the PRC and secretary general of the Party. Although he may continue to serve as chair of the CMC after the Sixteenth Party Congress, it is difficult to imagine that a leader who is neither head of state nor a standing committee member of the Politburo can overrule decisions made by the Politburo.

Third, one can be reasonably suspicious about how important and relevant the post of chair of the CMC is at this particular time and how effective Jiang would be in commanding the army by himself. While the military is always important to the leadership, the scenario that China's military will interfere in politics has become increasingly remote. The departure from the CMC of paramount military figures such as Yang Shangkun and his brother, Yang Baibing, in the early 1990s; the successful ban of the Chinese military's involvement in business in the late 1990s; regular reshuffling of military leaders; and the two-decade-long effort to "professionalize" the military all support this assessment.[16] It is true that none of the four rising stars of the Fourth Generation is associated with the military, but, meanwhile, no strong military man has emerged among the new generation of leadership. It is in the shared interest of Hu, Wen, Zeng, and Li to work together to prevent the emergence of a strong military figure. Of course, the military may return to a central role in the political life of the country, but this would take place only under truly extraordinary circumstances.

And fourth, any state leader who is about to transfer power is likely concerned about his legacy and security. As U.S. President Clinton and Russian President Yeltsin were concerned about these matters before they left office, Jiang Zemin will be as well. Jiang needs to know: (1) what achievements he can claim during his tenure and (2) what protection he can receive after his retirement. As for the first, Jiang and his associates have already boasted about what they call "the Jiang Zemin Theory." In contrast to Marx's original notion that the Communist Party is the "vanguard of the proletarian class," Jiang argues that the CCP should now represent "the developmental need of production," "the forward direction of advanced culture," and "the fundamental interests of the majority of the Chinese people." This new concept has broadened the CCP's base of power to include entrepreneurs, intellectuals, and especially technical specialists. "The Jiang Zemin Theory" has been endorsed by the recently held Sixth Plenum of the Central Committee and will likely be amended to the CCP constitution during the Sixteenth Party Congress.

On the foreign policy front, despite his initial failure to meet core nationalist goals of gaining new leverage over the Taiwan issue and dealing with the growing tensions in Sino-U.S. and Sino-Japan relations, Jiang's moderate approaches to "crises," such as Taiwan's 2000 presidential election, the Belgrade embassy bombing, and the EP-3 airplane crash, have now proved to be wise policy decisions. Beijing's successful bid to host the 2008 Olympics is seen as a great victory of Jiang's diplomacy and foreign policy.

As for concern about his political security after retirement, Jiang will certainly appoint as many as possible of his protégés to the Sixteenth Politburo and its standing committee. Jiang's lenient treatment of corruption charges against Deng's children may also indicate that Jiang and his family members will be exempt from this kind of charge, if any should surface in the future.

Conclusion: Toward a Peaceful and More Institutionalized Power Transition?

What does all this mean for China's future? What patterns and trends can one find in terms of the characteristics of rising stars in the Fourth Generation and the institutional developments that they may embody? Can one make some basic assumptions about the upcoming Chinese political succession—will it be violent and abrupt, or peaceful and predictable?

In response to these questions, I have three interrelated observations. First, in present-day China no individual, no faction, no institution, and no region can dominate power. Everyone has to compromise, and those who are skillful in coalition building are often favored. This explains why the four top contenders of the Fourth Generation are all capable political tacticians. This may also indicate that the upcoming political succession will more likely feature compromise and power-sharing, rather than vicious factional fighting.

Second, informal networks often have overlapping memberships, for example, many prominent members of the "Shanghai Gang" also belong to the "Qinghua Clique," thus forming a complex interdependence among various factions. As new leaders move into the highest level of authority, patron-client ties that previously enabled them to succeed may become a liability. Their legitimacy, therefore, should rely on something besides their political networks. The Fourth Generation leaders will be more concerned about their performance and achievements than their predecessors were. They will also be under pressure to make China's political institutionalization more effective.

And third, there is no indication at present that Hu, Wen, Zeng, and Li have any fundamentally different views regarding either domestic or foreign policies. But one can reasonably believe that there are radicals and moderates, conservatives and liberals, hardliners and softliners among the Fourth Generation leaders. The new leaders will deal with a long list of daunting economic and sociopolitical challenges: economic disparity, the negative impact (especially on China's farmers) of China's entry into the WTO, urban unemployment, rampant official corruption, ethnic tensions, large-scale industrial accidents, and environmental disasters. None of these problems has an easy solution. Thus, one can expect a high level of contentiousness and conflict to persist in China in the years to come. Consequently, it is likely that some cleavages within the Fourth Generation of leaders, especially the lack of consensus on major social and economic policies, are so fundamental that compromise will become very difficult, if not impossible. On the international front, while the September 11 terrorist attack reduced the tension in United States–China relations, China has been surrounded by an extremely unstable and increasingly unpredictable external environment. Furthermore, the issues of Taiwan and other problems in United States–China relations, though no longer imminent, have largely remained. But one can also argue that, as they face these daunting challenges both at home and abroad, China's new leaders will unite rather than divide.[17]

Paradoxical and uncertain as they are, these developments demonstrate the tensions and dynamism within the politics of China today. This will make the next several years a period of political experimentation that will not only test the wisdom and skill of the new leaders, but also test the effectiveness of the new institutional developments.

Notes

1. For a theoretical discussion of the concept of political generation, see Karl Mannheim, "Consciousness of Class and Consciousness of Generation," in *Essays on the Sociology of Knowledge*, ed. Mannheim (London: RKP, 1952).

2. Earlier studies based on generational analysis include Michael Yahuda, "Political Generations in China," *China Quarterly* 80 (December 1979): 795; W. William Whitson, "The Concept of Military Generation," *Asian Survey* 11, no. 11 (November 1968); and Carol Lee Hamrin, "Perspectives on Generational Change in China," unpublished scope paper for the workshop organized by the Paul H. Nitze School of Advanced International Studies, Johns Hopkins University, June 1993.

3. For example, Chen Zhili, minister of education and a rising star of the fourth generation, wrote in 1999: "the great calamity that the CR (Cultural Revolution) inflicted upon my family and myself made me first wander and wonder, and then wake up to reality, becoming politically and intellectually mature." The Cultural Revolution experience, in Chen's view, also influenced the way in which she handles her leadership job now. "I want to constantly deal with imminent work and issues instead of thinking too much about the long-term future." See *Zhonghua yingcai* (China's talents), no. 5 (March 1999): 12.

4. For a more detailed discussion of their experiences during the Cultural Revolution, see Yang Zhongmei, *Zhonggong kuashiji jiebanren: Hu Jintao* (The cross-century successor of China: Hu Jintao) (Taibei: Shibao chubanshe, 1999); Ren Zhichu, *Hu Jintao: Zhongguo kuashiji jiebanren* (Hu Jintao: China's first man in the twenty-first century) (Hong Kong: Mirror Books, 1997); Xiao Chong, *Zhonggong disidai mengren* (The fourth generation of leaders of the Chinese Communist Party) (Hong Kong: Xiafeier guoji chubangongsi, 1998); He Pin and Gao Xin, *Zhonggong "Taizidang"* (China's Communist "princelings") (Taipei: Shih-pao ch'u-pan kung-ssu, 1992); and

Gao Xin, *Xiangfu Guangdong bang* (Taming the Guangdong gang) (Hong Kong: Mingjing chubanshe, 2000). For their official biographies, see Shen Xueming et al., comp., *Zhonggong di shiwujie zhongyang weiyuanhui zhongyang jilü jiancha weiyunahui weiyuan minglu* (Who's who of the members of the Fifteenth Central Committee of the Chinese Communist Party and the Fifteenth Central Commission for Discipline Inspection) (Beijing: Zhonggong wenxian chubanshe, 1999); and Liao Gailong and Fan Yuan, *Zhongguo renming da cidian xiandai dangzhengjun lingdaorenwujuan* (Who's who in China, the volume on current party, government, and military leaders) (Beijing: Foreign Languages Press, 1994).

5. For a detailed study of the Qinghua Clique, see Cheng Li, *China's Leaders: The New Generation* (Lanham, MD: Rowman and Littlefield Publishers, 2001). Between 1995 and 2000, a total of 1,800 ministerial and provincial-level leaders attended training programs organized by the Central Party School, the State Public Administration Institute, and the National Defense University. In addition, over 1,000 young and middle-aged leaders attended a one-year program at the Central Party School, *People's Daily*, May 14, 2001, pp. 1, 6.

6. *China Daily*, June 20, 1998, p. 1.

7. For a detailed study of provincial leaders in present-day China, see Cheng Li, "After Hu, Who? China's Provincial Leaders Await Promotion," *China Leadership Monitor*, no. 1 (Fall 2001).

8. For the institutional connections among Qinghua University, the CCYL, and CPS, see "University Networks and the Rise of Qinghua Graduates in China's Leadership," *Australian Journal of Chinese Affairs*, no. 32 (July 1994): 1–32.

9. For more discussion on Jiang's network in the propaganda circle in the central government, see Paul Cavey, "Building a Power Base: Jiang Zemin and the Post-Deng Succession," *Issues and Studies* 33, no. 11 (November 1997): 13.

10. See John P. Burns, "Strengthening Central CCP Control of Leadership Selection," *China Quarterly* 138 (June 1994): 472.

11. *Qianshao yuekan* (Advance guard monthly) (October 1997): 16–17.

12. Willy Wo-Lap Lam, "All the President's Men," *South China Morning Post*, March 18, 1998, p. 1; Vivien Pik-Kwan Chan, "Strong Opposition as Jiang's Man Gets Top Law Job," *South China Morning Post*, March 18, 1998, p. 1; and *Shijie ribao* (World journal), March 20, 1998, p. A9.

13. In the municipalities where one full CC member concurrently holds the positions of both Party secretary and mayor—for example, Jia Qinglin in Beijing or Zhang Lichang in Tianjin—usually a deputy Party secretary in the city also holds a full membership on the Fifteenth Central Committee.

14. *Shijie ribao*, February 11, 2001, p. A1.

15. See www.chinesenewsnet.com, August 19, 2001.

16. James Charles Mulvenon, *Soldiers of Fortune: The Rise and Fall of the Chinese Military-Business Complex, 1978–1998* (Armonk, NY: M.E. Sharpe, 2001).

17. Paul Heer, "A House United: Beijing's View of Washington," *Foreign Affairs* 79, no. 4 (July/August 2000): 22.

3

Hu Jintao's Succession

Prospects and Challenges

Murray Scot Tanner

In just about a month or so, the Chinese Communist Party (CCP) is expected to hold its Sixteenth Party Congress. Presently, most China-watchers anticipate that Hu Jintao will accede to the post of CCP general secretary at that time, although a recent flurry of reports suggesting that Jiang Zemin is trying to cling to this post have raised some last minute questions.[1] Hu is also widely expected to be named president of China the following spring at the National People's Congress. The final major question in this "incomplete" succession scenario, according to most analysts, concerns whether or not General Secretary Jiang Zemin will attempt to emulate Deng Xiaoping by clinging to the chairmanship of the Central Military Commission for another five years (until the Seventeenth Party Congress in 2007) and continuing to rule to some degree from "behind the curtain." The confidence of outside analysts in this succession scenario has been reinforced by Hu Jintao's dramatic and steady rise to power, coupled with the failure of a credible rival to Hu to emerge. Hu was appointed to the Politburo Standing Committee, in charge of Party affairs and personnel in 1992, at the remarkably youthful age of 49. There followed his appointment as Jiang's vice president in early 1998 and his crucial appointment as the only civilian vice chairman of the Central Military Commission in 1999. The prominence China's official media have afforded him on key issues such as the U.S. bombing of China's Belgrade embassy, Jiang's controversial effort to reduce the People's Liberation Army's involvement in business, and Hu's highly-touted trip to Washington this past spring all testify to Hu's growing influence. The widely rumoured failure of Jiang Zemin to promote Zeng Qinghong—Jiang's longtime deputy and Hu's only obvious potential rival for the post of General Secretary—to the Politburo Standing Committee at successive Central Committee Plenary Sessions since October 2000 may be the greatest source of confidence in Hu's succession prospects among foreign analysts.[2]

The purpose of this chapter is to assess, admittedly very speculatively, Hu Jintao's succession prospects and challenges from several perspectives:

1. This chapter very briefly reviews Hu's rise to power, especially his capacity to win the support of various political patrons, and the state of his relationship with General Secretary Jiang Zemin. The personal and power relations among Jiang, Hu, and the other Fourth Generation leaders will be pivotal in determining the pace of change in China.
2. Next, this chapter will evaluate Hu's efforts to put in place his own power base, one that is relatively independent from Jiang.
3. Hu Jintao's policy views and the agenda he may pursue as General Secretary have been the object of considerable speculation and rumor. As a "baseline" and a check, this chapter takes a rather speculative first cut at analyzing Hu's policy views on a variety of issues. This section also considers Hu's manipulation of issues that could strengthen his appeal to key power constituencies where he has not yet established his power through personnel appointments.
4. More speculatively, this chapter will close with a few comments on Hu's capacity to develop new, less traditional sources of power that might sustain him in the event—seemingly likely—that China's political system undergoes substantial changes in the next five to ten years.

Any worthwhile analysis of succession prospects must be extremely frank about the limits of our knowledge. In places, the best we can do is to highlight key questions about current leadership politics that require further research and close monitoring in the next couple of years.

Courting Jiang While Building Support: Hu and the Successor's Dilemma

Hu Jintao's meteoric twenty-three-year rise from deputy chief of construction in desperately poor Gansu Province to the youngest member of the Politburo Standing Committee in 1992 clearly demonstrates an exceptionally skilled politician. But, as I have written elsewhere, Hu will need all of these skills to beat the "successor's dilemma" that plagues all authoritarian systems without institutionalized rules of leadership succession.[3] The "successor's dilemma" is a rational puzzle of power-building. Simply stated: the successor must try to maintain the trust and active support of the current top leader who chose him so long as that leader remains alive and politically influential. But simultaneously, as a hedge against the day when his patron will be gone, the successor must also build his own independent power base. Such future-oriented power-building efforts, however, risk leaving the current leader feeling so threatened and fearful of his successor that the current leader may attempt to undermine the successor or promote rival alternative successors. Thus, any action the designated successor takes to strengthen his future power risks threatening his main current source of power—his patron's trust. But actions designed to re-assure the current leader risk leaving the successor weak and exposed when the current leader passes from the scene. Conversely, the current leader faces a mirror-image dilemma: how to strengthen one's successor and "legacy" with-out inadvertently creating a political Frankenstein.[4] In a system such as China's that faces rapid change and a desperate need for reform, the successor's di-lemma takes on an issue dimension as well. To protect his "legacy" and current power, the present leader may demand extreme issue loyalty from the succes-sor, or may insist on foreclosing certain policy options or reforms that the successor sees as essential to the health of the country and the successor's own long-term survival. Even efforts by the successor at "normal" policy change may be misinterpreted by the current leader as attacks on his legacy.

Rapid political change can further compound the successor's dilemma by transforming the nature of leadership power, especially in reforming Leninist systems such as China. The process of reform and collapse in the European Leninist states a decade ago revealed that the power bases that Leninist leaders use in their successful rise to power—such as control of appointments, prop-aganda, and coercion—may lose their capacity to sustain those leaders in power through the reform process. Reform often causes these classic "Leninist" power resources to be supplanted by new more decisive power bases—some-times requiring new skills of issue manipulation, populism, use of mass media, or even plebicitory and electoral skills.[5]

Given the extraordinary complexity of this multilayered succession game of traditional power acquisition, policy management, and possible power tran-sition, it is little wonder that the "successor's dilemma" has defeated many of the most skillful and ruthless politicians in the history of the CCP. The logic of the "successor's dilemma" lays out the criteria by which analysts can eval-uate the progress of Hu Jintao: (1) his capacity to build the support and trust of current leaders and patrons; (2) his simultaneous capacity to build indepen-dent power sources; and (3) his ability to use issues to strengthen his capacity to survive if the bases of regime power shift in the course of reform.

Hu Jintao's Rise: The Management of Multiple Patrons

A close examination of Hu Jintao's rise to power might make us optimistic about his chances for working with Jiang, even though Hu is by no means a

"Jiang protégé." Hu has repeatedly demonstrated an impressive skill for attracting the dedicated support of multiple senior patrons from all across the political spectrum. Many sources have retold the story of how Hu Jintao graduated from Qinghua University, but like many educated youth was shipped off to obscure rural posts (in Hu's case, Gansu Province) in the early years of the Cultural Revolution. Hu quickly won the patronage of provincial CCP Secretary Song Ping, who sent him to the Central Party School, where he impressed Hu Yaobang, Hu Qili, Wang Zhaoguo, and other reformers who placed Hu in charge of the Communist Youth League.[6] In an effort to avoid criticism for his rapid promotion, Hu Jintao reportedly requested a classic "tempering" appointment to a provincial post, and thus was assigned as China's youngest provincial CCP secretary, to Guizhou (1985) and then to Tibet (1988).[7]

Even more impressive was Hu Jintao's capacity not merely to survive, but to accelerate his rise within the Party, even as the reformist leadership coalition of the early 1980s splintered and deep splits emerged among Hu Jintao's various patrons. Hu Yaobang's dismissal in 1987 and death in 1989, followed by the demotion of Hu Qili and Wang Zhaoguo for their behavior during the 1989 student-worker uprisings, suddenly deprived Hu Jintao of his most powerful patrons. Intense ideological and personal struggles also revealed the growing chasm among Hu Jintao's various supporters—the reformists Hu Yaobang, Hu Qili, and Wang Zhaoguo, the shifting Deng Xiaoping, and the increasingly conservative Song Ping, who was soon put in charge of the Central Organization Department.

In retrospect, one reason Hu Jintao's career did not stall after Tiananmen (unlike many young appointees of the 1980s) is almost certainly that from early spring 1989 onward, he was forced to focus on suppressing the Tibetan uprisings, and thus was spared from having to take sides in the Beijing intrigues of summer 1989. But it is harder to say exactly how Hu reinvigorated his connections with more conservative patrons without raising the suspicions of leaders such as Deng who still supported economic reform. Some Hong Kong press sources from this period stress Song Ping's patronage, and tend to portray Hu Jintao as a conservative, even a stalking horse for Song and arch-conservative Deng Liqun.[8] But this is too simple a solution to a very complex puzzle. Other sources claim that even though Song recommended Hu to Deng, it was Hu's ruling strategy in Tibet—combining economic growth and reform with political toughness and repression—that convinced Deng that Hu had what it took to be a successor, and caused Deng to "personally" mark Hu for promotion. The story is made all the more complex by the growing divide between Deng and Song after Deng insisted on accelerating economic reforms during his late 1991 to early 1992 "Southern Tour."[9] It was during the Southern Tour that Deng reportedly complimented Hu Jintao in public as a model successor and "a good man." Within the year, Hu jumped all the way from Central Committee member to the pivotal successor's post—Politburo Standing Committee member in charge of party affairs and organization.[10] In assuming the organization portfolio, Hu effectively took over from Song Ping. Once again, at a time of great ideological and personal division among the top Party leadership—and specifically among his own patrons—Hu Jintao again demonstrated his ability to appeal to both supporters and critics of reform, maintain ties with each, appear personally nonthreatening, and yet still impress top leaders that he can be entrusted with additional highly sensitive assignments.[11] All of these are crucial skills for the young leader attempting to beat the successor's dilemma.

Hu and Jiang Zemin

Most of the reports questioning Hu's prospects for beating the successor's dilemma have wondered how enthusiastically Jiang supports Hu, and even paint their relations in relatively adversarial or zero-sum terms. Since the mid-1990s, however, Hu Jintao has, for the most part, survived or surpassed all of the figures who were pivotal in his early promotion—a risky and exposed position for a potential successor. Certainly, Jiang Zemin is not one of Hu's historic patrons, and there is no evidence that they even worked together before 1992. And indeed, most journalistic reporting on the succession stresses that, within Beijing political society, it is generally accepted that Hu Jintao is not even Jiang's first choice to succeed him as general secretary. For nearly two years now, many well-connected Beijing political sources have been telling Hong Kong and Western analysts that Jiang would prefer to strengthen Zeng Qinghong's position. At the 1997 Fifteenth Party Congress, shortly after Deng's death, Jiang promoted Zeng to head of the Central Organization Department, the ideal position from which to build a power base to challenge Hu. (Hu Jintao, however, apparently continued as the Politburo Standing Committee member leading Party Affairs work—indicating a clear rivalry for control of personnel.)

But many sources report that at both the October 2000 and October 2001 Central Committee Plenary sessions, Jiang encountered too much resistance to promote Zeng to full membership in the Politburo or its Standing Committee. Assuming that Jiang did, in fact, fail twice in a serious effort to promote his close follower—particularly one with such a strong presumptive claim to membership as the head of the Organizational Department—it could indeed signal that Jiang's power within the Politburo is significantly less than when he impressively dispatched his rivals for power (especially Qiao Shi) in 1997–98. (Even if the reports are not true, they have become so universally accepted that they could still undermine Jiang's reputation and authority.) This, in turn, would raise doubts about Jiang's future capacity to influence Hu Jintao from "behind the screen," which, in any case, seems certain to be far less than Deng's capacity to do so with Hu Yaobang, Zhao Ziyang, and Jiang himself.

But it may not be necessary to accept these highly adversarial, zero-sum portrayals of the Jiang-Hu relationship contained in so much recent reporting. There is also substantial evidence that, even if Jiang Zemin is not wildly en- thusiastic about Hu Jintao as a successor, Jiang, like several senior Party lead- ers before him, nevertheless places substantial faith in Hu. The most obvious counterargument to the "zero-sum" view is that Hu Jintao's rise in power continued even during those periods (late 1997–98, for example), when Jiang Zemin was clearly at the height of his powers. We can also note several oc- casions in recent years in which Jiang has entrusted Hu with a number of sensitive and even risky political assignments.

- Hu has reportedly been placed in charge of the leadership group making personnel arrangements for this year's Sixteenth Party Congress.[12] Based on guidelines for promotion and retirement age, the Congress is expected to involve a 50–60 percent turnover in the full and alternate members of the Central Committee, and perhaps a change of five out of six members of the Politburo Standing Committee.[13]
- In the wake of the NATO bombing of the Chinese embassy, Jiang selected Hu to deliver the official televised address to the nation. The speech re- flected Beijing's conspiratorial interpretation of the bombing and endorsed the "legality" of the widespread demonstrations outside U.S. diplomatic facilities. It was also, however, the first public government statement to make the case to the Chinese people—however obliquely and gently— that because of the fundamental importance of the "opening up" policy and the United States–China relationship, the two countries would even- tually have to find some way of getting past the emotional crisis.[14]
- Hu has played an important role in one of Jiang Zemin's most sensitive policy initiatives—his efforts to substantially reduce the involvement of the People's Liberation Army and the civilian security and judicial organs in business activities.[15]
- In recent years, Jiang has apparently decided to increase Hu Jintao's vis- ibility and prestige. Hu has become something of a globetrotter, repre- senting Jiang on a large number of state visits. The same is true in military affairs. Since Hu's promotion to vice chairman of the Central Military Commission, and, particularly in the past six months, Jiang has had Hu accompany him on many of Jiang's ceremonial visits and inspections of People's Liberation Army (PLA) units. Jiang has also allowed Hu to an-

nounce a number of official military policy decisions, including permitting him the politically pleasant task of announcing the promotion of key officers to the rank of general.

- Hu has been a key figure in the investigation of several of the massive scandals currently plaguing the leadership. Hu has personally been involved in reorganizing the Communist Party Committees and governments of Beijing and Fujian Province, and some reports indicate that Song Defu was specifically in charge of the investigation of military cadres implicated in the Xiamen smuggling scandal. In the Fujian case, Hu's long-time Youth League associate, Song Defu, was recently chosen to take over as Party secretary in the revenue-rich province.[16]
- During the height of the United States–China crisis over the EP-3 reconnaissance plane, Jiang felt sufficiently confident in Hu that he left China for a prearranged trip to Latin America, leaving Hu and other members of the Politburo and Central Military Commission behind to deal with many of the smaller aspects of the crisis.
- Finally, in October–November 2001, Hu was dispatched on a high-profile visit to five European countries where he conveyed Beijing's reassurances about its role in the war on terrorism and its commitment to responsible World Trade Organization (WTO) membership. Quite predictably, Hu received terrific publicity and state receptions befitting China's next leader.

This list of important political assignments imposes a heavy burden on those holding to a strong "zero-sum" interpretation—that Jiang strongly desires to supplant Hu Jintao with Zeng Qinghong or other allies to whom he is personally much closer. It may indeed be the case that Hu Jintao is not Jiang Zemin's dream candidate for successor. Nevertheless, this evidence argues powerfully that, as with Song Ping, Hu Yaobang, and Deng Xiaoping before him, Hu Jintao has won at least a substantial measure of Jiang Zemin's respect.

For his part, Hu Jintao has gone to great lengths to reassure Jiang, at least publicly, that he respects Jiang's authority. In contrast to the succession jockeying of the mid-1990s, when Jiang's rivals often demurred from referring to him as the "core" of the new leadership, Hu Jintao has at times been terrifically fulsome in his public approbation for Jiang. In particular, Hu has lavished praise on Jiang Zemin's self-styled theoretical contributions to Marxism-Leninism such as the theory of the "Three Represents."

Still, in the successor's dilemma, the question of whether Jiang gives Hu his "respect" rather than his "enthusiastic support" could determine the amount of tension in the relationship if and when Jiang steps aside as general secretary. Certainly, looming over all of Hu Jintao's calculations is the spectre of Deng Xiaoping's withdrawal of support for Hu Yaobang and Zhao Ziyang during political crises in 1987 and 1989. In the end, however, we must frankly recognize the limitations on our information, and accept that a number of incidents in Jiang and Hu's relationship are equally compatible with two very different interpretations of their relationship—that Jiang trusts and respects Hu enough to support his promotion, or simply that whatever Jiang's reservations and preferences, he lacks the power to dislodge Hu as designated successor and build sufficient support for an alternative candidate in Hu's place. Thus, for Western analysts, one of our greatest questions in assessing Hu's prospects will continue to be Jiang's willingness to stand strongly behind Hu and to grant him the political power to operate during a significant future political crisis.

Building His Own Independent Power Base

Relations with the Military

What, then, of Hu's ability to beat the successor's dilemma by placing his own allies in positions of power, and perhaps eventually even being able to supplant Jiang Zemin? If Jiang's willingness to back Hu Jintao in a pinch is among the greatest questions looming over the succession, another must surely be Hu Jintao's relations with the People's Liberation Army. As noted, at present, the available sources overwhelmingly suggest that Jiang intends to cling to the chairmanship of the CCP's Central Military Commission (CMC) for another five-year term, until the Seventeenth Party Congress in 2007. Hu Jintao would presumably continue as first vice chairman. The current military leadership on the CMC all rose to power under Deng Xiaoping, and owe their present positions to the patronage of Deng and Jiang, not Hu. Jiang has probably devoted more effort to consolidating his control over the PLA than over any other political institution, and has lavished budgets, technological buildups, policy deference, promotions, and pay increases on them in order to secure that support.

There is no evidence of widespread military hostility to Hu Jintao, and, unlike the powerful hesitancy Deng Xiaoping encountered in trying to secure military support for a civilian leader like Hu Yaobang in the 1980s, the PLA seems to have accepted that, for the foreseeable future, they will be ruled by men like Jiang and Hu with no personal military experience. Still, Hu remains an unknown quantity to the military, unlike their avid long-term suitor Jiang Zemin. As the former Party secretary of Tibet during martial law, Hu probably worked more closely with military officers (in the Chengdu Military Region [MR] and the Tibet Military District [MD]) than did any other provincial secretary. Still, rather strikingly, this does not seem to have translated into any noteworthy following in the PLA. Indeed, it is difficult to identify any senior military officers whose closest leadership ties are clearly to Hu Jintao. Although Fu Quanyou—the Chengdu MR Commander during Hu's first years in Tibet—rose to chief of the General Staff, virtually every other identifiable senior PLA and People's Armed Police (PAP) officer who served in the Tibet MD during Hu's four years there had retired by 1996 or well before.[17] Based on presently available information, we have to conclude that Hu's influence over party personnel matters has not translated into any noteworthy power base within the PLA, and Jiang Zemin has hoarded those vital personnel resources away from his successor.

On the other hand, the age of the seniormost officers in the CMC (over 70 years) makes it almost certain that they will be replaced by the Sixteenth Congress or soon thereafter. We may yet see the emergence of some officers who served at lower levels in the Tibet MD during Hu's period there. Thus, one of the first key tests of Hu's personal power—ongoing as this chapter goes to press—will concern the struggle over appointing new officers to the CMC and new commanders and commissars to the key armies and military regions. It will bear close watching whether Hu can win Jiang's acquiescence in gradually appointing officers more closely tied to him than to Jiang.

Building Power Within the Party

Since becoming the Politburo Standing Committee Member in charge of party affairs and organization in 1992, how effectively has Hu Jintao exploited this opportunity to place his key supporters in positions of power? Has he positioned himself to effect the classic "circular theory of power" for Leninist general secretaries whereby these leaders select and promote the Central Committee members and other party-state leaders who, in effect, "select" them?[18]

At present, the best we can do is focus on those rising Party leaders who had demonstrable professional and personal ties to Hu in the past, most notably during his years in the national Communist Youth League (CYL) leadership and as provincial Party secretary.[19] Based on this limited pool, we can say that Hu apparently has already been able to promote a noteworthy but hardly overwhelming cadre of allies to significant Party and State posts. Viewed in historical terms, Hu's body of clients is probably greater than Jiang Zemin's network of clients was in Jiang's first couple of years as general secretary. But it pales in comparison to the enormous number of former Youth League allies Hu Yaobang was able to promote during the early to mid-1980s. (Of course, the fact that Jiang nevertheless beat the successor's dilemma while Hu Yaobang did not is a cautionary tale to analysts trying to infer too much about succession prospects solely from the ability to promote supporters!)

As a recruitment strategy, Hu Jintao seems to be making fairly effective use of China's numerous corruption investigations and scandals to place long-time associates in important positions that have been vacated by officials purged for malfeasance.

- In late 1994, Hu reportedly visited Guangdong to consult and arrange the succession and reshuffle of the Guangdong Provincial and Guangzhou City Party Committees and Governments.[20] Hu helped arrange the promotion of Liao Hui to governor and Yu Youjun and mayor.
- Hu also helped to reorganize the Beijing City Party Committee after the Wang Baosen/Chen Xitong case, chairing the meeting and delivering the speech to local cadres in which the new leadership was unveiled.[21] Other reports suggest that Hu has recently pushed the corruption investigation of later Beijing Party secretary and long-time Jiang ally Jia Qinglin and his wife.
- Since at least May 1995, Hu has made repeated prolonged investigations of Fujian Province, investigating corruption, and, in particular, the recent smuggling scandal there.[22] In the last months of 2000 his long-time CYL associate Song Defu was appointed Party secretary there.
- When Minster of Justice Gao Changli was suddenly removed from his post this past fall, he was replaced by Zhang Fusen, reportedly a former associate of Hu's from the CYL.

Those among the new appointees we can identify as previously having served with Hu Jintao in the leadership of the CYL or as his provincial deputies are shown in Table 3.1.

A couple of trends are apparent in Hu's emerging power base. Hu's provincial power base is growing, but is still rather limited, and is focused mostly in the interior, poorer, heavily minority provinces (although with allies recently promoted in Fujian and Jiangsu). Just as Hu lacks apparent supporters in the PLA, his influence in the civilian political-legal system is only slightly stronger (Justice and Civil Affairs), with few apparent clients or associates in the most powerful institutions (Public Security, State Security, the Supreme Court, Supreme Procuratorate).[23] Hu's associates appear to be strongest in the Party's propaganda sector (especially Xinhua) and in the Party's various united front organizations. These latter can be significant. They are, however, hardly the stuff out of which Leninist general secretaries have classically built successful power bases.

Any assessment of Hu's emerging power base must be cautious. Hu reportedly headed personnel arrangements for the Fifteenth Central Committee (CC) selected in 1997, and is reportedly in charge of similar arrangements for

Table 3.1

Rising Leaders with Ties to Hu Jintao

Name	Current post	Past association to Hu Jintao
Song Defu	Fujian CCP secretary; former personnel minister	Communist Youth League (CYL)
Mao Rubai	Ningxia CCP secretary	Tibet
Li Keqiang	Hunan governor	CYL
Linghu Jihua	CCP CC General Office deputy director	CYL/Tibet?
Danzim	Tibet CCP deputy secretary	Tibet
Zi Cheng	Tibet CCP deputy secretary/political-legal secretary	Tibet
Tian Congming	Xinhua Press Agency president; former director of the State Radio, Film, and TV Administration	CYL/Tibet
Zhang Baoshun	Vice president, Xinhua	CYL
Zhang Fusen	Minister of justice	CYL
Doje Cering	Minister of civil affairs	Tibet
Wang Zhaoguo	Secretary, CCP United Front Work Department (UFWD)	CYL
Liu Yandong	Department Secretary CCP UFWD	CYL
He Guangwei	Director general, National Tourism Administration	CYL
Li Haifeng	Department director State Council Overseas Chinese Office	CYL
Chen Haosu	President, Chinese Friendship, Peace and Development Foundation	CYL
Li Yuanchao	Jiangsu CCP department secretary (since November 2001); former vice minister of culture (to November 2000)	CYL

the Sixteenth Congress. Although a very large proportion of the current CC members selected in 1997 are expected to step down next year, a large percentage of those who are reelected for a second term are likely to be those whom Hu Jintao helped promote in 1997. There is no way to know how many of the currently emerging generation of officials owe their new positions to the patronage of Hu Jintao, Jiang Zemin, Zeng Qinghong, or others. Doubtless, many who will emerge are as yet unidentified as Hu supporters or clients.

In addition to his CYL and regional bases, Hu appears to be making extensive use of two other traditional recruitment bases. Reminiscent of both Hu Yaobang's tactics for building his Party support base and Jiang Zemin's tactics for building his military support base, Hu Jintao has made numerous grassroots inspection trips that permit him to meet and size up young cadres for potential patronage. According to available media reports, since January 1999, Hu has conducted inspection tours to at least nineteen of China's thirty-three provincial-level units, several of them more than once.[24] In particular, Hu has visited interior, impoverished, and ethnic minority regions. Aside from these inspections, as president of the Central Party School, Hu has held frequent meetings with the short-term specialized training classes for provincial cadres that are held at the school. These meetings likewise allow him to meet, select, and patronize promising young cadres. While there is no way for Western analysts to identify the cadres Hu met through these two channels in advance of the Sixteenth Congress, we must "flag" these possible promotion paths when performing background analysis on the new officials after the Congress.[25]

In sum, basing our judgments solely on those officials with identifiable past ties to Hu Jintao, it seems that he still has a good deal of work to do if he is to build the kind of support base in the Party Central offices, the State Council Ministries, and in the provinces that would assist him in beating the successor's dilemma. But based on his active efforts to meet top young cadres, there is strong reason to forecast that by this fall Hu will have significant numbers of additional clients on the Central Committee, quite possibly a good deal more than Jiang or Zeng Qinghong will.

Hu Jintao's Policy Views: An Initial Assessment

Assuming Hu Jintao successfully assumes the general secretaryship, what might his accession to that post mean for the CCP in terms of policy? How might Hu attempt to use issues and reform to strengthen his power base in the face of growing political and economic challenges to the CCP's leadership? At present, any answers to this question can only be extremely tentative, for two reasons. First, the degree of autonomy Hu will enjoy for promoting his policy preferences will be shaped by his as-yet undetermined relationship with

Jiang Zemin after Jiang steps to "the second line." Second, as innumerable reporters and analysts have noted, Hu Jintao plays his cards very close to his chest even by the high standards of Chinese succession politics. Nevertheless, some Western analysts have attempted to ascribe strong "hidden" policy views to Hu Jintao on several key subjects—with characterizations ranging from conservative Leninist to hard-line nationalist (some have even hinted "fascist") to closet Gorbachev—implicitly forecasting that Hu will act upon these views as soon as his power base permits.

The more extreme of these characterizations rest on alleged "insider accounts," which cannot be evaluated here, particularly among Hu's advisers at the Central Party School. At the same time, this chapter will attempt a "first cut" at Hu Jintao's policy views based on a close review of his speeches and writings over the past several years.

Political Reform

As general secretary, how Hu Jintao addresses the CCP's problems of indiscipline and corruption—perhaps the greatest threat to the Party's legitimacy—could prove to be the most important aspect of his leadership. Publicly, however, Hu has thus far betrayed little sign of crisis or panic about the state of the Party's cadres. He has referred to problems of corruption, predatory behavior, indiscipline, and becoming "divorced" from the masses only relatively briefly, and seldom in tones that would suggest a very deep sense of concern.

Perhaps as a consequence, Hu has not yet shown much public enthusiasm for reforming political institutions—not even by embracing several institutional changes that have long been a part of the Party's established policy under Jiang Zemin. He has spoken generally about the need to "further expand the scope of democratic and mass participation in cadres work." But even on the rare occasions when he has discussed elections for local cadres, he has primarily couched this in terms of promoting new, young, and female cadres— a necessity given the impending generational turnover. He has not, for the most part, portrayed elections in terms of their value for strengthening popular oversight of errant cadres.[26]

Given the fates of Hu Yaobang and Zhao Ziyang, Hu's policies toward maintaining social control and order will be pivotal in reassuring Party elders and consolidating his rule. Hu will ascend to the general secretaryship at the time when even official sources are frankly admitting that protest and disorder are rapidly increasing, and as China is forced to adopt policies required by WTO accession that will probably further exacerbate strikes, protests, and unrest. Susan Lawrence of the *Far Eastern Economic Review* has speculated that Hu will follow a social control strategy that is more sophisticated, albeit riskier, than those of his predecessors Jiang and Deng, and will be more willing to tolerate social unrest and protest as a "safety valve," or attempt to turn such unrest to the CCP's benefit. She points to the fact that Hu was the "public face" of the Party's moderately bold decision after the Belgrade embassy bombing to permit a limited period of channeled anti-U.S. protest right on the eve of the tenth anniversary of Tiananmen. In his official televised speech, Hu both voiced sympathy for such protests "according to the law," and annunciated their limits. Lawrence cites one article in the official media that lauded the strategy and specifically Hu's role in it, claiming that it reflected "the maturity and sobriety of China's leadership and people."[27]

In his speeches, Hu has approvingly cited Deng Xiaoping to the effect that:

> Stability is of overriding importance. Without a stable environment we can accomplish nothing, and may even lose what we have gained. This is a major principle for running the country, which overrules many minor principles.[28]

In quoting Deng, however, Hu has indeed suggested a willingness to consider more sophisticated approaches toward social control and stability. He has argued that the leadership needed to "keep a cool head . . . and enhance its political flair and acuity in handling contradictions among the people . . . particularly ones that emerge as a result of economic development."[29]

Although Hu Jintao may be a supporter of "safety valve" and "containment" strategies rather than stern deterrence and swift suppression for handling social order, the available evidence suggests that these views do not extend to his policies toward minority regions. In recent years, in a series of speeches in Tibet, Xinjiang, and in meetings with minority NPC delegations, Hu has reaffirmed in the strongest tones his intolerance of any "illegal" and "splittist" religious activities. Hu underscored this point when he represented the Party Center in the 2001 commemoration of the liberation of Tibet.

Relatedly, Hu Jintao has expressed little public support for accelerated reform of China's legal/coercive system and the building of "rule by law"—a body of reform that even Jiang has supported sporadically and for brief periods since 1997. He has not chosen to speak on legal issues very often. But when he has, he has been a vigorous advocate of China's most recent "stern blows" (*yanda*) anticrime campaigns. Hu has voiced no criticism of the abuses of these campaigns nor shown any awareness of the growing consensus within the Party's own political-legal sector that these campaigns have very little sustained effect in lowering crime rates. By contrast, Hu has not shown any sign that he intends to vigorously support even the modest measures toward giving judges greater professional autonomy and independence. Such policies are essential if China is to develop a legal system that can better strengthen "rule by law," fight corruption, protect the rights of apolitical citizens, and enforce China's legal obligations under the WTO. Instead, he has tended to mildly reaffirm the control of local CCP committees over legal organs—the major institutional obstacle to such judicial professionalism and autonomy.[30]

Economic Policy

In stark contrast to former General Secretary Zhao Ziyang (or even Jiang Zemin), Hu Jintao has taken little part in publicly debating or annunciating economic policy decisions, let alone putting forward a detailed "policy package" that could be identified with his candidacy for general secretary. Indeed, he has not even given many speeches that simply elaborated his support for mainstream Party policy efforts. At best, we can point to a number of economic issues about which Hu has expressed significant "concern," but embraced only the most general of principals for addressing them.[31] Extrapolating solely from this, we could speculate that Hu Jintao may not plan to be a very "hands-on" general secretary concerning economic policy—certainly not in the style of Zhao Ziyang, and perhaps not even to the same degree as Hu Yaobang.

Hu's apparent lack of interest in serving as "his own prime minister" on economic issues underscores the vital importance of the battle over who accedes to the premiership in early 2003. It also reminds us of the dangerously ill-defined relationship between the premier and the general secretary on important economic policy questions. As Zhu Rongji, Zhao Ziyang, Zhou Enlai, and others discovered when they held this post, Party leaders who normally held back from economic policymaking have often intervened in unpredictable and even destabilizing ways to undercut the premier when they feared the political risks of sensitive economic reforms.

Some Western analysts have tried to create the impression that Hu is an economic nationalist, significantly less committed to opening to the outside world and globalization than his predecessors.[32] There is, as yet, no clear public evidence to confirm such a view. On his recent trip to Europe, Hu gave very mixed signals on this score. In his widely reported November 5 speech before the French International Relations Institute, Hu noted that "globalization has become an inevitable trend" in the world economy, but surely heartened economic nationalists by claiming that "the developed nations benefit most from the economic globalization, while developing nations are facing the danger of being marginalized."[33] At the same time, in meetings with business groups, Hu endeavoured to allay their concerns about China's recent WTO accession, stressing that "China would earnestly fulfill it rights and obligations, and play its due part in promoting economic development and trade around the world."[34]

There is one noteworthy exception to Hu's general reticence on economic policy. Not surprisingly, given his long postings to Gansu, Guizhou, and Tibet, Hu Jintao has emerged as one of Beijing's most prominent spokesmen for efforts to develop impoverished inland and minority regions. In the past year, Hu has made several inspection tours to poor interior provinces including Tibet, Xinjiang, and the rustbelt and ethnic minority regions of Jilin.

Hu has used his visits to light a fire under local cadres to improve the income of local citizens. In minority regions, Hu has insisted repeatedly that dramatic increases in economic growth rates are essential to ensure long-term social stability. However, Hu has not, for the most part, used these inspection trips to display Central largesse in transferring resources to these impoverished regions. Instead, he has repeatedly stressed the need for these regions to further reform their own economies, exploit their resources bases, their tourism prospects, and their potential for trade ties with bordering countries.[35] In particular, he has called for intensifying policies of structural adjustment in agriculture.[36]

Tibet has been a bit of an exception to this relatively self-reliant strategy, however. During his fall 2001 visit to commemorate the 1951 "peaceful liberation" of Tibet, Hu stressed the economic importance of strengthening transport and communication links between Tibet and the rest of China, in particular, the Qinghai-Tibet railway. In his highly publicized speeches, Hu also underscored that during a spring 2001 Central leadership conference on policy toward Tibet, Beijing passed a blueprint requiring that "the Central Government and all localities" would "intensify their support" for Tibet, which was considered a "priority region" under the policy for developing the interior regions of the country. The goal, in Hu's words, was to move the Tibetan economy from "step-by-step" development to "leaps-and-bounds" development, and Tibetan society from "relative stability" to "lasting peace and stability."[37]

On balance, Hu's stated policy views to date have been studiedly—sometimes even painfully—within the Party's current mainstream, and hardly support the notion of either a new Gorbachev or an extreme hardliner. At this early stage, there are any number of ways that we could explain the relative lack of boldness in many of Hu's stated policy views—as a restrained but genuine reflection of his views, as a carefully crafted image to avoid frightening his "selectorate," and so on. It is certainly possible that Hu may be hiding a more reformist light under a bushel of moderation until political circumstances and his power base embolden him to act upon these convictions. On the other hand, even if Hu, at some level, envisions someday promoting a more radical vision of change for the CCP, and is just being very cautious, we must still ask ourselves how long such a cautious leader would be inclined to wait before seriously grasping the major problems China faces? He may be over-learning the negative lessons of Hu Yaobang and Zhao Ziyang's failed succession bids (even the quintessentially cautious Jiang Zemin allowed himself to drift from Deng's economic policies for a brief period in the early 1990s). If Hu remains overly deferential to a backstage Jiang for two or three years or longer, the risks could be substantial, and China could suffer from a prolonged period of indecisiveness, paralysis, drift, or unrest. More important, China's social and economic circumstances almost certainly will not permit Hu the luxury of mainstream policymaking for very long.

New Sources of Power?

Hu Jintao, like his predecessors, appears to be rising to the top by drawing on some very traditional sources of a general secretary's power—the patronage of their predecessors, their personnel support bases in the PLA, Party, government, and the like. But as traditional sources of power and social control erode in contemporary China, Hu will almost certainly have to think about forging new bases of power to sustain and expand his rule—for example, trying to build greater popular support or legitimacy, but without resorting to popular election. This topic of new sources of power has received very little discussion from scholars of reforming Communist systems. Perhaps the fates of formerly Communist and post-Communist leaders in the formerly Leninist states of Eastern Europe and central Eurasia will yield some interesting hypotheses here.

For now, we can only speculate on how Hu might use policy initiatives to generate new sources of power that could assist him in ruling through the major political changes and social upheavals that seem almost inevitable if he does indeed rule China for much of the next five to ten years. As noted above, based on the available information we simply cannot say if Hu has some "secret plan" for reviving the political structural reforms that Jiang Zemin has so carefully avoided. A number of recent Western and Hong Kong press reports have claimed that Hu has mobilized his own political reform think tanks at Qinghua University, the Central Party School, and elsewhere, and tasked them to study political reforms ranging from the incremental (gradual extension of the current village election system up to the township or even village/city level) to the radical (the prospect of reorganizing the Chinese Communist Party into a European-style "social democratic party"). This latter rumor may herald great changes. It may also be a deliberate bit of disinformation designed to fascinate and disarm potential Western critics (cf. "General Secretary Andropov speaks good English, and loves Western novels and jazz music"). At a more sophisticated level, such reports may also represent Hu's desire to emulate Zhao Ziyang in establishing a wide array of advisers who could assume the entrepreneurial risks of promoting reform policies, while the general secretary retains the autonomy to pick and choose among these initiatives when the political mood for change seems propitious.

However, if Hu Jintao wants to take an intermediate step to strengthen his popular support without crossing the "electoral Rubicon," he has at his disposal some key issues that would certainly play well with most Chinese citizens. Hu has shown, for example, a willingness to support tough crackdowns on crime. Although research has shown that anti-crime campaigns are not effective in fighting crime, as populist issues they are proven winners. Hu has also been willing to flirt with nationalist appeals, though, to date, hardly in a manner that needs to really worry Westerners. He has demonstrated this not only during the NATO bombing, when he spoke on national television and made a very emotional display of meeting the slain Xinhua reporters' bodies at the airport (in the company of his CYL allies who now head Xinhua). Hu has also occasionally given speeches to anniversary commemorations of the anti-Japanese war, and shown some skill at exploiting that always popular hotbutton issue. Finally, Hu's heavy involvement in the current anticorruption campaign is the ultimate populist issue, and Hu could win substantial popular support if he can find a self-sustaining, effective method for cracking down on official corruption that does not simply look like another leader "using" the issue as a weapon to attack his political rivals and their followers. This, of course, has always been the flaw in Jiang Zemin's and Zeng Qinghong's use of the corruption issue—that it simply looks like a ruse to demote their rivals. Whether Hu would be able and willing to effectively use it as a base for greater popular involvement in and support for the current regime is yet another question.

Notes

1. Shortly before the October 2000 Central Committee Plenum, Jiang reportedly told a meeting of Politburo members that he would step down as general secretary in 2002 and as president in 2003. Jiang declared that "the goals of the third generation have basically been achieved." Willy Wo-Lap Lam, *South China Morning Post*, October 4, 2000, p. 16. See also the *Straits Times* (Singapore), September 18, 2000, p. 62. For one of the many reports suggesting Jiang is trying to hang on, see Wen Huang and Chen Xiaoping, "Jiang Clings to His Throne," *Asian Wall Street Journal*, August 1, 2002.

2. This version of the Central Committee Plenum events has been reported in a number of sources. See "Ready for the Fourth Generation," *Economist*, October 28, 2000; David Hsieh, "He Was Not Promoted," *Straits Times*, October 22, 2000, p. 49; Li Chao, "Zeng Qinghong Has the Chance to Rise to the Core of the Party's Leadership," *Ching Chi Jih Pao* (Hong Kong), October 21, 2000, trans. *BBC Summary of World Broadcasts*, October 31, 2000. For a report from before the Plenum indicating Jiang's desire to promote Zeng Qinghong, see *Straits Times* (Singapore), September 18, 2000, p. 62.

3. I have discussed the "successor's dilemma" at greater length in "After Jiang, Hu? Can Hu Jintao Beat 'the Successor's Dilemma'?" in *China's Political Succession and Its Implications for the United States*, Woodrow Wilson International Center for Scholars, Asia Program Special Report, June 2001. Portions of this chapter have been revised and expanded from that article.

4. Several sources have sketched out this dilemma. For a particularly clear discussion with reference to China, see David Bachman "Institutions, Factions, Conservatism and Leadership Change in China" in *Leadership Change in Communist States*, ed. Raymond Taras (Boston: Unwin Hyman, 1989).

5. Nowhere was this point more dramatically illustrated than in the former Soviet Union, where Gorbachev initially did an impressive job of consolidating the traditional sources of power; but, by late 1991, he looked pathetic and irrelevant as he handed over power to Boris Yeltsin—a popularly elected Russian president whom Gorbachev had once dismissed from the traditional seat of Soviet power, the Politburo. Men like Yeltsin and Eduard Shevardnadze perfectly timed their "jump" away from relying on the "old" power sources to relying on "new" sources of power—had they turned their back on the Party leadership a few years earlier, they might well have been consigned to the kind of permanent political irrelevance China's Zhao Ziyang suffers under today. Gorbachev, by contrast, recognized the changing bases of power too late.

6. On Hu's early careers, see *South China Morning Post*, December 1, 1994, p. 13, and September 25, 1992, p. 12; *Jiushi niandai*, August 1, 1997, pp. 72–75; *New York Times*, October 20, 1992, p. A1; *Xin bao* (Hong Kong) April 14, 1997, p. 18; *New York Times*, September 23, 1985, p. A3; *Kyodo* (Hong Kong) December 10, 1984; *Xinhua*, June 25, 1985; *Straits Times* (Singapore), September 26, 1996, p. 40.

7. On Hu requesting provincial assignment to avoid criticism, see "Three New Faces for Standing Committee," *South China Morning Post*, September 25, 1992, p. 12.

8. Hsin Erh-ke charges that Hu Jintao and Organization Department Director Zhang Quanjing were both handpicked by Song and Deng Liqun and acted at their behest (*Xin bao*, April 14, 1997, p. 18). Willy Lam also stresses Song Ping as Hu's patron as well as their conservative links (*South China Morning Post*, December 1, 1994, p. 13). Another source reports that Hu returned to Beijing and began working with Song in the Organization Department by early 1992. See "Three New Faces for Standing Committee," p. 12.

9. Richard Baum contends that Song Ping was a focus of Deng's criticism during and after the Southern Tour in *Burying Mao* (Princeton: Princeton University Press, 1994), pp. 336, 344, 347.

10. On Deng's support, see, for example, James Kynge, "Aura of Dynastic Change Permeates Party," *Financial Times*, November 13, 2000, p. 2; also *Jiushi niandai*, August 1, 1997, pp. 72–75; Jiang An, *Straits Times*, September 26, 1996, p. 40.

11. In this regard, an interesting comparison can be made to the late leftist Politburo member Wang Hongwen, who rose to the top with even greater alacrity, but was unable to stay there because he had hitched his wagon to a single leftist "star."

12. Willy Lam has reported Jiang's choice of Hu to lead Congress personnel arrangements, interpreting it as a sign of Jiang's increased support for Hu since his failure to promote Zeng Qinghong. See Lam, "Waiting for Hu Jintao to Shake Off His Image as an Ornament and Reverse the Declining Reform Tendency," *Ping kuo jih pao* (Apple daily), January 31, 2001, p. A18, trans. *BBC Summary of World Broadcasts* (BBC/SWB), February 5, 2001.

13. On the turnover percentages in the Central Committee and Politiburo Standing Committee, see Willy Wo-Lap Lam, *South China Morning Post*, October 4, 2000, p. 16; *Straits Times*, September 18, 2000, p. 62; *Economist*, October 28, 2000.

14. The official text of Hu's televised speech after the embassy bombing is in Beijing Xinhua English, May 9, 1999, trans. BBC/SWB, May 9, 1999.

15. See "Vice President Hu Jintao Delivers Speech on Army, Business," Beijing, Xinhua Domestic Service, April 26, 1999, trans. BBC/SWB, May 1, 1999; also Susan Lawrence, "A Model People's Army," *South China Morning Post*, July 13, 2000.

16. On Hu's role in these cases, see the report from *Sing tao jih pao*, August 16, 2000, trans. BBC/SWB, August 17, 2000; also Mary Kwang, "Hu Jintao Leads Probe," *Straits Times*, January 22, 2000, pp. 30–31.

17. This includes two Chengdu MR Commanders (Fu Quanyou and his successor Zhang Taiheng), two Tibet Military District Commanders, two Tibet MD commissars, and more than ten other officers at the deputy-commander/commissar level in the PLA and PAP between 1988 and 1992. Based on Lexis-Nexis search of these officers' public appearances.

18. This "circular theory of power" for general secretaries was first described for the Soviet system. The classic work was Robert V. Daniels, "Soviet Politics Since Khrushchev" in *The Soviet Union Under Brezhnev and Kosygin*, ed. John W. Strong (New York: Van Nostrand-Reinhold, 1971); also Jerry F. Hough, "Gorbachev Consolidating Power," *Problems of Communism* 36, no. 4 (July–August 1987): 21–43.

19. While such biographical analysis is the staple of this kind of research, it has always rested on some shaky assumptions. Most notably, it tends to assume that any two current leaders who worked together in the same department in the past must have gotten along reasonably well with one another, and one of them probably served as patron for the other.

20. Hong Kong, *Lien ho pao*, November 29, 1994, p. 1.

21. *Ta kung pao*, April 29, 1995.

22. See, for example, the report on Hu's inspections there in 1995 (*Xinhua*, May 19, 1995).

23. In his excellent biographical analysis of the "Fourth Generation" leadership, Cheng Li correctly points out that Minister of Public Security Jia Chunwang shares a common CYL background with Hu Jintao. Still, Jia's rise to power as Minister of State Security, and later Public Security, actually predated Hu Jintao's real emergence as a Central leader. Thus, while the two men may be close, it seems very unlikely that Jia primarily owes his career to Hu.

24. I am grateful to Western Michigan University doctoral candidate Wang Jianfeng for carefully performing the computer searches necessary to compile this data.

25. According to press reports, in the past two years, Hu has paid inspection visits to Zhejiang, Jilin, Sichuan, Shanghai, Xinjiang, Hebei, Shanxi, Tibet, Hong Kong, Fujian, Henan, Shandong, Jiangsu, and Anhui.

26. See Hu's Zhejiang speech, *Xinhua*, May 8, 2001.

27. Susan Lawrence, "Primed for Power," *Far Eastern Economic Review*, February 22, 2001.

28. *Xinhua*, March 6, 1997.

29. *Xinhua*, March 6, 1997.

30. *Xinhua*, May 3, 1996, October 3, 1996, November 29, 1996, and August 24, 2001.

31. See, for example, his general comments at the Central Party School on the need to reform the financial system, noting only that the Center's percentage of revenue was

too low, and the system still too "loose" and "irrational," *Financial Times Asia Wire,* January 13, 2000; *Xinhua,* January 12, 2000.

32. Martin Sieff, "Analysis: Is China Due for Fascism?" United Press International, March 16, 2001.

33. *Xinhua,* November 5, 2001.

34. *Xinhua,* October 29 and 30, 2001.

35. See, for example, Hu's speech during his inspection of Xinjiang, *Xinhua,* June 16, 2001.

36. *Xinhua,* August 23, 2001.

37. *Xinhua,* July 19, 2001.

———— 4 ————

The Provinces

Training Ground for National Leaders or a Power in Their Own Right?

Zhiyue Bo

The purpose of this chapter is fourfold. First, it will evaluate the extent to which provinces in China serve as a training ground for national leaders.[1] Based on the demographic and political data of more than 2,600 provincial leaders in the years 1949–2001,[2] this study attempts to discover historical patterns of using provinces as a training ground for future central leaders and to predict possible future trends. Second, it explores the ties between provincial leaders and central leaders. It not only examines formal ties, such as formal meetings of significance, but also informal ties such as family connections, school networks, and work experiences in the same organizations or areas. Third, it explains some formal rules that the central leadership has used to transfer provincial leaders to the center and examines the commonalities of the past provincial leaders who are currently serving in the central leadership. Finally, the chapter tries to predict which current provincial leaders are likely to be called back to Beijing to serve in the central leadership after the Sixteenth Party Congress.

Provinces as Training Ground

The Chinese Communist Party (CCP) began to send central cadres to local governments as early as 1949 when the People's Republic of China (PRC) was founded. The composition of these "Chinese prefects," however, varies over time. In the late 1940s and early 1950s, for instance, the CCP tended to send cadres back to their home provinces. Li Xiannian, the president of the PRC between 1983 and 1988, for example, was sent back to his home province of Hubei in 1949 and served as both governor and party secretary. Other

examples include Huang Kecheng of Hunan, Zhang Dingcheng and Ye Fei of Fujian, Ye Jianying of Guangdong, and Zhou Baozhong[3] of Yunnan. In view of a well-established tradition of "avoidance" in China, this practice of sending cadres back to their home provinces seems puzzling. According to the tradition, officials were not allowed to work in their home provinces in order to avoid their family members, relatives, friends, and classmates.[4] This tradition, however, was substantially weakened in the late Qing Dynasty when the Qing court authorized Zeng Guofan to organize a Xiang army, a military force based on local connections. From this system of local militia ensued a system of warlords, who were dominant in various localities in the 1920s. Consequently, the central concern for the CCP after 1949 was no longer that local officials who worked in their home provinces might abuse their power in favor of their family members, relatives, friends, or classmates. Rather, it was how to ensure the CCP's control over the provinces. Because local forces were very strong in many provinces, the CCP sent cadres back to their home provinces to extend its control.

From the mid-1950s to the mid-1960s, the CCP called many provincial leaders back to Beijing[5] but sent very few central cadres to provinces. The exceptions were Chen Yu and Hu Yaobang. Chen was minister of Fuel In-

Table 4.1

Basic Statistics of China's Provinces, 1995

Provinces	Size	Population	GDP	GDP per capita	Agricultural output	Industrial output	Foreign investment
Beijing	16.80	12.51	139.40	11,150	16.40	173.30	1,106
Tianjin	11.30	9.42	92.00	9,767	13.30	172.50	1,586
Hebei	130.00	64.37	284.90	4,426	114.70	258.90	613
Shanxi	156.00	30.77	109.20	3,550	29.90	112.10	93
Inner Mongolia	1,280.00	22.84	83.20	3,646	37.30	64.80	88
Liaoning	145.70	40.92	279.30	6,826	76.10	354.40	1,568
Jilin	180.00	25.92	112.90	4,356	49.00	123.30	481
Heilongjiang	469.00	37.01	201.40	5,443	67.00	195.10	624
Shanghai	6.43	14.15	246.20	17,403	18.20	470.30	3,005
Jiangsu	100.00	70.66	515.50	7,295	168.60	898.70	5,325
Zhejiang	100.00	43.19	352.40	8,161	89.10	449.70	1,289
Anhui	130.00	60.13	200.30	3,332	98.00	206.30	516

Fujian	120.00	32.37	216.00	6,674	76.50	174.70	4,149
Jiangxi	166.60	40.63	120.50	2,966	63.10	99.00	345
Shandong	150.00	87.05	500.20	5,746	185.70	568.60	2,764
Henan	167.00	91.00	300.20	3,299	130.40	276.30	649
Hubei	180.00	57.72	239.10	4,143	98.80	278.50	886
Hunan	200.00	63.92	219.50	3,435	104.60	164.60	560
Guangdong	178.00	68.68	538.10	7,835	144.50	718.90	10,669
Guangxi	230.00	45.43	160.60	3,535	74.30	114.00	708
Hainan	34.00	7.24	36.40	4,988	20.20	15.40	1,184
Sichuan	570.00	113.25	353.40	3,120	152.00	322.90	619
Chongqing	82.00	30.02	47.30	1,575	n.a.	n.a.	n.a.
Guizhou	170.00	35.08	63.00	1,796	34.40	47.60	90
Yunnan	390.00	39.90	120.60	3,024	47.40	103.80	119
Tibet	1,200.00	2.40	5.60	2,332	3.50	0.80	n.a.

Table 4.1 *(continued)*

Provinces	Size	Population	GDP	GDP per capita	Agricultural output	Industrial output	Foreign investment
Shaanxi	200.00	35.14	100.00	2,845	38.10	94.80	392
Gansu	450.00	24.38	55.30	2,269	28.90	69.40	82
Qinghai	720.00	4.81	16.50	3,436	5.50	14.20	2
Ningxia	66.00	5.13	16.90	3,309	5.60	18.20	6
Xinjiang	1,600.00	16.61	83.40	5,024	41.50	76.40	188

Notes: size = 1,000 square kilometers; population = million; gross domestic product (GDP) = 1 billion yuan (current prices); GDP per capita = yuan; agr. output = gross output value of farming, forestry, animal husbandry, and fishery (1 billion yuan); industrial output = gross output value of industry at township level and above (1 billion yuan); foreign investment = total foreign capital and investment actually aquired in US$ million; n.a. = not available.

Source: Adapted from Table 1.1 in Peter T.Y. Cheung, Jae Ho Chung, and Zhimin Lin, ed., *Provincial Strategies of Economic Reform in Post-Mao China* (Armonk, New York: M.E. Sharpe, 1998), 8–9.

dustries[6] between 1949 and 1957. He was sent back to Guangdong in 1957 when Tao Zhu, an outsider governor and Party secretary, shifted his focus to the Party work. The case of Hu Yaobang, however, is noteworthy. Hu, a prominent figure in Chinese politics in the 1980s, was born in Hunan in 1915. He ran away from home and joined the Red Army when he was 14. He participated in the legendary Long March (1934–35) as a "little red devil" (*hong xiao gui*). In the 1950s, Hu was the leader of the New Democratic Youth League (it was renamed the Communist Youth League in 1957). He was sent to his home province of Hunan in 1962 as a deputy secretary. After two years, he was promoted to secretary of Shaanxi province. Evidently, this was the first case in which a potential candidate for an important position in the center was sent to the provinces for work experience. Unfortunately, he soon fell victim to the Cultural Revolution.

During the Cultural Revolution (1966–76), the center sent mostly military leaders to the provinces. Examples include Huang Yongsheng (Guangdong), Ding Sheng (Guangdong), Li Desheng (Anhui), Liang Xingchu (Sichuan), Liu Xingyuan (Qinghai, Guangdong, and Sichuan), Xu Shiyou (Jiangsu), Zeng Siyu (Hubei), and Zeng Yongya (Tibet). These leaders were not necessarily all from the central government, but they had close ties to certain central leaders. Huang Yongsheng and Ding Sheng,[7] for instance, were certainly Lin Biao's men, Liu Xingyuan and Li Desheng[8] were close to Mao's wife, Jiang Qing, and Xu Shiyou was absolutely loyal to Mao. Clearly, the Cultural Revolution was not the time to have long-term plans, and no central cadres were sent out as part of a grooming process.

In the aftermath of the Cultural Revolution, CCP leaders, especially Hu Yaobang, Deng Xiaoping, and Chen Yun, recognized the significance and urgency of succession. Hu Yaobang was probably the first central leader who raised the issue of selecting middle-aged and young cadres. In a series of report sessions on selecting excellent middle-aged and young cadres, between August 16 and September 21, 1978, Hu, the director of the Central Organization Department, emphasized the strategic importance of selecting and promoting middle-aged and young cadres.[9] On July 21, 1979, in his meeting with the standing members of the Shanghai Party Committee, Deng Xiaoping indicated that succession was a major issue, an issue for all localities and departments; that selecting relatively young cadres was a strategic and fundamental task of the Party; and that selection of cadres should be based on merit instead of seniority.[10] In his meeting with the standing members of the Navy's Party Committee on July 29, Deng stressed the importance of having a new organization line. In establishing a new organization line, Deng pointed out, the most important, most difficult, and most urgent task was to select good successors.[11] With Deng Xiaoping's instructions, the Organization Department, under the direction of Song Renqiong, held a major national organization conference from September 5 to October 7, 1979. The conference decided that the most urgent task was to strengthen the construction of leading bodies, select and foster middle-aged and young cadres, and reform the cadre system.[12] On September 29, Ye Jianying, chairman of the Standing Committee of the National People's Congress, suggested that the cadre corps should gradually be built using young people with specialized knowledge in order to fit the political task of the four modernizations.[13]

In 1980, Deng Xiaoping stressed the importance of selecting middle-aged and young cadres on two important occasions. In his speech to a cadre conference on January 16, Deng indicated that modernization construction was the core of all important tasks of the Party and that, in order to realize the four modernizations, one of the conditions was to have a contingent of cadres with socialist orientation, specialized knowledge, and capabilities.[14] At an expanded Politburo meeting on August 18, Deng presented his ideas on the reform of the Party and the State leadership system. He urged the Party to locate, foster, and promote a large number of relatively young individuals with specialized knowledge that strongly supported socialist modernization construction, and adhered to the four cardinal principles.[15]

Chen Yun raised the issue of training middle-aged and young cadres and proposed the idea of cadres on reserve, though he did not yet use the exact wording for this, *houbei ganbu*.[16] On May 8, 1981, Chen mentioned in his article, "Selecting and Fostering Middle-aged and Young Cadres Is a Task of Top Priority," that the Party should initiate a practice of selecting and fostering thousands of middle-aged and young cadres, providing them opportunities to work at different levels and offering them training and mentoring from the old cadres. The goal was to cultivate a large number of middle-aged and young cadres who would become an important reserve force from which the Party could select leading cadres at any time.[17] Chen's suggestion was strongly endorsed by Deng Xiaoping.[18]

According to Song Renqiong, the director of the Central Organization Department between December 1978 and February 1983, the four requirements—more revolutionary, younger, more knowledgeable, and professionally more competent—were formulated by Deng Xiaoping, Ye Jianying, and Chen Yun from 1978 to 1981. These requirements became the Party's policy in 1981 at the Sixth Plenary Session of the Eleventh Central Committee.[19] In order to implement this policy, the Central Organization Department produced a plan for selecting and fostering cadres including those on reserve. The most systematic presentation of this plan was a handbook published in January 1983, entitled "Questions and Answers on Party Organization Work."[20] According to this handbook, the Party not only needed to select qualified middle-aged and young cadres for current leadership posts but also to identify those who could be trained for leading posts at various levels. "To prepare a leading cadre reserve list," the handbook says, "is a major means of developing outstanding young and middle-aged cadres and choosing and identifying rightful successors. By doing this, we can have more initiative in appointing and deploying cadres and ensure the process by planned arrangement."[21]

Once a candidate is selected for a leading post, he or she will be given appropriate training. Candidates are classified into two categories and training plans are designed accordingly. For those who have extensive work experience but lack theoretical knowledge, a period of study is necessary to "fill in gaps in their theoretical, scientific, and general knowledge." Those who have good theoretical knowledge but lack practical experience should be transferred to lower levels "for tempering in order to enhance their ability in handling practical work."[22]

To provide theoretical training for cadres, the Party restored and strengthened the Party school system and gradually established a system of training. In February 1980, the Central Committee issued a memorandum on a national meeting of Party school work, indicating that the task of Party schools at all levels was to regularly train cadres in rotation and rearm cadres with the basic theories of Marxism–Leninism–Mao Zedong Thought in order to ensure the unity of the Party in ideological line and political line.[23] In February 1983, the Second National Conference of Party School Work made a decision to reform Party schools so that they could shift their focus from short-term training to regular training and produce Party and government cadres that would meet the four requirements. On May 3, 1983, the Central Committee issued a decision with regard to regular training in Party schools. According to the decision, during the Seventh Five-Year Plan period (1986–90), the Party would accomplish the following goals: (1) leading cadres of the Party and government at the provincial and perfectural levels would receive training in the Central Party School; (2) leading cadres of the Party and government at the country level would receive training at Party schools of the provinces, centrally administered municipalities, or autonomous regions; and (3) leading cadres of the Party and government under the management of the Party committees of prefectures, cities, or counties would receive training at Party schools of prefectures, cities, or counties.[24] In December 1984, the Central Committee decided to establish a central leading group of cadre education to strengthen the work of cadre training.[25]

To provide practical training for leading cadres, the Party gradually instituted a system of sending cadres down to lower levels on a regular basis.[26] Since the provincial level (including provinces, centrally administered municipalities, and autonomous regions) is the immediate lower level of the central government, the Party usually sends future leaders of the central government to the provincial units. The examples in the early 1980s include Hu Qili, Li Ruihuan, and Li Lanqing. Hu was born in 1929 in Shaanxi Province. He joined the Chinese Communist Party in 1948, when he was only 18 years old. He was a graduate of Beijing University and became an alternate secretary of the Chinese Youth League in 1964 (when Hu Yaobang was the first secretary). After the Cultural Revolution, he was elected as a secretary of the Chinese Youth League (CYL). In 1980, he was sent to Tianjin, one of the centrally administered municipalities, as mayor and secretary (there was a first secretary then). After two years, he was transferred back to Beijing to become a secretary of the Secretariat of the Central Committee of the CCP. His experience in Tianjin was preparation for his later responsibility in the center.[27] Li Ruihuan was born in 1934 in Tianjin. He started as a carpenter and joined the Party in 1959. Between 1979 and 1981, he was a secretary of the Secretariat of the Central Committee of the CYL and a vice president of the National Youth Association. He was sent to Tianjin in March 1981 as a vice mayor. He later became mayor and Party secretary of Tianjin. He was elevated to Politburo member in 1987. He was called back to Beijing in 1989 as a secretary of the Secretariat of the Central Committee of the CCP and a standing member of the Politburo. Li Lanqing was born in 1932 in Jiangsu Province. He joined the Party in 1952 and graduated from Fudan University. He was director of the Bureau of Foreign Capital Management in the Ministry of Foreign Trade and Economic Cooperation before he was transferred to Tianjin as a vice mayor in 1983. Three years later, he became a vice minister of the Foreign Trade and Economic Cooperation in Beijing.[28]

In the mid- to late 1980s, more central leaders were sent to the provinces for practical experience. This group includes Hu Jintao, Wang Zhaoguo, Zhu Rongji, Li Ximing, Song Ruixiang, Wan Shaofen, and many others. As is well known, Hu Jintao was born in 1942 in Anhui Province. He studied hydraulic engineering at Qinghua University and joined the Party in 1964. From 1974 to 1982, his position changed from a secretary (*mishu*) in the Commission of Construction in Gansu Province to secretary of the Youth League of Gansu Province. He was transferred to Beijing in 1982 as a secretary of the Secretariat of the Central Committee of the CYL. In the following year, he was elected president of the National Youth Association. After a one-year tenure as first secretary of the Central Committee of the CYL between 1984 and 1985, he was appointed Party secretary of Guizhou Province. Three years later, he was transferred to Tibet as Party secretary. In 1992, at the First Plenary Session of the Fourteenth Central Committee of the CCP, he was elevated to standing member of the Politburo and member of the Secretariat. Wang Zhaoguo was born in 1941 in Hebei Province. He joined the Party in 1965 and graduated from Harbin Industrial University. He was "discovered" by Deng Xiaoping in 1981 when Deng visited the No. 2 Motor Vehicle Plant in Wuhan where Wang was the Party secretary. Wang was subsequently transferred to Beijing as first secretary of the Central Committee of the CYL. He was appointed director of the Central Office of the Central Committee of the CCP in 1984 and promoted to member of the Secretariat of the Central Committee of the CCP in 1985. In September 1987, he was sent down to Fujian Province as acting governor (and then governor) and deputy secretary. Three years later, he was transferred back to Beijing as director of the Office of Taiwan Affairs of the State Council. Zhu Rongji was born in 1928 in Hunan, Mao Zedong's home province. He joined the Party in 1948 and graduated from Qinghua University. His political career was filled with ups and downs. He was demoted from a deputy section chief to a teacher in 1958 because of his outspokenness, and he was a victim of the Cultural Revolution. In the late 1970s and early 1980s, he worked on the Economic Commission in various capacities until he became a vice chairman of the Commission in 1983. He was transferred to Shanghai as a deputy secretary in December 1987 and became mayor in April 1988. After a year, he succeeded Jiang Zemin as Party secretary of Shanghai. And in 1991, he was called back to Beijing as a vice premier.

Not everyone who was sent to the provinces in the late 1970s and 1980s was sent for training purposes, however. Some central leaders were sent to the provinces for other purposes. Among this group are Chen Guodong, Wang Daohan, Wan Li, Lin Hujia, Xiang Nan, Jiang Zemin, Rui Xingwen, and many others. Chen Guodong and Wang Daohan were transferred to Shanghai because Shanghai was a stronghold of the Gang of Four and they were needed there to control the situation. Jiang Zemin and Rui Xingwen were sent to the same municipality with a new mission, to revive its economy.[29] Wan Li was sent to Anhui, Lin Hujia first to Tianjin and then to Beijing,[30] and Xiang Nan[31] to Fujian in order to ensure that reformers were in control of these areas.

In the 1990s, especially after the Fourteenth National Congress of the CCP (1992), massive transfers from the center to the provinces took place. Between 1990 and 1999, twenty-five cases of transfers from the center to the provinces can be identified (Table 4.2). These central leaders came from various ministries and central organizations and went to seventeen provincial units (including twelve provinces, three centrally administered municipalities, and two autonomous regions). Five of them served as Party secretaries, nine governors (including mayors of centrally administered municipalities), six deputy secretaries, and five vice governors (including vice mayors of centrally administered municipalities and vice chairmen of autonomous regions). These leaders, however, can be classified into three subgroups. One subgroup consists of central leaders who were sent to provinces for training purposes. This subgroup in-

Table 4.2

Transfers from the Center to the Provinces (1990–1999)

Name	From Ministry	Title	To Province	Title	Date
Zhang Dejiang	Civil Affairs	vice minister	Liaoning	deputy secretary	November 1990
Lin Yongsan	CPPCC	vice minister	Neimeng	vice governor	October 1991
Chen Shineng	Light Industry	vice minister	Guizhou	vice governor	January 1992
Hu Fuguo	Coal Mine Co.	minister	Shanxi	governor	August 1992
Hui Liangyu	Policy Research	vice minister	Hubei	deputy secretary	October 1992
Ma Zhongchen	Agriculture	vice minister	Henan	governor	December 1992
Ruan Chongwu	Labor	minister	Hainan	secretary	January 1993
Gao Dezhan	Forestry	minister	Tianjin	secretary	March 1993

Name	Ministry	Title	Province	New Role	Date
Linghu An	Labor	vice minister	Yunnan	deputy secretary	October 1993
Xu Yongyue	Advisory	vice minister	Hebel	deputy secretary	March 1994
Liu Qi	Metallurgy	minister	Beijing	deputy secretary	April 1994
Zheng Silin	Foreign Trade	vice minister	Jiangsu	governor	September 1994
Jiang Zhuping	Civil Aviation	vice minister	Hubei	governor	February 1995
Wei Jianxing	Discipline	secretary	Beijing	secretary	April 1995
Jin Renqing	Finance	vice minister	Beijing	vice governor	November 1995
Qu Weizhi	Electronics	vice minister	Tianjin	vice governor	January 1996
Wu Yixia	Agriculture	vice minister	Guizhou	governor	July 1996
He Guoqiang	Chemical Industry	vice minister	Fujian	governor	October 1996
Xu Youfang	Forestry	minister	Heilongjiang	secretary	July 1997
Mao Rubai	Construction	vice minister	Ningxia	secretary	August 1997
Zhang Fusen	Justice	vice minister	Beijing	deputy secretary	December 1997

Table 4.2 *(continued)*

Name	From Ministry	Title	To Province	Title	Date
Wang Qishan	People's Bank	vice minister	Guangdong	vice governor	January 1998
Li Keqiang	Youth League	minister	Henan	governor	June 1998
Niu Maosheng	Water	minister	Hebel	governor	February 1999
Bao Xuding	Planning	minister	Chongqing	mayor	August 1999

Notes: 1. Vice governors include vice mayors of cities under central control and vice chairmen of autonomous regions.
2. Ministers and vice ministers refer to ranks instead of specific titles.

Sources: Updated from Zhiyue Bo, "Managing Political Elites in Post-Deng China," *Asian Profile* 28, no. 5 (October 2000): Appendix 3.

cludes Xu Yongyue, Ma Zhongchen, Jin Renqing, Wang Qishan, Linghu An, and Li Keqiang. Another group consists of provincial leaders who had been transferred to the center for experience in the central government and then transferred back to the provinces. In this subgroup are Zhang Dejiang, Hui Liangyu, Mao Rubai, and others. And the third subgroup includes central leaders who were sent to the provinces to solve problems. One good example is Wei Jianxing. He was sent to Beijing in 1995 when the former Party secretary, Chen Xitong, was involved in corruption scandals. He was transferred back to the center two years later when another appropriate candidate for the post of Party secretary of Beijing was identified.

The trend of sending central leaders to the provinces continued in 2000 and 2001 (Table 4.3). Between January 2000 and December 2001, nine cases of transfers from the center to the provinces can be identified. These central leaders were sent to nine different provinces either as deputy secretary or secretary. Five cases are noteworthy: Wang Xudong, Li Yuanchao, Song Defu, Bai Keming, and Yu Zhengsheng.

Wang was born in 1946 in Jiangsu Province. He joined the Party in 1972 and had experience in the People's Liberation Army (PLA) and the Ministry of Electronics. He was transferred from Tianjin to the center in 1993 as a deputy director of the Central Organization Department and then to Hebei as the Party secretary in June 2000. His transfer to the province was a transfer back to the provinces.

Li was born in 1950 in Jiangsu Province. He joined the Party in 1978, graduated from Fudan University in 1982 (with a major in mathematics), and obtained his master's degree in economic management from Beijing University in 1986. He was a secretary in the Secretariat of the Central Committee of the Chinese Youth League in the 1980s (when Song Defu was the first secretary) along with Li Keqiang and Zhang Baoshun.[32] He was identified as a deputy director of the Information Office of the State Council in 1995 and, concurrently, responsible for the Fourth World Women's Conference in Beijing. He was soon promoted to vice minister of Culture in January 1996. He was transferred to Jiangsu Province in October 2000 as deputy secretary.

Song was born in 1946 in Hebei Province. He joined the Party in 1965 and spent his early career in the Air Force. He became the first secretary of the Central Committee of the CYL in 1985 and worked in the Ministry of Personnel, the Central Organization Department, and Central Editorial Office in the following years. He was transferred to Fujian Province in December 2000 as Party secretary. His transfer was probably for training purposes.

Bai was born in 1943 in Shaanxi Province. His experience in the center includes the National Education Commission, the State Council, the Central Propaganda Department, the General Office of the Central Committee of the

Table 4.3

Transfers from the Center to the Provinces (2000–2001)

Name	From Ministry	Title	To Province	Title	Date
Zhou Yongkang	Resources	minister	Sichuan	secretary	January 2000
Wang Xudong	Organization	vice minister	Hebel	secretary	June 2000
Li Yuanchao	Culture	vice minister	Jiangsu	deputy secretary	October 2000
Shi Xiushi	State Council	vice minister	Guizhou	deputy secretary	December 2000
Song Defu	Personnel	minister	Fujian	secretary	December 2000
Xu Rongkai	Flood control	vice minister	Yunnan	deputy secretary	May 2000
Bai Keming	People's Daily	minister	Hainan	secretary	August 2000
Zhang Baoshun	Xinhua News Agency	vice minister	Shanxi	deputy secretary	September 2000
Yu Zhengsheng	Construction	minister	Hubei	secretary	December 2000

Notes: 1. Vice governors include vice mayors of cities under central control and vice chairmen of autonomous regions.
2. Ministers and vice ministers refer to ranks instead of specific titles.

Sources: People's Daily, www.people.com.cn, January 1, 2000–December 7, 2001.

CCP, and *People's Daily*. He was sent to Hainan in August 2001 as Party secretary.[33]

Finally, Yu Zhengsheng was born in 1945 in Zhejiang Province. He joined the Party in 1964 and graduated from Harbin Military Engineering College in 1968. He worked in the Ministry of Electronic Industries from 1975 to 1985 and became the mayor of Yantai in November 1985. After twelve years in Shandong Province as mayor of Yantai and Qingdao, he was transferred back to the center as vice minister of Construction in September 1997. He was soon promoted to minister of Construction in March 1998. Yu was appointed Party secretary of Hubei on December 7, 2001 to replace the retiring Jiang Zhuping.

It is very likely that the current trend of sending promising young central leaders to the provinces will continue after the Sixteenth National Party Congress.

Maintaining Ties with Central Leaders

Membership in the CCP Central Committee

Provincial leaders maintain their ties with Beijing in several ways. First, many provincial leaders are also members of the Central Committee of the CCP (either full members or alternate members) and have contact with central leaders when they attend plenary sessions of the Central Committee (CC). This is the case for deputy secretaries and vice governors as well if they are also members of the Central Committee (mostly alternate members). Between September 1982 and October 2001, there were four national congresses of the CCP, twenty-nine plenary sessions, and one national conference (Table 4.4). Those provincial leaders with CC membership had opportunities to interact with central leaders on these occasions. Moreover, some provincial leaders are in fact central leaders in their capacity as members of the Politburo. Their contact with other central leaders is much more frequent than that of other provincial leaders.

It should be indicated, however, that not every provincial Party secretary or governor is a full member of the Central Committee. In the past twenty years (1982–2001), the Party center has been trying to install full members of the Central Committee as either provincial Party secretaries or governors.[34] It has been more successful with Party secretaries than with governors. As Figure 4.1 indicates, out of twenty-nine to thirty-one provincial Party secretaries each year, there have been between nineteen and thirty-one full members of the Central Committee. During these twenty years, full member provincial Party secretaries were 85.5 percent of the total on average, with a range between 66

Table 4.4

The National Congresses of the Chinese Communist Party (CCP) and the Plenums of the Central Committees (CCs) (1982–2001)

CCP Twelfth National Congress, Beijing	September 1–11, 1982
First Plenum, Twelfth CC, Beijing[a]	September 12–13, 1982
Second Plenum, Twelfth CC, Beijing	October 11–12, 1983
Third Plenum, Twelfth CC, Beijing	October 20, 1984
Fourth Plenum, Twelfth CC, Beijing	September 16, 1985
CCP National Conference, Beijing	September 18–23, 1985
Fifth Plenum, Twelfth CC, Beijing	September 24, 1985
Sixth Plenum, Twelfth CC, Beijing	September 28, 1986
Seventh Plenum, Twelfth CC, Beijing	October 20, 1987
CCP Thirteenth National Congress, Beijing	October 25–November 1, 1987
First Plenum, Thirteenth CC, Beijing[a]	November 2, 1987
Second Plenum, Thirteenth CC, Beijing	March 15–19, 1988
Third Plenum, Thirteenth CC, Beijing	September 26–30, 1988
Fourth Plenum, Thirteenth CC, Beijing	June 23–24, 1989
Fifth Plenum, Thirteenth CC, Beijing	November 6–9, 1989
Sixth Plenum, Thirteenth CC, Beijing	March 9–12, 1990
Seventh Plenum, Thirteenth CC, Beijing	December 25–30, 1990
Eighth Plenum, Thirteenth CC, Beijing	November 25–29, 1991
Ninth Plenum, Thirteenth CC, Beijing	October 5–9, 1992
CCP Fourteenth National Congress, Beijing	October 12–18, 1992
First Plenum, Fourteenth CC, Beijing[a]	October 19, 1992
Second Plenum, Fourteenth CC, Beijing	March 5–7, 1993
Third Plenum, Fourteenth CC, Beijing	November 11–14, 1993
Fourth Plenum, Fourteenth CC, Beijing	September 25–28, 1994
Fifth Plenum, Fourteenth CC, Beijing	September 25–28, 1995

Sixth Plenum, Fourteenth CC, Beijing	October 7–10, 1996
Seventh Plenum, Fourteenth CC, Beijing	September 6–9, 1997
CCP Fifteenth National Congress, Beijing	September 12–18, 1997
First Plenum, Fifteenth CC, Beijing[a]	September 19, 1997
Second Plenum, Fifteenth CC, Beijing	February 25–26, 1998
Third Plenum, Fifteenth CC, Beijing	October 12–14, 1998
Fourth Plenum, Fifteenth CC, Beijing	September 19–22, 1999
Fifth Plenum, Fifteenth CC, Beijing	October 9–11, 2000
Sixth Plenum, Fifteenth CC, Beijing	September 24–26, 2001

Note:
[a]First Plenums are usually held immediately after national congresses for the purpose of electing new Politburo and other central organs.

percent and 100 percent. There are significant historical variations, however. In the early 1980s, for instance, only 66–86 percent of Party secretaries were full members of the CC. The rest were nonmembers. In 1982, six Party secretaries (20.7 percent) were not CC members. Two years later, the number of nonmembers increased to ten—more than one-third of the total number of Party secretaries at the time. The Thirteenth National Party Congress (1987) reduced the number of nonmember Party secretaries to zero, but subsequent changes brought in a number of alternate CC members and nonmembers in the following years. The Fifteenth Party Congress (1997) managed to install full CC members as Party secretaries in all but one case (Ruan Chongwu of Hainan). But in three years, first alternate members and then nonmembers were appointed Party secretaries. In 2001, there were twenty-two full members, eight alternate members, and one nonmember among provincial Party secretaries.

It is more difficult to install full CC members as governors because the Party does not have complete control over the process of selecting governors.[35] During the past twenty years, full-member governors comprised only about 54 percent of the total on average, with 1983 and 1984 the lowest at 31 percent and 1987 the highest at 83 percent (Figure 4.2). In other words, the probability that a governor is not a full member of the CC is much higher than that of a Party secretary. In fact, in some years (especially in the 1980s and early 1990s), the majority of governors were not even alternate members of the CC. In 1983 and 1984, for instance, nineteen out of twenty-nine governors (65.5 percent)

Figure 4.1. **Provincial Party Secretaries in the Central Committee (1982–2001)**

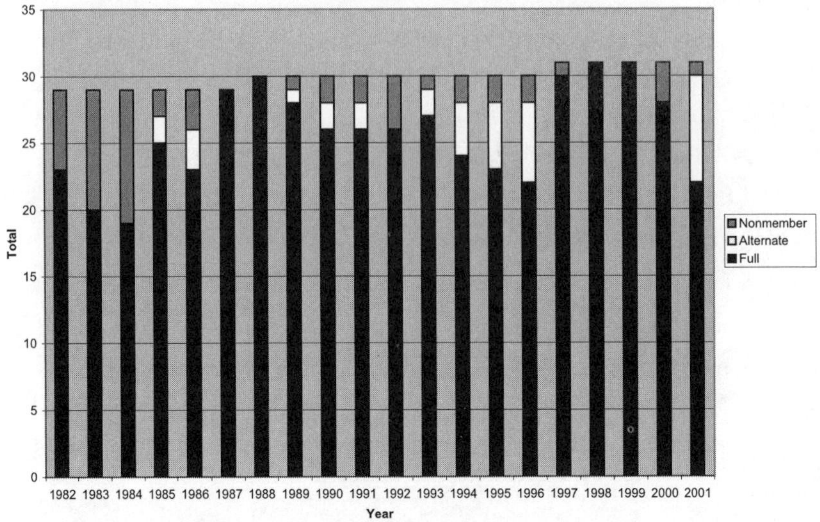

were not members of the Central Committee, full or alternate. In 1990 and 1991, twelve out of thirty governors (40 percent) were not members of the Central Committee. In the following years, the number of nonmembers was somewhat reduced, but the number of full members did not increase significantly. A noticeable pattern for both Party secretaries and governors in these years is that the number of full members tended to peak around the year when the National Party Congress was held (1987, 1992, and 1997) and then declined in subsequent years. In 2001, there were fifteen full members, nine alternate members, and seven nonmembers among governors.

National People's Congress Meetings

Second, provincial leaders also go to Beijing to attend meetings of the National People's Congress (NPC) as deputies. Between June 1983 and October 2001, there were four congresses and nineteen meetings (Table 4.5). Provincial Party secretaries and governors usually use the press conferences on these occasions to impress central leaders with their accomplishments and ambitious plans. At the most recent meeting (March 5–15, 2001), for instance, there was a forum of provincial Party secretaries and governors in *People's Daily*, the mouthpiece of the CCP.[36] Lu Ruihua, governor of Guangdong, indicated that this year was a year of regulating market economic order in the province. Li Changchun, Party secretary of the province

Figure 4.2. **Governors in the Central Committee (1982–2001)**

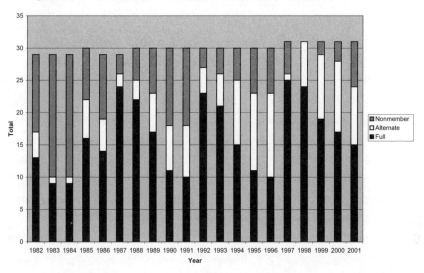

and a Politburo member, stressed the primacy of increasing peasants' income. Li Keqiang, a young governor for a large province (Henan), revealed his plan for the province in the new century. Liu Qi, mayor of Beijing, vowed to turn Beijing into a world-class metropolitan city. Xu Kuangdi, mayor of Shanghai, emphasized the importance of strengthening comprehensive capacity for Shanghai through a new round of development. Since these meetings are open to the media, provincial leaders tend to get more publicity at them than they do at Party meetings. Moreover, non-CC member provincial leaders usually are not excluded from NPC meetings. For instance, Bo Xilai (governor of Liaoning), Zhang Yunchuan (governor of Hunan), and Zhang Zhongwei (governor of Sichuan) were non-CC members, but they were deputies to the NPC. Shi Xiushi, governor of Guizhou, was neither a CC member nor a deputy, but he showed up at the NPC meeting and announced his plan for Guizhou's development in the next five years.

Training Courses in Beijing

Third, provincial leaders may have contacts with central leaders when they are enrolled in training courses in Beijing. As mentioned earlier, Party schools were restored in the late 1970s in order to train cadres in theories of Marxism–Leninism–Mao Zedong Thought. In recent years, the theories have also included Deng Xiaoping's theory and Jiang Zemin's theoretical construct, the "Three Represents."[37] Provincial leaders received their training at the Central

Table 4.5

The National People's Congresses (NPCs) and Their Meetings (1983–2001)

Sixth National People's Congress, Beijing	
First Meeting, Sixth NPC, Beijing	June 6–21, 1983
Second Meeting, Sixth NPC, Beijing	May 15–31, 1984
Third Meeting, Sixth NPC, Beijing	March 27–April 10, 1985
Fourth Meeting, Sixth NPC, Beijing	March 25–April 12, 1986
Fifth Meeting, Sixth NPC, Beijing	March 25–April 11, 1987
Seventh National People's Congress, Beijing	
First Meeting, Seventh NPC, Beijing	March 25–April 13, 1988
Second Meeting, Seventh NPC, Beijing	March 20–April 4, 1989
Third Meeting, Seventh NPC, Beijing	March 20–April 4, 1990
Fourth Meeting, Seventh NPC, Beijing	March 25–April 9, 1991
Fifth Meeting, Seventh NPC, Beijing	March 20–April 3, 1992
Eighth National People's Congress, Beijing	
First Meeting, Eighth NPC, Beijing	March 15–31, 1993
Second Meeting, Eighth NPC, Beijing	March 10–22, 1994
Third Meeting, Eighth NPC, Beijing	March 5–18, 1995
Fourth Meeting, Eighth NPC, Beijing	March 1–17, 1996
Fifth Meeting, Eighth NPC, Beijing	March 1–15, 1997
Ninth National People's Congress, Beijing	
First Meeting, Ninth NPC, Beijing	March 5–19, 1998
Second Meeting, Ninth NPC, Beijing	March 5–16, 1999
Third Meeting, Ninth NPC, Beijing	March 5–16, 2000
Fourth Meeting, Ninth NPC, Beijing	March 5–15, 2001

Party School, the National College of Administration, and National Defense University in Beijing. According to the decision issued by the Central Committee in March 1983, provincial leaders would be trained in the Central Party School starting from the Seventh Five-Year Plan Period (1986–90). Beginning in the mid-1980s, provincial leaders, along with ministerial leaders, were trained in classes specially designed for them (*shengbu ji ganbu jinxiuban*). In the past fifteen years (1985–2001), thirty classes of provincial and ministerial cadres have graduated from the Central Party School. Moreover, the Central Committee also organized other special classes for provincial and ministerial leaders. After the Fourteenth Party Congress was held, for instance, the Central Committee started a series of special training classes for chief leading cadres at the provincial (ministerial) level on Deng Xiaoping's theory of building socialism with Chinese characteristics. Between October 1993 and May 1994, four classes graduated. Between 1997 and 2000, two more classes on Deng Xiaoping's theory and one class on the spirit of the Fifteenth Party Congress were designed for newly elected members of the Central Committee, many of whom were provincial leaders.

Provincial leaders also attend classes at the National College of Administration and National Defense University. In the past two years, the National College of Administration has held special classes for provincial and ministerial cadres on finance, administration in accordance with the law, implementing the strategy of developing the West, and other topics.

During the Ninth Five-Year Plan Period (1996–2000), provincial and ministerial leaders attended classes in these three schools more than 1,800 people-times.[38] In these five years, more than 1,000 people-times of provincial and ministerial cadres attended twenty-two classes on special topics such as finance and revenue and taxation. Among them, two classes were specially designed for chief provincial and ministerial leaders and were attended by chief provincial and ministerial leaders 500 people-times. These classes have provided ample opportunities for provincial leaders to interact with central leaders.

Provincial Inspection Tours

Finally, provincial leaders may have contacts with central leaders when central leaders take inspection tours of their provinces. Jiang Zemin, for instance, visited Guangdong, Jiangsu, Zhejiang, Shanghai, Beijing, Ningxia, Gansu, Heilongjiang, Jilin, Anhui, and Shanxi between June 2000 and August 2001. Leaders in these provincial units had opportunities to report to Jiang directly.

Groups with Stronger Central Ties

It is hard to locate identifiable factions among central leaders because it is a taboo in China to form factions. Yet several groups of provincial leaders have stronger ties to central leaders than do other provincial leaders. The first is a group of "Chinese prefects," a group of provincial leaders with central origins.

They started their careers in the central government and were sent to provincial units to gain experience for more important positions in the center. In this group, a particular subgroup is noteworthy: youth league cadres. A list of familiar names appears in this subgroup: Song Defu (Party secretary of Fujian), Li Keqiang (governor of Henan), Li Yuanchao (deputy secretary of Jiangsu), and Zhang Baoshun (deputy secretary of Shanxi). Zhang is the most recent example of sending promising young cadres to the provinces for training purposes. Zhang was born in 1950 in Qinghuangdao, Hebei Province, and joined the Party in 1971 (the Cultural Revolution generation). He was transferred to Beijing in 1978 as a secretarial worker in the Central Committee of the CYL. He was promoted to alternate secretary of the Secretariat of the CYL in 1982 and to secretary in 1985. He became president of the National Youth Association (a title Hu Jintao held in 1983) in 1991 and was appointed vice director of the Xinhua News Agency in 1993. In September 2001, he was transferred to Shanxi as deputy secretary. Neither Li Yuanchao nor Zhang Baoshun are members of the Fifteenth Central Committee, but both are likely to enter the Sixteenth Central Committee and will be called back to the center in the future.

The second is a group of princelings, children of an older generation of revolutionary cadres. In this group, are Xi Jinping (governor of Fujian) and Bo Xilai (governor of Liaoning). The third group consists of directors of organization departments of provincial Party committees. They have more frequent contacts with the Central Organization Department (COD) than provincial leaders themselves. Finally, cadres from Shanghai are connected to Jiang Zemin either directly or through other central leaders of Shanghai origin.[39]

Transferring to the Center

Groups Most Likely to Transfer

Three groups of provincial leaders are likely to be called back to serve in the central leadership. The first is the group of "Chinese prefects," provincial leaders with central origins. This group of cadres has been groomed for central leading posts, and their experience in the provinces is a part of this grooming process. Among current chief provincial leaders, sixteen can be identified as "Chinese prefects": eight Party secretaries and eight governors (Table 4.6). The second is a group of provincial leaders from elite provinces,[40] provinces that have representation in the Politburo. In particular, cadres from Shanghai have very good chances to land central leadership posts. Between 1987 and 2001, eight provincial units were represented in the Politburo at one time or another. In addition to three centrally administered municipalities (Beijing,

Table 4.6

China's Provincial Leaders (October 2001)

Provinces[a]	Party secretary	Birth	Center	Governor[b]	Birth	Center
Beijing	Jia Qinglin	1940	center	Liu Qi	1942	center
Tianjin	Zhang Lichang	1939	province	Li Shenglin	1946	province
Hebei	Wang Xudong	1946	center	Niu Maosheng	1939	center
Shanxi	Tian Chengping	1945	center	Liu Zhenhua	1943	province
Inner Mongolia	Chu Bo	1944	province	Wuyunqimuge	1942	province
Liaoning	Wen Shizhen	1940	province	Bo Xilai	1949	province
Jilin	Wang-Yunkun	1942	province	Hong Hu	1940	center
Heilongjiang	Xu Youfang	1939	center	Song Fatang	1940	province
Shanghai	Huang Ju	1938	province	Xu Kuangdi	1937	province
Jiangsu	Hui Liangyu	1944	province	Ji Yunshi	1945	province
Zhejiang	Zhang Dejiang	1946	province	Chai Songyue	1941	province

Table 4.6 (continued)

Provinces[a]	Party secretary	Birth	Center	Governor[b]	Birth	Center
Anhui	Wang Taihua	1945	province	Xu Zhonglin	1943	province
Fujian	Song Defu	1946	center	Xi Jinping	1953	center
Jiangxi	Meng Jianzhu	1947	province	Huang Zhiquan	1942	province
Shandong	Wu Guanzheng	1938	province	Li Chunting	1936	province
Henan	Chen Kuiyuan	1941	province	Li Keqiang	1955	center
Hubei	Jiang Zhuping	1937	center	Zhang Guoguang	1945	province
Hunan	Yang Zhengwu	1941	province	Zhang Yunchuan	1946	center
Guangdong	Li Changchun	1944	province	Lu Ruihua	1938	province
Guangxi	Cao Bochun	1941	province	Li Zhaozuo	1944	province
Hainan	Bai Keming	1943	center	Wang Xiaofeng	1944	province
Chongqing	He Guoqiang	1943	province	Bao Xuding	1939	province

Sichuan	Zhou Yongkang	1942	center	Zhang Zhongwei	1942	province
Guizhou	Qian Yunlu	1944	province	Shi Xiushi	1942	center
Yunnan	Bai Enpei	1946	province	Xu Rongkai	1942	center
Tibet	Guo Jinlong	1947	province	Legqog	1944	province
Shaanxi	Li Jianguo	1946	province	Cheng Andong	1936	province
Gansu	Song Zhaosu	1941	province	Lu Hao	1947	province
Qinghai	Su Rong	1948	province	Zhao Leji	1957	province
Ningxia	Mao Rubai	1938	province	Ma Qizhi	1943	province
Xinjiang	Wang Lequan	1944	province	Abulati Abdurexit	1942	province

Notes:

[a]This refers to provinces, centrally administered cities, and autonomous regions. Hong Kong, Macao, and Taiwan are excluded.
[b]This includes governors, mayors of centrally administered cities, and chairmen of autonomous regions.

Tianjin, and Shanghai), there were four provinces (Sichuan, Shandong, Guangdong, and Henan) and one autonomous region (Tibet). Tibet's representation in the Politburo in 1992 was largely due to the holder of the position of its Party secretary, Hu Jintao. Therefore, it is unlikely that Tibet will have Politburo representation in the future. Henan is in a similar situation. It had Politburo representation in 1997 simply because of Li Changchun, who was soon transferred to Guangdong. At the Politburo of the Sixteenth Central Committee, the following provincial units are likely to retain their seats: Beijing, Shanghai, Shandong, and Guangdong. In addition, Tianjin and Chongqing might be added to the list. It is less likely for Sichuan to regain its lost seat at the Politburo, and it is even less likely for Henan to regain its status as an elite province. Therefore, future elite provinces would include four centrally administered municipalities (Beijing, Shanghai, Tianjin, and Chongqing) and two provinces (Guangdong and Shandong). Finally, a group of senior provincial leaders reaching the retirement age of 65 will also likely be called back to the center to serve in either the National People's Congress (NPC) or the Chinese People's Political Consultative Conference (CPPCC). Since China's cadre system has been institutionalized, it is rare that a provincial leader could stay in power beyond his or her retirement age. As these provincial leaders are political assets with extensive knowledge of various provinces, they are often mobilized to the center to serve as decision makers in the NPC or advisors in the CPPCC.

Commonalities in Background

It is becoming increasingly difficult to generalize about the background of the past provincial leaders who are currently serving in the central leadership. This is because provincial experience has become such an important credential for central leaders that almost everyone has to have such experience. For instance, among seven standing members of the current Politburo, only Li Peng has no provincial experience. All the others (Jiang Zemin, Zhu Rongji, Li Ruihuan, Hu Jintao, Wei Jianxing, and Li Lanqing) have served in the provinces, and, except for Li Lanqing, all were provincial Party secretaries in the past. Among these six standing members with provincial experience, five were from centrally administered municipalities (Shanghai, Beijing, and Tianjin). Over half of the Politburo members (14 out of 21)[41] have provincial experience or are currently provincial leaders, and the two alternate Politburo members have both served in provincial units before. Over half (4 out of 7) of the members of the Secretariat of the Central Committee have previous working experience in the provinces. Half of the vice premiers have worked in provinces, and 60 percent (3 out of 5) of the State Councilors have provincial experience. And more than one-third (12 out of 29) of ministers in the State Council have served either on provincial Party committees or provincial governments. In the Standing Committee of the NPC, however, relatively fewer have provincial experience: 23.5 percent (4 out of 17) of the vice chairmen have served in the provinces and 16.9 percent (23 out of 136) of the standing members have provincial experience. In the Standing Committee of the CPPCC, on the other hand, half of the vice chairmen have served in the provinces but only 11 percent (33 out of 299) of standing members have worked as provincial leaders previously.

Nevertheless, the current central leaders who have served as provincial leaders before do have some interesting patterns in their backgrounds (Table 4.7). In the following section, these leaders are presented in terms of age, gender, Party affiliation, number of years as a Communist Party member, education, nationality, home province, and provincial experience.

Generally Old

First, these leaders are generally old, with a wide range of ages. In 2002, the average age of the group will be 67.5 years old, with the youngest at 53 (Zhou Shengxian) and the oldest (Ngapoi Ngawang Jigme) at 92. Therefore, the group as a whole is over the retirement age for chief provincial leaders (65). Of course, this is not surprising because many of them, especially standing members of the NPC and the CPPCC, came to Beijing after their retirement. Among different age groups, 66 (60.55 percent) were born between 1930 and 1939 and 16 (14.68 percent) between 1920 and 1929 (Table 4.8). In other words, 77 percent of the total will be 63 years old or older in 2002, and only 22.94 percent (twenty-five leaders) will be 62 years old or younger in 2002.

Predominantly Male

Second, this group is predominantly male. Among 109 leaders, 102 (93.6 percent) are males and only 7 (6.4 percent) are females. On average, males are older (67.8 years old) than females (63 years old). Among these 7 female central leaders with provincial experience, 5 (71.4 percent) are standing members of either the NPC or the CPPCC and only 2 (28.6 percent) are in the executive part of the central government.

Veteran Chinese Communist Party Members

Third, although the majority of the central leaders are Chinese Communist Party (CCP) members, some are noncommunists. Fourteen people (12.8 percent) in this group do not belong to the CCP. Clearly, it is easier to find a

Table 4.7

Current Central Leaders with Provincial Experience

Name	Title	Provincial experience
Jiang Zemin[a]	General secretary and president	Shanghai, mayor and secretary
Zhu Rongji[a]	Premier	Shanghai, mayor and secretary
Li Ruihuan[a]	Chairman of the Chinese People's Political Consultative Conference (CPPCC)	Tianjin, mayor and secretary
Hu Jintao[a]	Vice president	Guizhou, secretary Tibet, secretary
Wei Jianxing[a]	Secretary of the Commission of Disciplinary Inspection	Beijing, secretary
Li Lanqing[a]	Vice premier	Tianjin, vice mayor
Wu Bangguo[b]	Vice premier	Shanghai, secretary
Li Tieying[b]	President of the Chinese Academy of Social Sciences	Liaoning, deputy secretary
Jiang Chunyun[b]	Vice Chairman of the Ninth National People's Congress (NPC)	Shandong, secretary
Luo Gan[b]	Secretary of the Secretariat	Henan, deputy secretary
Jia Qinglin[b]	Politburo member	Beijing, secretary
Li Changchun[b]	Politburo member	Guangdong, secretary
Wu Guanzheng[b]	Politburo member	Shandong, secretary
Huang Ju[b]	Politburo member	Shanghai, secretary
Zeng Qinghong[c]	Secretary of the Secretariat and Director of the Central Organization Department	Shanghai, deputy secretary
Wu Yi[c]	State Councilor	Beijing, vice mayor
Ismail Amat	State Councilor	Xinjiang, chairman

Name	Title	Provincial experience
Wang Zhongyu	State Councilor and Director of Central Office of the State Council	Jilin, governor
Chen Zhili	Minister of Education	Shanghai, deputy secretary
Li Dezhu	Minister of Nationality Affairs	Jilin, vice governor
Jia Chunwang	Minister of Public Security	Beijing, deputy secretary
Xu Yongyue	Minister of National Security	Hebei, deputy secretary
Doje Cering	Minister of Civil Affairs	Tibet, chairman
Zhang Fusen	Minister of Justice	Xinjiang, deputy secretary Beijing, deputy secretary
Zhang Xuezhong	Minister of Personnel	Gansu, vice governor Tibet, deputy secretary
Tian Fengshan	Minister of National Resources	Heilongjiang, governor
Wu Jichuan	Minister of Information Industry	Henan, deputy secretary
Du Qinglin	Minister of Agriculture	Hainan, secretary
Sun Jiazheng	Minister of Culture	Jiangsu, deputy secretary
Zhang Weiqing	Chairman of the National Family Planning Commission	Shanxi, vice governor
Tian Congming	Director of Xinhua News Agency	Neimeng, deputy secretary Tibet, deputy secretary
Wan Xueyuan	Director of Foreign Experts Bureau	Zhejiang, governor
Chen Bangzhu	Director of National Survey Bureau	Hunan, governor

Table 4.7 *(continued)*

Name	Title	Provincial experience
Wang Qishan	Director of the Economic Reform Office	Guangdong, vice governor
Zhou Shengxian	Director of National Forest Bureau	Ningxia, vice governor
Jin Renqing	Director of the National Tax General Bureau	Yunnan, vice governor Beijing, vice mayor and deputy secretary
Liu Jianfeng	China Civil Aviation General Bureau	Hainan, governor
Pagbalha Geleg Namgyai	Vice chairman of the Ninth NPC	Tibet, vice chairman
Buhe	Vice chairman of the Ninth NPC	Inner Mongolia, chairman
Tomur Dawamat	Vice chairman of the Ninth NPC	Xinjiang, chairman
Wan Shaofen	Standing member of the Ninth NPC	Jiangxi, secretary
Wang Chaowen	Standing member of the Ninth NPC	Guizhou, vice governor Guizhou, governor
Yin Kesheng	Standing member of the Ninth NPC	Qinghai, vice governor Qinghai, secretary
Bai Qingcai	Standing member of the Ninth NPC	Shanxi, vice governor Shaanxi, governor
Wu Jinhua	Standing member of the Ninth NPC	Tibet, secretary
Gyaincain Norbu	Standing member of the Ninth NPC	Tibet, deputy secretary Tibet, chairman
Ruan Chongwu	Standing member of the Ninth NPC	Shanghai, vice mayor Shanghai, deputy secretary Hainan, governor and secretary

Name	Title	Provincial experience
Li Boyong	Standing member of the Ninth NPC	Sichuan, vice governor
Wang Jialiu	Standing member of the Ninth NPC	Beijing, deputy secretary
Zhang Haoruo	Standing member of the Ninth NPC	Sichuan, governor
Chen Guangyi	Standing member of the Ninth NPC	Gansu, governor Fujian, secretary
Chen Kuizun	Standing member of the Ninth NPC	Jiangxi, vice governor
Feng Henggao	Standing member of the Ninth NPC	Guangxi, vice governor
Luo Shangcai	Standing member of the Ninth NPC	Guizhou, vice governor
Zhao Di	Standing member of the Ninth NPC	Henan, deputy secretary
Huanjue Cenam	Standing member of the Ninth NPC	Qinghai, deputy secretary
Gu Jinchi	Standing member of the Ninth NPC	Sichuan, vice governor Sichuan, deputy secretary Gansu, secretary Liaoning, secretary
Gao Dezhan	Standing member of the Ninth NPC	Jilin, vice governor Jilin, governor Tianjin, secretary
Guo Zhenqian	Standing member of the Ninth NPC	Hubei, vice governor Hubei, deputy secretary Hubei, governor
Ge Hongsheng	Standing member of the Ninth NPC	Zhejiang, governor
Pu Chaozhu	Standing member of the Ninth NPC	Yunnan, governor Yunnan, secretary
Wang Xueping	Standing member of the Ninth NPC	Hainan, vice governor

Table 4.7 *(continued)*

Name	Title	Provincial experience
Jia Zhijie	Standing member of the Ninth NPC	Gansu, deputy secretary Gansu, governor Hubei, governor Hubei, secretary
Ye Xuanping	Vice chairman of the Ninth CPPCC	Guangdong, vice governor Guangdong, governor
Yang Rudai	Vice chairman of the Ninth CPPCC	Sichuan, vice governor Sichuan, deputy secretary Sichuan, secretary
Wang Zhaoguo	Vice chairman of the Ninth CPPCC	Fujian, governor
Ngapoi Ngawang Jigme	Vice chairman of the Ninth CPPCC	Tibet, vice chairman Tibet, chairman
Li Guixian	Vice chairman of the Ninth CPPCC	Liaoning, vice governor Liaoning, secretary Anhui, secretary
Chen Junsheng	Vice chairman of the Ninth CPPCC	Heilongjiang, deputy secretary
Sun Fuling	Vice chairman of the Ninth CPPCC	Beijing, vice mayor
Hu Qili	Vice chairman of the Ninth CPPCC	Tianjin, mayor
Chen Jinhua	Vice chairman of the Ninth CPPCC	Shanghai, vice mayor
Cho Namgi	Vice chairman of the Ninth CPPCC	Jilin, vice governor Jilin, deputy secretary

Name	Title	Provincial experience
Mao Zhiyong	Vice chairman of the Ninth CPPCC	Hunan, deputy secretary Hunan, governor Hunan, secretary Jiangxi, secretary
Bai Lichen	Vice chairman of the Ninth CPPCC	Liaoning, vice governor Ningxia, chairman
Zhou Tienong	Vice chairman of the Ninth CPPCC	Heilongjiang, vice governor
Wang Wenyuan	Vice chairman of the Ninth CPPCC	Liaoning, vice governor
Wang Julu	Standing member of the Ninth CPPCC	Liaoning, deputy secretary
Wang Senhao	Standing member of the Ninth CPPCC	Shanxi, governor
Uliji	Standing member of the Ninth CPPCC	Inner Mongolia, deputy secretary Inner Mongolia, chairman
Senqin Losanglisam	Standing member of the Ninth CPPCC	Tibet, vice chairman
Feng Yuanwei	Standing member of the Ninth CPPCC	Sichuan, deputy secretary
Quan Shuren	Standing member of the Ninth CPPCC	Liaoning, governor Liaoning, secretary
Zhuang Gonghui	Standing member of the Ninth CPPCC	Tianjin, vice mayor
An Zhendong	Standing member of the Ninth CPPCC	Heilongjiang, vice governor
Keyim Bahawdun	Standing member of the Ninth CPPCC	Xinjiang, vice chairman Xinjiang, deputy secretary

Table 4.7 *(continued)*

Name	Title	Provincial experience
He Zhukang	Standing member of the Ninth CPPCC	Henan, vice governor Henan, governor Jilin, governor Jilin, secretary
Shen Zulun	Standing member of the Ninth CPPCC	Zhejiang, vice governor Zhejiang, governor
Song Hanliang	Standing member of the Ninth CPPCC	Xinjiang, vice chairman Xinjiang, secretary
Song Defu	Standing member of the Ninth CPPCC	Fujian, secretary
Zhang Boxing	Standing member of the Ninth CPPCC	Shaanxi, vice governor Shaanxi, governor Shaanxi, secretary
He Zhiqiang	Standing member of the Ninth CPPCC	Yunnan, governor
Yue Qifeng	Standing member of the Ninth CPPCC	Hebei, deputy secretary Hebei, governor Liaoning, governor Heilongjiang, secretary
Jin Jian	Standing member of the Ninth CPPCC	Beijing, deputy secretary
Jin Jipeng	Standing member of the Ninth CPPCC	Qinghai, governor
Hu Ping	Standing member of the Ninth CPPCC	Fujian, vice governor Fujian, deputy secretary Fujian, governor
Hou Jie	Standing member of the Ninth CPPCC	Heilongjiang, vice governor Heilongjiang, deputy secretary Heilongjiang, governor

Jiang Xinzhen	Standing member of the Ninth CPPCC	Shaanxi, vice governor
Xu Caidong	Standing member of the Ninth CPPCC	Guizhou, vice governor
Gao Zhanxiang	Standing member of the Ninth CPPCC	Hebei, deputy secretary
Huang Huang	Standing member of the Ninth CPPCC	Anhui, secretary Jiangxi, vice governor Ningxia, secretary
Liang Jinquan	Standing member of the Ninth CPPCC	Yunnan, deputy secretary
Jiang Minkuan	Standing member of the Ninth CPPCC	Sichuan, vice governor Sichuan, deputy secretary Sichuan, governor
Fu Xishou	Standing member of the Ninth CPPCC	Anhui, governor
Xie Lijuan	Standing member of the Ninth CPPCC	Shanghai, vice mayor
Lu Ming	Standing member of the Ninth CPPCC	Gansu, vice governor
Lu Rongjing	Standing member of the Ninth CPPCC	Anhui, deputy secretary Anhui, governor Anhui, secretary
Zhang Rongming	Standing member of the Ninth CPPCC	Liaoning, vice governor
Shu Shengyou	Standing member of the Ninth CPPCC	Jiangxi, vice governor Jiangxi, governor

Notes:
[a]Standing member of the Politburo
[b]Member of the Politburo
[c]Alternate Member of the Politburo
NPC = National People's Congress
CPPCC = Chinese People's Political Consultative Conference

noncommunist in this group of leaders than to find a female. However, those noncommunist leaders are generally older (70 years old) than communist leaders (67 years old). And two out of seven female leaders are noncommunists.

Fourth, these central leaders are mostly veteran party members (Table 4.9). About 16 percent of them joined the Party before 1949 (between 1940 and 1948), and 71 percent of them joined the Party before the Cultural Revolution (between 1949 and 1965). In other words, more than 87 percent of the current central leaders with provincial experience joined the Party before the Cultural Revolution. Only about 12 percent of them joined the Party during the Cultural Revolution (1966–76). And even fewer (1 percent) have joined the Party ever since. In fact, only Wang Qishan, former vice governor of Guangdong Province, joined the Party in the 1980s (1983 in his case). Therefore, in terms of their Party experience, these leaders belong to the pre–Cultural Revolution generation.

Well Educated

Fifth, this group of central leaders is well educated. Among those with known educational background, 77 (82.8 percent) received at least three years of college education (*dazhuan*) and 16 (17.2 percent) do not have any college education. Among those who received college education, 18 (23.4 percent) were educated either in foreign countries or in graduate schools.

Minorities Overrepresented

Sixth, Han leaders are dominant but minorities are overrepresented. The majority (81.7 percent) of the leaders in this group are of Han origin. But given the percentage of Han people in the total population in China (91.9 percent), Han leaders are in fact underrepresented. Minority leaders, on the other hand, are overrepresented because they represent 18.3 percent of the total leaders in this group, while the minority population comprises only 8.1 percent of the total population. In particular, Tibetan (6), Uygur (3), Mongolian (2), and Korean (2) groups are all well represented. It is interesting to note that six Tibetan leaders with experience in local government are currently central leaders and they occupy very important positions. Out of the six Tibetan leaders, one (Pagbalha Geleg Namgyai) is vice chairman of the NPC, one (Ngapoi Ngawang Jigme) is vice chairman of the CPPCC, one (Doje Cering) is minister, two (Gyaincain Norbu and Huanjue Cenam) are standing members of the NPC, and one (Senqin Losangjisam) is a standing member of the CPPCC. This indicates that the central government is willing to utilize minority leaders in order to forge a strong link between these minority regions and the central

Table 4.8

Distribution of Birth Years of the Central Leaders with Provincial Experience

Birth	Number	Percentage	Valid percentage	Cumulative percentage
1910–1919	2	1.83	1.83	1.83
1920–1929	16	14.68	14.68	16.51
1930–1939	66	60.55	60.55	77.06
1940–1949	25	22.94	22.94	100.00
Total	109	100.00	100.00	—

government. By moving these powerful leaders to Beijing, on the other hand, the central government is also able to ward off potential localist deviations in these sensitive regions.

Geographically Diverse

Seventh, these central leaders are from all provincial units but two: Shanghai and Taiwan (Table 4.10). It is not surprising that no one is from Taiwan, but it is shocking that no one among this group of central leaders with provincial experience has Shanghai as his or her hometown.[42] This seriously conflicts with our impression of the strong presence of the "Shanghai Gang"[43] in the center. The fact that none of the "Shanghai Gang" (such as Jiang Zemin, Zhu Rongji, Wu Bangguo, Huang Ju, Zeng Qinghong, and many others) have Shanghai as their hometown points to the recent undue overemphasis on the significance of home provinces.[44] It is very important, therefore, to distinguish between home provinces and political origins (faji).[45]

As for the patterns of distributions of home provinces of the central leaders with provincial experience in provincial units other than Taiwan and Shanghai, it is interesting to note that, instead of Shandong, Hebei stands out with 12 people (11 percent),[46] Zhejiang and Jiangsu follow with 10 (9.2 percent) and 9 (8.3 percent) leaders, respectively. Three prominent coastal provinces, Shandong (4), Guangdong (2), and Fujian (2), are not very productive in supplying members of this group. In terms of distributions of home provinces in different regions, the East region ranks first with 29 leaders (26.6 percent), followed by the North region with 23 leaders (21.1 percent) and the Central region with

Table 4.9

Distribution of Party Years of the Central Leaders with Provincial Experience

		Number	Percentage	Valid percentage	Cumulative percentage
Valid	1940–1948	15	13.76	16.13	16.13
	1949–1965	66	60.55	70.97	87.10
	1966–1976	11	10.09	11.83	98.92
	1980–1989	1	0.92	1.08	100.00
	Total	93	85.32	100.01	
Missing	System	16	14.68		
Total		109	100.00		

17 leaders (15.6 percent). The South region has the least representation in this group with only 4 leaders (3.7 percent).

Diverse Backgrounds

Finally, and most important, this group of central leaders has very diverse backgrounds in their provincial experience, with some well-established patterns. First, it is quite clear that the central leaders at the core—members of the Politburo—have strong Shanghai connections. Jiang Zemin, Zhu Rongji, Wu Bangguo, Huang Ju, and Zeng Qinghong have all been Shanghai leaders. Moreover, Beijing, Tianjin, and Shandong are also very well represented. The vice chairmen of the NPC with provincial experience, however, are all from minority regions (Tibet, Inner Mongolia, and Xinjiang). The vice chairmen of the CPPCC with provincial experience, moreover, have much broader representation.

Second, these central leaders have served in different numbers of provincial units. Although the majority (85.3 percent) of the leaders in this group worked in one provincial unit, sixteen (14.7 percent) served in two or three provincial units. Li Guixian, for instance, worked as a vice governor in Liaoning Province in the early 1980s and then was promoted to the post of Party secretary of the

Table 4.10

Distribution of Home Provinces of the Central Leaders with Provincial Experience

	Number	Percentage		Number	Percentage
North			*South*		
Beijing	5	4.59	Guangdong	2	1.84
Tianjin	2	1.84	Guangxi	1	0.92
Hebei	12	11.01	Hainan	1	0.92
Shanxi	2	1.84	subtotal	4	3.68
Inner Mongolia	2	1.84	*Southwest*		
subtotal	23	21.12	Sichuan	5	4.59
Northeast			Guizhou	2	1.84
Liaoning	6	5.51	Yunnan	2	1.84
Jilin	6	5.51	Xizang (Tibet)	2	1.84
Heilongjiang	2	1.84	subtotal	11	10.11
subtotal	14	12.86	*Northwest*		
East			Shaanxi	4	3.67
Shanghai	0	0.00	Gansu	1	0.92
Jiangsu	9	8.26	Qinghai	1	0.92
Zhejiang	10	9.17	Ningxia	2	1.84
Anhui	4	3.67	Xinjiang	3	2.75
Fujian	2	1.84	subtotal	11	10.10
Shandong	4	3.67			
Taiwan	0	0.00			
subtotal	29	26.61			

Table 4.10 *(continued)*

	Number	Percentage	Number	Percentage
Central				
Jiangxi	6	5.50		
Henan	4	3.67		
Hubei	3	2.75		
Hunan	4	3.67		
subtotal	17	15.59		
Total	109	100.07		

province in 1985. He was transferred to Anhui in 1986 as Party secretary. In 1988, he was promoted to the center as a state councilor and governor of the Central Bank, the People's Bank of China. Gu Jinchi, as another example, started his political career in Sichuan. He was a vice governor and then a deputy secretary of the province in the 1980s (1982–90). In 1990, he was promoted to Party secretary of Gansu Province. Three years later, he was transferred to Liaoning Province as Party secretary. The fact that many provincial leaders have worked in more than one provincial unit is a result of rotations (*jaoliu*), a practice by which provincial leaders were exchanged among different provinces. It is likely that those provincial leaders with experience in multiple provincial units tend to be more cosmopolitan than those with experience in one province. Hu Jintao, for instance, served as Party secretary of both Guizhou (1985–88) and Tibet (1988–92). His experiences in these two different provincial units, especially in Tibet, must have helped him to better understand the advantages and challenges facing different provincial units.[47]

Third, the members of this group of central leaders have worked in all provincial units. Again, Shanghai and Beijing are prominent. Nine leaders (8.3 percent) have worked in Shanghai, and seven (6.4 percent) in Beijing.

Fourth, some of these leaders have worked in various positions in provinces, while others just in one provincial post. Among these 109 leaders, more than 50 percent (52.3 percent) have worked in more than one position.[48] Some climbed

Table 4.11

Distribution of Provincial Positions of the Central Leaders with Provincial Experience

Positions	Number	Percentage	Valid percentage	Cumulative percentage
Governors	30	27.52	27.52	27.52
Party secretaries	32	29.36	29.36	56.88
Vice governors	24	22.02	22.02	78.90
Deputy secretaries	23	21.10	21.10	100.00
Total	109	100.00	100.00	—

the ladder of success in one provincial unit, while others moved up through transfers. Zhang Boxing, for instance, was elected vice governor of Shaanxi Province in 1985. He was appointed acting governor about one year later. In 1987, he was further promoted to Party secretary of the same province.[49]

He Zhukang, as an example of a leader with experience in several provinces, started his provincial leadership career as a vice governor in Henan Province in 1980. He was promoted to governor of the same province in 1983. He was transferred to Jilin Province as governor in 1987 and was promoted to Party secretary of the province one year later.

Fifth, if we use the last position the leader held before his or her departure to Beijing, we find that they were evenly distributed over four categories. Thirty leaders (27.5 percent) were governors before they became central leaders, 32 (29.4 percent) were secretaries, 24 (22 percent) vice governors, and 23 (21.1 percent) deputy secretaries (Table 4.11).

Future Central Leaders from the Provinces

After the Sixteenth Party Congress, several current provincial leaders are likely to be called back to serve in the central leadership. Among provincial Party secretaries, likely candidates include four current Politburo members (Huang Ju, Li Changchun, Wu Guangzheng, and Jia Qinglin), provincial leaders with central origins (Wang Xudong[50] of Hebei, Xu Youfang of Heilongjiang, Song Defu of Fujian, and He Guoqiang of Chongqing), and provincial party secretaries from the Western area (Li Jianguo of Shaanxi)[51] (Table 4.6). These predictions can be classified into three groups. First, being a Politburo member places one as a central leader already. In addition, three of the four current Politburo members who are concurrently provincial leaders will be close to their retirement age of 65 in 2002. Both Huang Ju and Wu Guangzheng will be 64 years old in 2002, and Jia Qinglin will be 62. Only Li Changchun can afford to wait for another five years since he will be only 58 years old in 2002. It is not clear whether all of them will be elevated to the center in 2002, but their replacements would also likely be candidates for Politburo membership in case they retire. Second, the "Chinese prefects" may be called back for different reasons. Xu Youfang has been out in the province Heilongjiang[52] for four years and he will be 63 years old in 2002. If he is to be called back for any substantial central post, this is the only chance. Otherwise, he will be retired in 2004. Wang Xudong could be a good candidate for director of the Central Organization Department, if Zeng Qinghong is selected for other more important jobs.[53] With experience in several ministries and departments in the center and a long-time full member of the Central Committee (since 1987), Song Defu could be a candidate for Politburo membership. And He Guoqiang might enter the Politburo in his current position because of the status of Chongqing as the fourth centrally administered city, as the center is shifting its focus from the coastal areas to the inland regions. Li Jianguo might be called back for some learning experience in the center.

Among governors, likely candidates include Li Keqiang, Xi Jinping, and Bo Xilai. Li Keqiang has been a rising star in Chinese politics since 1997. He became a full member of the Central Committee in 1997 from nonmember, skipping the step of alternate membership. In June 1998, he was appointed acting governor of the second largest province in China, Henan (with a population of 92 million in 1996). At the age of 42, he was the youngest governor of all provincial units at the time (even today, only Zhao Leji of Qinghai is younger than he). As a member of the "Chinese prefects," and, in particular, a member of the youth league subgroup, he has close ties with central leaders, especially Hu Jintao. However, he still needs to prove himself a capable governor. A large fire accident last year[54] in Luoyang resulting in 309 deaths was not good for his career.[55] If he were to follow the career path of Hu Jintao, he would need to get promoted to Party secretary of a province before he could be elevated to the center for important jobs.

Although a graduate of Qinghua University, Xi Jinping does not necessarily belong to the same group as Hu Jintao does. Xi entered Qinghua in 1975 as a "Worker-Peasant-Soldier" student probably without many academic credentials, while Hu was admitted to the same institution of higher education in 1959 through rigorous college entrance examinations. Xi's credential as a Qinghua graduate does not carry much weight, while Hu's is considered "genuine." However, as the son of veteran revolutionary and former governor and

Party secretary of Guangdong Province, Xi Zhongxun, Xi Jinping landed a job with the General Office of the State Council after his graduation from Qinghua. After several positions at the county and city levels, he was elevated to deputy secretary of Fujian Province in October 1995 and to acting governor in August 1999. As the alternate member of the Fifteenth Central Committee who received the least votes, he needs to prove that he is not only the son of a veteran revolutionary but also a leader in his own right. Similarly, Bo Xilai, a son of Bo Yibo, another veteran revolutionary and longtime central leader, also attributes his political career to his family background in some measure.[56] But Bo's academic credentials are much stronger. He was admitted to Beijing University in 1977 by examination and soon was admitted as a graduate student to the Chinese Academy of Social Sciences. He has been recognized as a charismatic speaker.[57] With the experience of more than ten years as a top leader in Dalian, he is very well qualified for the position of governor in Liaoning. He is likely to enter the Central Committee in 2002 and to be called to the center a few years after the Sixteenth Party Congress.

Other provincial leaders are also likely to be selected for central jobs. These include provincial Party secretaries and governors who have reached (or are about to reach) their retirement age of 65, but are regarded as powerful leaders (Zhang Lichang of Tianjin, Jiang Zhuping of Hubei, Mao Rubai of Ningxia, Xu Guangdi of Shanghai, Li Chunting of Shandong, Cheng Andong of Shaanxi, Lu Ruihua of Guangdong, Niu Maosheng of Hebei, and Bao Xuding of Chongqing). Since these leaders are going to retire from their provincial positions, they may be called back to Beijing to serve in either the National People's Congress or the Chinese People's Political Consultative Conference. Because of the elite status of their provincial units, Xu Kuangdi[58] (age 65 in 2002), Li Chunting[59] (age 66 in 2002), Lu Ruihua (age 64 in 2002), and Zhang Lichang (age 63 in 2002) will likely get senior positions of vice chairmanships in either the NPC or the CPPCC. Jiang Zhuping,[60] Mao Rubai, Cheng Andong, Niu Maosheng, and Bao Xuding may join the NPC or CPPCC as standing members in 2003 or soon thereafter.

Conclusion

The Chinese Communist Party started to use the provinces as a training ground as early as 1962, when Hu Yaobang, one of the youngest central leaders at the time, was sent back to his home province of Hunan as a Party secretary. However, it was not until the 1980s that the center initiated the practice of systematically training future national leaders in the provinces. Under the instructions of Deng Xiaoping, Chen Yun, Ye Jianying, and Hu Yaobang, the

Central Organization Department implemented a plan in 1983 to train cadres for leading posts at various levels.

Candidates for future leading posts are usually classified into two categories and training plans are designed accordingly. For those who have extensive work experience but lack theoretical knowledge, a period of theoretical study is necessary; for those who have good theoretical knowledge but lack practical experience, a transfer to lower levels is necessary to enhance their abilities in handling practical work.

Since the provinces are the immediate lower level of the central government, future national leaders are usually sent to the provinces for practical training. Examples in the 1980s include Hu Qili, Li Ruihuan, Li Lanqing, Hu Jintao, Wang Zhaoguo, Zhu Rongji, Li Ximing, Song Ruixiang, Wan Shaofen, and many others. Many of these leaders are now at the top of the Chinese political system as members of the Politburo, vice president of the State, premier, vice premiers, and so on. In the 1990s, especially after the Fourteenth National Party Congress in 1992, more central leaders were sent to the provinces for training purposes. On this list are Xu Yongyue, Ma Zhongchen, Jin Renqing, Wang Qishan, Linghu An, and Li Keqiang. Moreover, in the past two years, the center has continued to send central leaders to the provinces. Among nine cases identified, five were obviously sent for training purposes: Li Yuanchao, Song Defu, Bai Keming, Zhang Baoshun, and Yu Zhengsheng.

Provincial leaders maintain their ties with Beijing in several ways. First, provincial Party secretaries and governors attend plenary sessions of the Central Committee of the CCP as members. Between September 1982 and October 2001, there were four national congresses of the CCP, twenty-nine plenary sessions, and one national conference. These meetings provided opportunities for provincial leaders with CC membership to interact with central leaders. However, not all provincial Party secretaries and governors are full members of the Central Committee. Between 1982 and 2001, about 85.5 percent of provincial Party secretaries were full members and only 54 percent of governors were full members. In fact, some provincial Party secretaries and governors are not even alternate members. In the past twenty years, 8.2 percent of provincial Party secretaries and 25.2 percent of governors were nonmembers. In 2001, there were twenty-two full members, eight alternate members, and one nonmember among provincial Party secretaries; and fifteen full members, nine alternate members, and seven nonmembers among governors.

Second, provincial leaders also go to Beijing to attend meetings of the National People's Congress as deputies. Between June 1983 and October 2001, there were four congresses and nineteen meetings. Provincial Party secretaries and governors usually use the press conferences held on these occasions to impress central leaders with their accomplishments and ambitious plans.

Third, provincial leaders may have contact with central leaders when they are enrolled in training courses in Beijing. Provincial leaders received their training at the Central Party School, the National College of Administration, and National Defense University in Beijing. Beginning in the mid-1980s, provincial leaders, along with ministerial leaders, were trained in classes specially designed for them (*shengbu ji ganbu jixiuban*). In the past fifteen years (1985–2001), thirty classes of provincial and ministerial cadres have graduated from the Central Party School. Moreover, the Central Committee also organized other special classes for provincial and ministerial leaders. Finally, the National College of Administration also held special classes for provincial and ministerial cadres on finance, administration in accordance with the law, implementing the strategy of developing the West, and other topics in the past two years.

Finally, provincial leaders may have contact with central leaders when central leaders take inspection tours of their provinces. Jiang Zemin, for instance, visited Guangdong, Jiangsu, Zhejiang, Shanghai, Beijing, Ningxia, Gansu, Heilongjiang, Jilin, Anhui, and Shanxi between June 2000 and August 2001. Leaders in these provincial units had opportunities to report to Jiang directly.

It is hard to locate identifiable factions among central leaders because it is a taboo in China to form factions. Yet several groups of provincial leaders have stronger ties to central leaders than do other provincial leaders. The first is a group of "Chinese prefects," a group of provincial leaders with central origins. They started their careers in the central government and were sent to provincial units to gain experience for more important positions in the center. In this group, a particular subgroup is noteworthy: youth league cadres. The second is a group of princelings, children of an older generation of revolutionary cadres. The third group consists of directors of organization departments of provincial Party committees. They have more frequent contacts with the Central Organization Department than do provincial leaders themselves. Finally, cadres from Shanghai are connected to Jiang Zemin either directly or through other central leaders of Shanghai origin.

Three groups of provincial leaders are likely to be called back to serve in the central leadership. The first is the group of "Chinese prefects." This group of cadres has been groomed for central leading posts, and their experience in the provinces is a part of this grooming process. The second is a group of provincial leaders from elite provinces, provinces that have representation in the Politburo. And the third group is composed of senior provincial leaders approaching the retirement age of 65. They are to be called back to the center to serve in either the NPC or CPPCC.

It is becoming increasingly difficult to generalize about the background of past provincial leaders who are currently serving in the central leadership. This is because provincial experience has become such an important credential for central leaders that almost everyone has to have such experience. Nevertheless, these leaders have some interesting patterns in their backgrounds. Generally speaking, they are old (67.5 years in 2002), predominantly male (93.6 percent), mostly Communist Party members (87.2 percent), well educated (82.8 percent have received at least a three years of college education), predominantly Han (81.7 percent), from all provinces but two (Taiwan and Shanghai), and have worked in all provincial units. People who have worked in Shanghai and Beijing are very visible at the top, but the current central leaders with provincial work experience have served in all the other provincial units. Because of the practice of rotations between the center and provinces and among different provincial units, it is getting harder to identify one particular provincial (or former provincial) leader with only one provincial unit because it is increasingly common for provincial leaders to serve in two or more provincial units.

After the Sixteenth National Party Congress, several current provincial leaders are likely to be called back to serve in the central leadership. Among provincial Party secretaries, likely candidates include four current Politburo members (Huang Ju, Li Changchun, Wu Guangzheng, and Jia Qinglin), provincial leaders with central origins (Wang Xudong of Hebei, Xu Youfang of Heilongjiang, Song Defu of Fujian, and He Guoqiang of Chongqing), and provincial Party secretaries from the Western area (Li Jianguo of Shaanxi). Among governors, likely candidates include Li Keqiang of Henan, Xi Jinping of Fujian, and Bo Xilai of Liaoning. Since many provincial leaders on this list are candidates for important jobs in the center, they are likely to be placed in either the Central Committee or the State Council.

Other provincial leaders are also likely to be selected for central jobs. These include provincial Party secretaries and governors who have reached (or are about to reach) the retirement age of 65, but are regarded as powerful leaders (Zhang Lichang of Tianjin, Jiang Zhuping of Hubei, Mao Rubai of Ningxia, Xu Guangdi of Shanghai, Li Chunting of Shandong, Cheng Andong of Shaanxi, Lu Ruihua of Guangdong, Niu Maosheng of Hebei, and Bao Xuding of Chongqing). Since these leaders are going to retire from their provincial positions, they may be called back to Beijing to serve in either NPC or CPPCC.

Notes

The author would like to thank Lori Wagner, Diane M. Lucas, Kimberly McCracken, Danielle Devault, Linda S. Mocejunas, and Bojana Zivanovic for their research assistance. He would also like to thank Dave Finkelstein and Maryanne Kivlehan of the CNA Corporation for organizing a conference on China's leadership transition at which this chapter was originally presented and to thank all the participants in the conference for their insights into Chinese politics.

1. Provinces (often referred to as provincial units) in this chapter mainly refer to twenty-two provinces, four centrally administered cities, and five autonomous regions in China. Excluded from the analysis are Taiwan, Hong Kong, and Macao. See Table 4.1 for basic information about these provincial units.

2. Unless otherwise noted, this study is based on my dataset of four types of leaders in thirty-one provincial units in China: Party secretaries (the first Party secretaries during certain periods), deputy Party secretaries, governors (including mayors of centrally administered municipalities and chairmen of autonomous regions), and vice governors (including vice mayors of centrally administered municipalities and vice chairmen of autonomous regions). This study does not include leaders from Hong Kong, Macao, and Taiwan.

3. Zhou had been involved in revolutionary activities in the Northeast before 1949. Mao Zedong met with him about his new assignment in his home province of Yunnan. See Liu Wenxin and Li Shuqing, *Zhou Baozhong Zhuan* (The biography of Zhou Baozhong) (Harbin: Heilongjiang renmin chubanshe, 1987), p. 288.

4. For a detailed study of the avoidance system during the Qing dynasty, see Wei Hsiu-mei, *Qingdai zhi huibizhidu* (The avoidance system of the Ch'ing dynasty) (Taipei: Institute of Modern History Academia Sinica, 1992).

5. Li Xiannian, for instance, was made minister of finance in 1954.

6. In 1955, the Ministry of Fuel Industries was split into three ministries, the Ministry of Coal (of which Chen continued to be Minister), the Ministry of Electricity, and the Ministry of Petroleum.

7. Ding Sheng later switched to the side of the "Gang of Four" after the demise of Lin Biao.

8. Li Desheng later became a victim of the "Gang of Four."

9. See "Zhongguo Gongchandang Bashinian Dashiji: 1978" (The chronology of the eighty years of the Chinese Communist Party: 1978), *People's Daily*, www.people. com.cn/GB/shizheng/252/5580/5581/20010611/486485.html.

10. See "Zhongguo Gongchandang Bashinian Dashiji: 1979," www.people.com. cn/GB/shizheng/252/5580/5581/20010612/487163.html.

11. Ibid.

12. Ibid.

13. Ye Jianying, "Speech to the Celebration Meeting of the Thirtieth Anniversary of the People's Republic of China" (September 29, 1979), *People's Daily*, September 30, 1979, p. 1.

14. Deng Xiaoping, "Muqian de xingshi he renwu" (Present situation and tasks), in *Selected Works of Deng Xiaoping*, Vol. 2, web.peopledaily.com.cn/deng/newfiles/ b1390.html, January 16, 1980.

15. These refer to adhering to Marxism-Leninism and Mao Zedong Thought, the socialist road, the arty leadership, and the proletarian dictatorship.

16. In the early 1980s, the more often used phrase was "the Third Echelon." For detailed studies of this concept, see Hong Yung Lee, *From Revolutionary Cadres to Party Technocrats in Socialist China* (Berkeley: University of California Press, 1991), 261–65; Ting Wang, "An Analysis of the P.R.C.'s Future Elite: The Third Echelon," *Journal of Northeast Asian Studies* 4, no. 2 (Summer 1985): 19–37; Hong Yung Lee, "Mainland China's Future Leaders: Third Echelon of Cadres," *Issues and Studies* 24,

no. 6 (June 1988): 36–57; and Cheng Li, *China's Leaders: The New Generation* (Lanham, MD: Rowman and Littlefield, 2001), pp. 43–45. However, the phrase "cadres on reserve" (*houbei ganbu*) has been more consistently used throughout the whole period of economic reforms in the People's Republic of China.

17. See Chen Yun, "Tiba peiyang zhongqingnian ganbu shi dangwu zhiji" (Selecting and fostering middle-aged and young cadres is a task of top priority), in *Chen Yun wen xuan* (Selected works of Chen Yun), Vol. 3 (Beijing: Renmin chubanshe, 1995), pp. 292–97.

18. Deng Xiaoping said, "For Comrade Chen Yun's suggestion, I raise both of my hands to support."

19. See Wang Leiming, "Song Renqiong fangtanlu" (Interview with Song Renqiong), *People's Daily*, www.people.com.cn/GB/shizheng/19/20010611/486460.html, June 11, 2001.

20. For detailed information, see Melanie Manion, ed., "Cadre Recruitment and Management in the People's Republic of China," *Chinese Law and Government* 17, no. 3 (Fall 1984). The following discussion is based on this work.

21. Ibid., p. 35.

22. Ibid., p. 36.

23. See "Zhongguo Gongchandang Bashinian Dashiji: 1980," *People's Daily*, www.people.com.cn/GB/shizheng/252/5580/5581/20010612/487172.html.

24. See "Zhongguo Gongchandang Bashinian Dashiji: 1983," *People's Daily*), www.people.com.cn/GB/shizheng/252/5580/5581/20010612/487211.html.

25. See "Zhongguo Gongchandang Bashinian Dashiji: 1984," *People's Daily*, www.people.com.cn/GB/shizheng/252/5580/5581/20010612/487216.html.

26. In practice, this is often done in conjunction with rotations. But this system is conceptually different from the system of rotations. Rotations are bidirectional, while training leading cadres at lower levels is unidirectional.

27. He later climbed the ladder of success all the way to standing member of the Politburo until 1989, when he was demoted because of his sympathy toward student demonstrators. He is currently a vice chairman of the Chinese People's Political Consultative Conference.

28. He is now a standing member of the Politburo and a vice premier now.

29. For a detailed study of different groups of Shanghai leaders and their missions, see Zhimin Lin, "Shanghai's Big Turnaround since 1985: Leadership, Reform Strategy, and Resource Mobilization," in *Provincial Strategies of Economic Reform in Post-Mao China*, ed. Peter T.Y. Cheung, Jae Ho Chung, and Zhimin Lin (Armonk, NY: M.E. Sharpe, 1998), pp. 49–88.

30. For a study of Lin Hujia in Beijing, see Zhiyue Bo, "Economic Development and Corruption: Beijing beyond 'Beijing'," *Journal of Contemporary China* 9, no. 25 (November 2000): 467–87.

31. Unfortunately, Xiang was wrongfully fired because of his alleged connection to a corruption scandal, the "Jinjiang Fake Medicine Scandal." For a detailed presentation of Xiang Nan, see Shawn Shieh, "Provincial Leadership and the Implementation of Foreign Economic Reforms in Fujian Province," in Cheung et al., *Provincial Strategies of Economic Reform in Post-Mao China*, pp. 309–13.

32. Zhang Baoshun will be discussed later in the chapter.

33. He is the only current Party secretary who is a nonmember of the Central Committee of the CCP.

34. For a detailed analysis of provincial representation in the Central Committee of the CCP between 1969 and 1997, see Zhiyue Bo, "Provincial Power and Provincial Economic Resources in the PRC," *Issues and Studies* 34, no. 4 (April 1998): 1–18.

35. For a detailed discussion of the relationship between the provincial party committee and the provincial people's congress in selecting a governor, see Zhiyue Bo, "Institutionalization of Elite Management in Post-Deng China," in *Holding China Together*, ed. Barry Naughton and Dali Yang (forthcoming).

36. The following presentation is based on the special forum for provincial party secretaries and governors in *People's Daily*, www.people.com.cn/GB/other4349/4364/index.html.

37. This is the idea Jiang Zemin articulated for the Chinese Communist Party in his inspection tour of Guangdong Province in March 2000. "As long as our Party will always be a true representative of the development request of China's advanced social productive forces, the future direction of China's advanced culture, and the fundamental interests of the broadest masses of Chinese people, our Party will always be in an invincible position and always receive sincere support from the people of all nationalities of the whole country and lead people to progress continuously." See "Anzhao 'sangedaibiao' de yaoqiu quanmian jiaqiang dang de jianshe" (Comprehensively strengthening the party construction in accordance with the requirement of the "Three Represents"), *People's Daily*, http://www.people.com.cn/GB/paper464/167/15118.html, March 10, 2000.

38. If one person attends one class, that is one person-time; if the same person attends two separate classes, it is counted as two people-times. See "Yixiang shiguan quanju de zhanluxing renwu" (A task of strategic significance concerning the overall situation), *People's Daily*, www.people.com.cn/GB/shizheng/19/20010513/463566. html, May 13, 2001.

39. "Origin" here does not refer to the birthplace (or home province) of a political leader. It refers to the place where the political leader's career (*faji*) took off. Jiang Zemin, for instance, was born in Yangzhou, Jiangsu, but his political origin is Shanghai, where his political career took off.

40. For a detailed description of this concept, see Zhiyue Bo, "Provincial Power and Provincial Economic Resources in the PRC," *Issues and Studies* 34, no. 4 (April 1998): 1–18.

41. Xie Fei, the former Party secretary of Guangdong Province, passed away on October 27, 1999.

42. It should be noted that home provinces (*jiguan*) are not necessarily always identical with birthplaces (*chushengdi*). Jia Qinglin, for instance, was born in Qingdao, Shandong Province, but his home province is Hebei. Since it is more difficult to find information on birthplaces than home provinces, it is more accurate to report home provinces here.

43. This term is borrowed from Cheng Li. See his book, *China's Leaders*.

44. Home provinces have been used in connection with localism. For such a usage, see Cheng Li and David Bachman, "Localism, Elitism, and Immobilism: Elite Formation and Social Change in Post-Mao China," *World Politics* 42, no. 1 (October 1989): 64–94; and Xiaowei Zang, "Provincial Elite in Post-Mao China," *Asian Survey* 31 (June 1991): 512–25. For an alternative approach, see Zhiyue Bo, "Native Local Leaders and Political Mobility in China: Home Province Advantage?" *Provincial China*, no. 2 (October 1996): 2–15.

45. See note 39 for distinctions.

46. Shandong is prominent for the Third and Fourth Generations of China's leaders. See Cheng Li, *China's Leaders*, p. 61.

47. As the only top central leader with firsthand experience in a minority region, Hu Jintao possesses unique political resources as a future prominent leader of China.

48. Since governors are all concurrently deputy secretaries by default, their positions are counted once. If a governor has been a deputy secretary prior to his/her governorship, however, it is counted as two positions.

49. Apparently, Zhang was not terribly popular in Shaanxi. His nickname was "Zhang Buxing" ("no good Zhang"). For a critical overview of Zhang's performance in Shaanxi, see Kevin P. Lane, "One Step Behind: Shaanxi in Reform, 1978–1995," in Cheung et al., ed., *Provincial Strategies of Economic Reform in Post-Mao China*, pp. 212–50.

50. Wang Xudong, as indicated earlier, is actually a provincial leader with local origins. But he is likely to be called back because of his central experience.

51. In my original predictions in October 2001, this list also included Linghu An, Party secretary of Yunnan, and Bai Enpei, Party secretary of Qinghai. As predicted, Linghu An was indeed called back to the center. He was replaced by Bai Enpei as Party secretary of Yunnan Province on October 25, 2001, and Linghu An was appointed deputy head of the Bureau of Auditing (with a ministerial rank) on December 6, 2001. Since Bai has already been transferred to a different province, it is less likely that he will be called back to the center soon.

52. Xu's assignment to Heilongjiang was very dramatic. Zhang Quanjing, the director of the COD at the time, accompanied him to the province and announced his appointment at a meeting of the provincial party committee in July 1997.

53. Of course, being the director of the Central Organization Department is very important. In this position, he has control over the most important posts in the center and provinces. In fact, even though the two men do not have any overlap in their local leadership experiences, the elevation of Meng Jianzhu, another member of the "Shanghai Gang," to the position of Party secretary of Jiangxi Province, was probably the work of Zeng Quinghong. When Meng started to work in the Shanghai municipal government in 1992, Zeng had been long gone to the center.

54. The fire occurred in a department store in Luoyang on December 25, 2000. It was the second largest fire accident in China since 1990.

55. He had to take more blame for the accident than both Party secretaries because the old Party secretary had just left Henan before the accident and the new Party secretary had only arrived recently. He was the most senior deputy secretary and the governor throughout this period.

56. According to Bo Xilai, his family background was in fact a barrier to his work. "For a quite long time," he recalled of his experience in Jin County, Liaoning Province, about sixteen years earlier, "people had reservations about me." See his interview, *People's Daily*, www.peopledaily.com.cn/GB/other4349/4355/20010314/417053.html, March 14, 2001.

57. He made quite a stir at Beijing University on October 19, 2001, when he visited the campus. "Governor Bo is coming! Governor Bo is coming!" one student shouted with excitement. See Luo Bing, "Liaoning yu Beida qianshu xieyi, Bo Xilai qingdao Beida xuezi" (Liaoning Province is signing an agreement with Beida, Bo Xilai captivated Beida students), *People's Daily*, www.peopledaily.com.cn/GB/other4788/20011022/586992.html, October 22, 2001. For a detailed presentation of Bo Xilai's

political career and his family's division of labor in politics, see Cheng Li, *China's Leaders*, pp. 131–34, 165–66.

58. At the Thirty-fourth Meeting of the Eleventh Standing Committee of the Shanghai People's Congress on December 7, 2001, Xu resigned as mayor of Shanghai and Chen Liangyu, a deputy secretary and vice mayor, was elected as acting mayor.

59. Li Chunting retired on December 6, 2001, as predicted. Zhang Gaoli, deputy secretary of Guangdong Province, secretary of Shenzhen Municipality, and chairman of the Shenzhen municipal people's congress, was transferred to Shandong to replace him.

60. Jiang Zhuping retired on December 7, 2001, as predicted. Yu Zhengsheng, minister of construction, was transferred to replace him. Apparently, Jiang was a transitional figure. He had just been appointed as the Party secretary of Hubei Province in January 2001.

—— III ——

Institutions in Transition

5

Leading Small Groups

Managing All Under Heaven

Taeho Kim

The enormous economic and social changes during the two-decade-long reform era notwithstanding, little has changed in the fundamental behavioral code of China's leaders: The maintenance of consensus and conformity remains the most crucial requirement for leadership unity, political stability, and economic development. Additionally, how well and in what manner China's current leaders handle the leadership transition could significantly affect not only political stability in China but also its future capability and behavior.

While the most significant and salient aspects of leadership changes in the upcoming Sixteenth Party Congress and thereafter—from Hu Jintao's succession to the rise of the Fourth Generation of leaders, to the new Party-army relationship—are extensively discussed in this volume, a key unknown that has a direct bearing on the leadership's unity, their management of State affairs (*guozheng*), and their own basis of power is how the new leadership will interact with the Party's Leading Small Groups (*lingdao xiaozu* or LSGs)—the central-level nonstanding policy deliberation and coordination bodies in charge of all major issues of the country.

This chapter throws some light on this little discussed yet potentially consequential aspect of leadership politics in China. The first section introduces an overview of the current LSGs and their equivalent central-level committees in terms of membership, structures, and processes. The second section looks into the likely changes in the relationships between the post-Congress leadership and the LSGs, including their possible members and their changing roles. The third and final section sums up the findings of this study and their implications for China and beyond.

Due to the nature of the topic, a few caveats are in order. The first and foremost challenge for the outside researcher is simply the invisibility of the LSGs from public purview. They do not appear in the Party's formal organizational charts, nor is their existence, let alone their workings, discussed in public. This super-secrecy reinforces the second problem, which is that the paucity of reliable data is often compounded by the inundation of poorly sourced, tabloid-quality press reports about their meetings, their presumed policy recommendations, and their relations with the top leadership.[1] Third, given the sensitive and closed nature of the topic, it should be acknowledged that complete information is rare and "hard evidence" is rarer still. In spite of the overall trend toward institutionalizing bureaucracies in China's reform era, the inner workings of such nonstanding bodies as LSGs are still heavily influenced or controlled by a handful of top leaders in China. The informal, closed, and often personalized operation of the LSGs not only speaks volumes about the nature of elite politics at the pinnacle of China's power hierarchy, but also making predictions based on research findings in other issue-areas to be increasingly difficult and risky. The following discussion notes only very recent trends and developments that can be corroborated by widely accessible sources and interviews in China, Hong Kong, and Taiwan in 2000–2001. Until more reliable sources become available, the analysis below should be regarded as tentative and inferential.

Leading Small Groups (LSGs) and Central-level Committees

An Overview

The People's Republic of China (PRC) is a "Party-State" ruled by the Chinese Communist Party (CCP), whose ultimate objective is to continue its rule by monopolizing all major power relationships in that country. As Figure 5.1 illustrates, political power in China is formally structured into the Party, the government, and the military. In addition to the vast bureaucratic organizations at the central level, there are thirty-one provincial-level units (as well as the Hong Kong Special Administrative Region) and numerous other subnational administrative units that cut cross the Party, the government, and the military. Contemporary as well as traditional China, in short, has long been a bureaucratic leviathan.

As Kenneth Lieberthal and other scholars have noted, however, at any moment in its existence, the PRC has been ruled by approximately twenty-five to thirty-five top leaders. Even if today's China enters the third decade of reform, these top leaders are still less defined by their formal positions than by their respective standing with the paramount leader, network of personal ties, and the "rules of the game" of their own making.[2] In relatively closed and hier-

Figure 5.1. **The Formal Organization of Political Power in China**

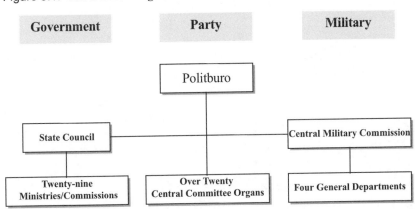

archical societies such as China's, information is often transmitted only through the complex web of personal connections called *guanxi*. Additionally, China's bureaucratic structure, organized along the vertical command system (*xitong*) with minimum horizontal coordination inhibits the proliferation of information beyond a small coterie of those who are directly involved with the issue.

Of particular importance to this study is the *xitong*, a grouping of functionally related bureaucracies that together address specific policy tasks. The six *xitong*s are military affairs; legal affairs (including legal, judicial, and law enforcement); administrative affairs (industrial, economic, foreign, education, and science affairs); propaganda (media and cultural issues); united front affairs (minorities, Hong Kong, Macao, and Taiwan); and mass organization affairs (unions, youth, and women).[3]

The basic role of the LSGs is to form a bridge between the top leadership and the major bureaucracies in terms of information processing and policy implementation. The LSGs bring together top bureaucrats from across the system who are in charge of the issues for policy deliberation and proposal before these issues are formally approved by the Politburo. The participation of relevant bureaucratic organizations in policy deliberation ensures cooperation among them during policy implementation. Headed by a Politburo or a Politburo Standing Committee (PBSC) member and composed mostly of ministerial or vice ministerial officials, it allows the top leadership to exercise direct control over all major issue-areas in the country, thus ensuring continued CCP rule. As shown in Figure 5.2, the LSGs are internal mechanisms that do not appear on the Party's organizational charts. They also have varying degrees of importance and duration, thus making it difficult to generalize.

Figure 5.2. **Organs Directly Under the Chinese Communist Party Central Committee**

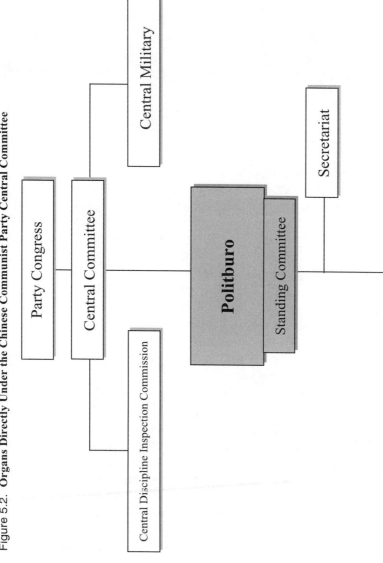

125

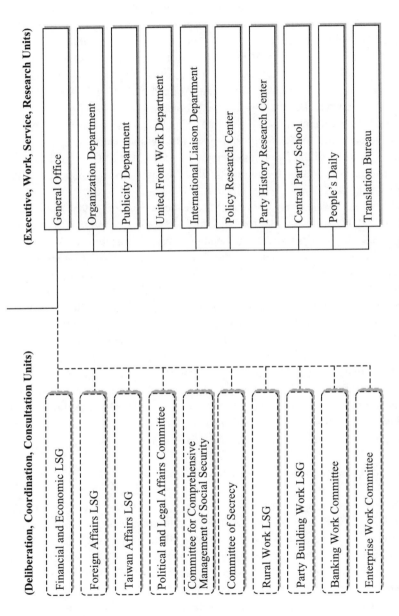

(Deliberation, Coordination, Consultation Units)

Financial and Economic LSG

Foreign Affairs LSG

Taiwan Affairs LSG

Political and Legal Affairs Committee

Committee for Comprehensive Management of Social Security

Committee of Secrecy

Rural Work LSG

Party Building Work LSG

Banking Work Committee

Enterprise Work Committee

(Executive, Work, Service, Research Units)

General Office

Organization Department

Publicity Department

United Front Work Department

International Liaison Department

Policy Research Center

Party History Research Center

Central Party School

People's Daily

Translation Bureau

Sources: Adapted from *China Directory 2001* (Tokyo: Radiopress, 2000); *Zhongguo dalu zongguan* (Comprehensive View of Mainland China) (Taipei: Gongdang wenti yanjiu zhongxin, 1998), p. 61.

The circumstances surrounding the creation of the LSGs are not adequately known. Most extant studies point to the June 1958 joint circular issued by the CCP Central Committee and the State Council as their founding document, entitled, *The Circular Concerning the Establishment of Financial and Economic, Political and Legal, Foreign Affairs, Science, and Cultural and Education Small Groups*.[4] At that time, the Great Leap Forward reached a new height in terms of mobilization, and Mao Zedong was probably unaware of his coming fate in April 1959, when he resigned as state president, and also in July 1959, when the landmark Lushan Conference was held. It was probably part of Mao's attempts to shift the center of political gravity from the government bureaucracy to the Party apparatus that prompted the creation of the major LSGs.[5] Like the Party system itself, however, the LSGs ceased to function during the Cultural Revolution (1966–76) and were only revived in the reform era.

While there were over a dozen LSGs at the end of the 1990s, their status and importance differ. Aside from such key LSGs as the Foreign Affairs Leading Small Group, Taiwan Affairs Leading Small Group, Financial and Economic Leading Small Group, and Political and Legal Affairs Committee and its related committees that are discussed below, there are other leading small groups tasked to handle specific issue-areas including rural affairs (Wen Jiabao), Party building (Hu Jintao), banking (Wen Jiabao), enterprises (Wu Bangguo), and publicity (Ding Guangen).[6]

The use of such different appellations as "leading small groups" and "committees" may imply that the latter have more enduring status and more direct guidance over subordinate units than the former. As Carol Hamrin has noted in her pathbreaking study on the LSGs, however, it has been a "distinction without a difference for most of the PRC's history."[7] Besides, as illustrated in the discussion of key LSGs below, their importance is largely determined by the membership and by the nature and scope of their work.

Foreign Affairs Leading Small Group

One of the most important leading small groups in the eyes of foreign governments is the Foreign Affairs Leading Small Group (*waishi lingdao xiaozu*) or FALSG. It currently consists of one head (Jiang Zemin), two deputy heads (Zhu Rongji and Qian Qichen), and five members (Foreign Minister Tang Jiaxuan, Party Central FAO Director Liu Huaqiu, ILD Director Dai Bingguo, Minister of State Security Xu Yongyue, and Defense Minister Chi Haotian).[8] Its membership composition reinforces the paramount leader's strong interest in controlling this foreign affairs *xitong*. The most influential figure under Jiang in this *xitong* is doubtless Qian Qichen, a former foreign minister (1988–98)

Figure 5.3. **Actual Foreign Policymaking Processes in China, 2001**

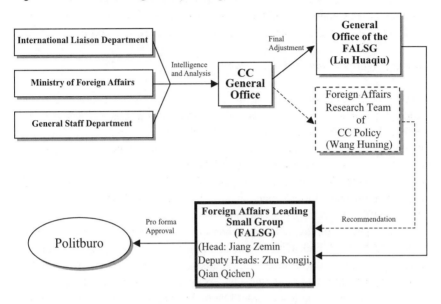

and vice premier in charge of foreign policy, who is assisted by Tang Jiaxuan and Liu Huaqiu. Due to a lack of experience or expertise or simply to different job responsibilities, other FALSG members such as Zhu Rongji, Dai Bingguo, Xu Yongyue, and Chi Haotian play lesser roles in policy deliberation. For reasons to be discussed below, however, its current composition could turn out to be highly problematic as most of its members are due to retire after the next congress in 2002.

The FALSG can better be illuminated by analyzing its functions and its place in China's overall foreign policy decision-making processes in 2001 (Figure 5.3). For any given foreign policy issue, the relevant units from the Party (e.g., International Liaison Department), the government (Ministry of Foreign Affairs), and the military (General Staff Department) provide the CC General Office with intelligence and analysis. The CC General Office, which is in charge of overall bureaucratic coordination, then sums up and processes those various reports and transmits them to the General Office of the FALSG *and* the CC Policy Research Center (i.e., its Foreign Affairs Research Team headed by Wang Huning), which is not an institutionalized channel in China's foreign policy decision-making processes.[9] In principle, it is the sole prerogative of the General Office of the FALSG to make policy recommendations to the FALSG. Once a consensus is reached at the FALSG on the pending issues, it is submitted to the unwieldy Politburo for pro forma approval. This modus operandi is further reinforced by the facts that the head of the FALSG is the paramount leader himself and the "recommendations" were supported by their own colleagues in the Politburo with foreign-policy responsibilities.

Taiwan Affairs Leading Small Group

Due to the critical importance of the unification task for the nation and for the leadership, Jiang Zemin took over the Taiwan Affairs Leading Small Group (*duiTai [gongzuo] lingdao xiaozu*) or TALSG early on—in June 1993. Besides its one deputy head (Qian Qichen), its members are United Front Work Director cum TALSG Secretary General Wang Zhaoguo, Association for Relations Across the Taiwan Strait Chairman Wang Daohan, Deputy Chief of the PLA General Staff Xiong Guangkai, Xu Yongyue, and Party Central Taiwan Affairs Office Director Chen Yunlin.[10] It is important to note, however, that because of the complex and comprehensive nature of the task, the TALSG's policy deliberation and implementation often bring in a large number of representatives from major bureaucratic units from across the system as well as other senior leaders and academic advisers. Whoever emerged in the next party congress as China's top leader would be highly likely to assume the leadership role over this critical LSG.

Of particular importance is the fact that Jiang Zemin serves as the head of both the FALSG and the TALSG, which would provide him with dominant influence over other leaders on China's foreign affairs in general and its U.S. and Taiwan policy in particular. More specifically, this also means that even if Jiang remains the primary channel for expressing China's overall strategy toward Taiwan, his actual role is to ensure support from other senior leaders and to manage a consensus-oriented policy process. As is the case with the FALSG, Qian is believed to be in overall charge of TALSG operations with the assistance of Wang Zhaoguo and Wang Daohan.

Financial and Economic Leading Small Group

This is the most important body for economic and trade decision-making deliberation and implementation in post-reform China. The ongoing reform drive focusing on economic development has also vastly broadened this LSG's policy responsibilities. In line with the launch of the reform and open-door policy, the Financial and Economic LSG (*caijing lingdao xiaozu*) was revived in 1980 with Zhao Ziyang as its head.[11] Currently led by Zhu Rongji with Vice Premier Wu Bangguo as its deputy head, this LSG includes in its membership NPC Vice Chairman Zou Jiahua, Chairman of the China Enterprise Management Association Chen Jinhua, Vice Chairman of the State Committee for Restructuring the Economic System (*guojia jingji tizhi gaige weiyuanhui*) Liu Zhongli, Vice Chairman of the NPC Financial and Economic Committee Zhou Zheng-qing, and Jiang Chunyun—all of whom have substantial experience and expertise on economic issues.[12]

Reflecting his towering role in all major issues regarding the Chinese economy, Zhu is believed to have almost complete control over the LSG, and his expertise is widely respected by other members of the Politburo.[13] However, not only could his expected departure from the scene create a vacuum in this critical LSG, but also China's accession to the World Trade Organization (WTO) is likely to enhance the authority and scope of the LSGs in such areas as domestic stability and foreign interactions.

Political and Legal Affairs Committee

Reconstituted with its present name in March 1990, the Political and Legal Affairs Committee (*zhengfa weiyuanhui*) has so far had only three secretaries in charge of its work: Qiao Shi (March 1990–November 1992), Ren Jianxin (November 1992–March 1998), and Luo Gan (March 1998–present).[14] It currently consists of the President of the Supreme People's Court Xiao Yang, Procurator General of the Supreme People's Procuratorate Han Zhubin, Public Security Minister Jia Chunwang, Xu Yongyue, Justice Minister Zhang Fusen, Deputy Director of the PLA General Political Department Zhou Ziyu, and Central Discipline Inspection Committee member, Wang Shengjun. The size of its membership varied throughout the 1990s.

Luo Gan concurrently heads both the Committee of Secrecy (*baomi weiyuanhui*) and the Committee for Comprehensive Management of Social Security (*shehui zhian zonghe zhili weiyuanhui*).[15] In light of an overlap in their memberships and roles as well as of the preeminent status of the Political and Legal Affairs Committee within the Party, however, the other two committees are subordinate to it. The Committee holds an annual conference, usually in December, and, as is done in national economic planning, it charts out a five-year plan. Its main tasks during the "9.5 Plan" (1996–2000) included continued social and political stability, a reduction in the growth of criminal cases, public order at the grassroots level, and a new legal basis for the socialist market economy.[16]

The Interaction Between the New Leadership Lineups and the LSGs

The upcoming Sixteenth Party Congress could bring about significant changes in the LSGs in terms of their membership, their role, and their relationship with the new leadership. This is primarily because of the ineluctable fact that, even if the control of the key LSGs remains crucial for the emerging leaders' political longevity, they must secure their formal positions in the CCP's hierarchy first. Once landed in the positions of responsibility, they can try gradually but surely to replace the remaining leaders anointed by the outgoing Third Generation leaders with their own.

While it is extremely difficult to predict the leadership alignment that will emerge after the congress, let alone the distribution of their portfolios, the extent of prospective leadership changes virtually guarantees the ensuing changes in the key LSGs. In particular, it is widely believed inside and outside of China that prior to the Fifteenth Party Congress in September 1997 there was an internal agreement on age limits for leading positions—that is, in principle, those leaders who were 65 or older would not be elected as CC members and those leaders who were 70 or older would not become members of the Politburo or the Central Military Commission (CMC).

If the agreed-upon age limit for leadership selection were to apply for the Sixteenth Party Congress, a large-scale turnover would occur in short order, for three reasons. As shown in Table 5.1, first, five out of the seven members of the Politburo Standing Committee, eleven out of the twenty-three members of the Politburo (including two alternate members), and seven out of the eleven CMC members will have reached 70 years of age or older by the time of the Sixteenth Party Congress in the fall of 2002.

Second, not all the remaining nine Politburo members aged 61 (Wu Bangguo) to 68 (Li Ruihuan) are likely to remain in the Politburo, as this would leave very little room for Fourth Generation leaders to move up, let alone for Fifth Generation leaders. Several members of this age group could be promoted to the PBSC, possibly together with Hu Jintao as Party general secretary and Wen Jiabao as premier, while others are under pressure to toe the principle of "making cadres younger" (*ganbu nianqinghua*).[17]

And third, the above analysis strongly indicates that the majority of the current Politburo and PBSC members are expected to retire after the congress. In particular, all seven leaders elected to the CMC at the Fifteenth Party Congress will be over 70 years of age by the fall of 2002, thus resulting in a significant turnover of the military top brass.[18]

Taken together, while the post-Congress leadership configuration is still a matter of conjecture and would gradually take shape in a drawn-out political struggle, the extent of leadership change and its impact on the new leadership lineup are likely to be so great as to constitute a new relationship between the top leadership and the LSGs. Several features would stand out.

First and foremost, the current dozen or so LSGs, particularly the major ones, are headed by a handful of top leaders and/or manned by their acolytes.

Table 5.1

Age Distribution of China's Top Leaders (as of September 2002)

	Politburo Standing Committee (seven)	Politburo (twenty-three)	Central Military Commission (eleven)
Over 75	(one)	(one)	(one)
	Jiang Zemin (August 1926)	Jiang Zemin (August 1926)	Jiang Zemin (August 1926)
70 to 75	(four)	(ten)	(six)
	Li Peng (October 1928)	Qian Qichen (January 1928)	Zhang Wannian (August 1928)
	Zhu Rongji (October 1928)	Zhang Wannian (August 1928)	Chi Haotian (July 1929)
	Wei Jianxing (January 1931)	Li Peng (October 1928)	Wang Ruilin (January 1930)
	Li Lanqing (May 1932)	Zhu Rongji (October 1928)	Fu Quanyou (November 1930)
		Tian Jiyun (June 1929)	Wang Ke (August 1931)
		Chi Haotian (July 1929)	Yu Yongbo (September 1931)
		Ding Guangen (September 1929)	
		Jiang Chunyun (April 1930)	
		Wei Jianxing (January 1931)	
		Li Lanqing (May 1932)	

Table 5.1 *(continued)*

	Politburo Standing Committee (seven)	Politburo (twenty-three)	Central Military Commission (eleven)
65 to 69	(one) Li Ruihuan (September 1934)	(four) Li Ruihuan (September 1934) Luo Gan (July 1935) Li Tieying (September 1936) Wu Guanzheng (August 1938)	(one) Cao Gangchuan (December 1935)
60 to 64		(five) Huang Ju (September 1938) Wu Yi (November 1938) Zeng Qinghong (July 1939) Jia Qinglin (March 1940) Wu Bangguo (July 1941)	(one) Guo Boxiong (July 1942)

	(one)	(two)	(three)
55 to 59	Hu Jintao (December 1942)	Hu Jintao (December 1942)	Wen Jiabao (September 1942)
		Xu Caihou (June 1943)	Hu Jintao (December 1942)
			Li Changchun (February 1944)

Note: Due to the above categorization of age cohorts and to the cut-off date of September 2002, those leaders who were born in 1932, 1938, and 1942 are borderline cases.

Sources: Adapted from Chien-wen Kou, "Zhonggong 'ganbu nianqinghua' yu zhengzhi jicheng" ("Making Cadres Younger" and Political Succession in China), *Zhongguo Dalu Yanjiu* 44, no. 5 (May 2001): 14; Shen Xueming et al., comp., *Zhonggong dishiwujie zhongyang weiyuanhui zhongyang jilu jiancha weiyuanhui weiyuan minglu* (Who's who of the members of the Fifteenth Central Committee [and of] the Central Discipline Inspection Commission) (Beijing: Zhonggong wenxian chubanshe, 1999).

The power handover to the new generation would inevitably necessitate a significant membership turnover in the newly constituted LSGs. Most notable are the departure of Jiang Zemin (head of both the FALSG and the TALSG), Zhu Rongji (head of the Financial and Economic LSG), and Qian Qichen (deputy head of both the FALSG and the TALSG) as well as of those members in the key LSGs who owe their patrons for their positions. Put differently, four leaders from the FALSG, three from the TALSG, three from the Financial and Economic LSG, and one from the Political and Legal Affairs Committee 70 years of age or older by the fall of 2002 would likely retire from service thereafter.[19]

Second, in light of the growing complexities in social and state management as well as in the external environment, it is entirely possible for the new leadership to set up new LSGs to cope effectively with them. A recent example that still needs further corroboration might be the alleged creation of the National Security Council–like body or LSG in the wake of the May 1999 embassy bombing.[20] Domestic and external challenges attending China's accession to the WTO could well lead to a strengthening of the LSGs in charge of security, trade, banking, and agriculture.

Third, depending on the relationship emerging after the next congress between Fourth Generation leaders and the retired elders, the latter may find that positioning their protégés into the LSGs rather than into high-profile party or state positions is a safer and more effective way to prolong their influence. In Jiang's case, Education Minister Chen Zhili, Wang Huning, and Shanxi Deputy Party Secretary Li Jingtian, among others, could belong to this category.

On the other hand, even Jiang's closest personal aides, if they had credentials acceptable to other leaders, could be promoted to higher positions of responsibility including seats in various LSGs. For instance, Zeng Qinghong's promotion to full membership in the Politburo or the PBSC would likely land him not only in the portfolio of party affairs but also assign him other broad responsibilities.[21] Other top leaders such as Hu Jintao, Zhu Rongji, and Li Peng also carry their own list of up-and-coming leaders.[22]

In early 2001, several press reports indicated that Vice Foreign Minister Li Zhaoxing had assumed the position of Party secretary of the Chinese Foreign Ministry, outflanking incumbent minister Tang Jiaxuan.[23] If true, this points to the doddering performance of Tang in the eyes of the top leadership and particularly of Qian Qichen, who would likely support Li Zhaoxing to land on the FALSG.

However, there are several important reasons supporting the continued work of the LSGs. First, the increasing functional differentiation and structural diversification throughout the system tend to result in gradual and incremental changes within each sector or issue-area, even if this observation needs to be qualified due to the nature of political struggle in China—which is basically unpredictable.

Second, in the case of the several LSGs currently headed by the leaders of the Fourth Generation, continuity will likely be the norm rather than an exception. Most notable are Luo Gan (political and legal affairs), Wen Jiabao (financial and rural affairs), and Wu Bangguo (enterprises). In particular, Luo Gan's elevation to the PBSC, which is highly likely for a variety of reasons, might ensure that he would continue to take overall charge of the political and legal *xitong*.

Third, and related to the first reason, is that the absence of a "strong man" in post-Deng China who can call several shots in a broad array of issue-areas would impel the contending leaders and groups to share power among themselves. Their limited personal status and authority would, under most of the circumstances, circumscribe their institutional power in a way and to an extent that leadership unity is upheld at any cost and a continued semblance of consensus and conformity is achieved.

Finally, the emergent relationship between the new generation of leaders and the key LSGs depends upon an array of political factors that are interpersonal, contingent, and changeable. A few questions suffice to make this point. What kind of relationship would the outgoing Third Generation of leaders, the so-called post-revolutionary elders, have with the Fourth Generation of leaders? What would be the arrangements or *quid pro quo* before their relinquishment of power to the next generation of leaders? Would the outgoing top leaders abide by the unprecedented yet widely accepted rule for the retirement age of 70 at the Fifteenth Party Congress in September 1997? More to the point, what would be the unknown and unknowable demands of Jiang and others for their retirement?

Conclusion and Implications

From the preceding analysis of the membership, structure, and role of the key LSGs and their prospective post-congress changes, several conclusions can be inferred. First, as earlier studies on the LSGs by Carol Hamrin, Lu Ning, and Michael Swaine have done,[24] this chapter has reaffirmed the continued critical importance of the LSGs in the management of state affairs as well as in leadership politics in China. It is entirely possible that, notwithstanding the overall trend toward bureaucratic institutionalization throughout the Chinese system, the future generation of the Chinese leadership will increasingly rely on the informal and closed party mechanisms—such as the LSGs—to keep state affairs under its management and therefore to prolong its rule.

Second, the current dominance over the key LSGs by a handful of Third Generation leaders in tandem with the apparent lack of expertise and experience of the incoming leadership could well pose a problem in policy formulation and implementation during the transition period. Moreover, as is the case elsewhere, new leaders in China often bring in a new set of ideas, styles, and faces. The prospects for policy changes, however, should be balanced by an equally strong tendency toward leadership unity, bureaucratic inertia, and broad-based policy consensus. China's overall strategy for economic development and its policy orientations toward the United States and Taiwan are such examples. In brief, no short-term changes are likely.

Third, China's new leaders, like their predecessors, will have to go through the long and difficult stages of power struggle. Without a set of institutional mechanisms for leadership change and without the aura of revolutionary achievements, new leaders must secure their position and status, first and foremost, in the closed circle of top leaders, and they must prove their policy performance. Control of the key LSGs, therefore, will be the crucial step for their political longevity.

Finally, beyond their initial positioning into the Party's top hierarchy, the post-congress leadership will arguably face more daunting tasks. Domestically, coping with the new and complex challenges in Chinese society unleashed by a two-decade-long reform drive will also be a Herculean task. Externally, the emerging leaders in China should not only remain engaged with the outside world but also address the widespread perceptions and worries about the long-term consequences of China's rise. It is this complex set of major domestic and external challenges that the new Chinese leadership will face for many years to come. How well and in what manner they handle the challenges could significantly affect not only political stability in China but also, to some degree, the future capability and behavior of China.

Notes

The author is deeply grateful for research assistance and interviews provided by anonymous individuals in China, Hong Kong, and Taiwan. Any inadequate analysis and factual errors that remain are the responsibility of the author.

1. There are notable exceptions to this pervasive problem. Some of the well-researched and well-informed background studies are Carol Lee Hamrin, "The Party Leadership System," in *Bureaucracy, Politics, and Decision-Making in Post-Mao China*, ed. Kenneth G. Lieberthal and David M. Lampton (Berkeley and Los Angeles: University of California Press, 1992), pp. 95–124; Lu Ning, *The Dynamics of Foreign-Policy Decisionmaking in China* (Boulder, CO: Westview, 1997), and "The Central Leadership, Supraministry Coordinating Bodies, State Council Ministries, and Party Departments," in *The Making of Chinese Foreign and Security Policy in the Era of*

Reform, 1978–2000, ed. David M. Lampton (Stanford: Stanford University Press, 2001), pp. 39–60; Michael D. Swaine, *The Role of the Chinese Military in National Security Policymaking*, rev. ed. (Santa Monica: RAND, 1998).

2. The informal nature of Chinese politics is best captured by a collection of articles in *China Journal* 45 (January 2001).

3. The above categorization of the six *xitong*s is from Lu Ning, "The Central Leadership," p. 40. Other scholars have offered a more detailed explanation of the functional division system among the top leaders, including the relationship between *kou* ("gateway") and its related concepts. See chapters 6 and 7 of Kenneth Lieberthal, *Governing China: From Revolution through Reform* (New York: Norton, 1995) for both the formal and informal aspects of political power in China, especially pp. 192–207.

4. The heads of the groups were Chen Yun, Financial and Economic Small Group; Peng Zhen, Political and Legal Small Group; Chen Yi, Foreign Affairs Small Group; Nie Rongzhen, Science Small Group; and Lu Dingyi, Cultural and Education Small Group, respectively. See Party History Research Center of the Central Committee of the Chinese Communist Party, *History of the Chinese Communist Party: A Chronology of Events (1919–1990)* (Beijing: Foreign Language Press, 1991), p. 272.

5. For a background on their formation and evolution, see Hamrin, "The Party Leadership System," pp. 95–124, especially pp. 99, 111–19.

6. Besides the party's LSGs and central-level committees, the State Council also operates a large number of "provisional organizations" (*linshi jigou*) for policy deliberation and coordination for a set of specific tasks such as the Three Gorges Project, development of the Western Region, implementation of the Chemical Weapons Convention, and placement of demobilized army officers. Their status and duration vary greatly from one organization to another, and they are beyond the scope of discussion.

7. Hamrin, "The Party Leadership System," p. 119.

8. Lu Ning did not list all members of the FALSG in his excellent study, but said its members "included" Wu Yi, Tang Jiaxuan, Chi Haotian, and Xu Yongyue. See Lu Ning, "The Central Leadership," p. 45. My own interviews conducted in 2001 indicate that Wang Huning, deputy director of the CC Policy Research Center, often sits in the body on behalf of Jiang Zemin who apparently is increasingly preoccupied with other national affairs. On several occasions in 2001, on the other hand, deputy chief of the General Staff Xiong Guangkai attended the meetings of the FALSG. It is not clear whether General Xiong was invited to the meetings or attended on behalf of his boss, CMC Vice Chairman and Defense Minister Chi Haotian. Interview with the editor of a military magazine, Hong Kong in January 2001 and interviews in summer 2001.

9. This practice of sending "comprehensive opinions" (*zonghe yijian*) of relevant units to Wang Huning, head of the Foreign Affairs Research Team of the CC Policy Research Center, is due to the fact that Wang is a de facto senior secretary for Jiang Zemin on foreign affairs. For Wang's background, see Cheng Li's contribution to this volume.

10. An excellent study on China's Taiwan policymaking is available. See Michael D. Swaine, "Chinese Decisionmaking Regarding Taiwan, 1979–2000," in *The Making of Chinese Foreign and Security Policy in the Era of Reform, 1978–2000*, ed. David M. Lampton (Stanford: Stanford University Press, 2001), 289–336. See also Guo Ruihua, *Zhonggong dui Tai gongzuo zhuzhi tixi gailun* (Introduction to the PRC's organizations and systems on Taiwan affairs) (Taipei: Fawubu diaochaju, 1996); Xu Zhijia,

Zhonggong waijiao juece moshi yanjiu: Deng Xiaoping shiqi de jianzheng fenxi (Study on the mode of the PRC's foreign policy and decisionmaking: Examination and analysis of the Deng Xiaoping era) (Taipei: Shuiniu chubanshe, 2000).

11. Wang Jingsong, *Zhonghua renmin gongheguo zhengfu yu zhengzhi, 1949.10– 1992* (The government and politics of the People's Republic of China, 1949.10–1992) (Beijing: Zhonggong zhongyang dangxiao chubanshe, 1994), pp. 340–41.

12. *China Directory* (Tokyo: Radiopress, 2000), p. 27. This source lists Wen Jiabao as its secretary general and Hua Jianmin as director of its General Office. The full list of its members should be corroborated with other independent sources, however.

13. Barry Naughton, "Changing Horses in Midstream? The Challenge of Explaining Changing Political Economy Regimes in China," in *China Rising: Implications of Economic and Military Growth in the PRC*, ed. Jaushieh Joseph Wu (Taipei: National Chengchi University Institute of International Relations, 2001), pp. 37–65.

14. Between May 1988 and March 1990 the committee was called the Political and Legal Affairs LSG, which was headed by Qiao Shi. Its origin goes back to the 1940s but its name, composition, and status have vastly changed over the years. For a comprehensive overview of the CCP's political and legal *xitong*, see Yang Shengchun, *Dalu zhengfa zhanxian de tongyuzhe: Zhonggong zhongyang zhengfa weiyuanhui zhi yanjiu* (The controller of the political and legal combat front in mainland [China]: Study of the CCP Central Political and Legal Affairs Committee) (Taipei: Yongye chubanshe, 2001).

15. During the reform years a host of political and legal affairs units were set up to deal with the increasing intelligence need for internal and external security. The Ministry of State Security (June 1983), the Committee for Comprehensive Management of Social Security (March 1991), and the Fourth Department of the General Staff Department (1993) are prime examples.

16. For the composition and activities of the Political and Legal Affairs Committee see the web page of the East Asian Bureau of Japan's External Intelligence Department at www2.odn.ne.jp/~cae02800/index.htm. This is not a part of Japan's Self-Defense Agency. It is operated by former agents and offers information on China's intelligence and public security operations.

17. Chien-wen Kou, "Zhonggong 'ganbu nianqinghua' yu zhengzhi jicheng" ("Making cadres younger" and political succession in China), *Zhongguo Dalu Yanjiu* 44 no. 5 (May 2001): 1–16.

18. Cao Gangchuan became a CMC member in 1998 and the remaining three (Hu Jintao, Guo Boxiong and Xu Caihou) in 1999.

19. They are Jiang Zemin, Zhu Rongji, Qian Qichen, and Chi Haotian in the FALSG; Jiang Zemin, Qian Qichen, and Wang Daohan in the TALSG; Zhu Rongji, Zou Jiahua, and Chen Jinhua in the Financial and Economic LSG; and Han Zhubin in the Political and Legal Affairs Committee.

20. For instance, a *Far Eastern Economic Review* column reported that the body was created in late 2000 for a swift response to national security crises, and that it was headed by Jiang Zemin and coordinated by Liu Huaqiu and Li Peng. It, however, raises several immediate questions as to the apparent delayed setup for the body after the bombing, inclusion of Li Peng, and no follow-up reportage of its meetings. See *Far Eastern Economic Review*, December 14, 2000, p. 10; *Qianshao* (Frontline), June 2001, pp. 6–7.

21. This presupposes Hu Jintao's assumption of the FALSG and the TALSG as the top leader, notwithstanding his lack of experience in these portfolios. For Zeng Qinghong's broad job experience and network of relationships, see Wen Yu, "Zeng Qinghong:

A Possible Contender for PRC Leadership," *China Brief* 1, no. 10 (November 21, 2001); Ting Wang, *Zeng Qing-hong and the Strong Men of the Sunset Race* (Hong Kong: Celebrities Press, 2000). See also Willy Wo-Lap Lam, "Post Beidaihe: No Consensus on PRC Leadership," *China Brief* 1, no. 5 (September 12, 2001).

22. Third generation leaders' patronage of the future generation of leaders is best described in Cheng Li, *China's Leaders: The New Generation* (Lanham, MD: Rowman and Littlefield, 2001).

23. Vice Foreign Minister Li Zhaoxing is a well-known figure in the United States for his long stint as Chinese ambassador to the United Nations and later to the United States throughout the 1990s, during which time he successfully performed his job requirements—promoting China's interests at the world body and at the center of the diplomatic battlefield in Washington at the time of a strained relationship between China and the United States. Due to his barrage of high-profile harangues on U.S. policy and policymakers alike, particularly after the May 1999 embassy bombing, most U.S. scholars and commentators saw him as a hard-line, conservative figure. It is interesting to note that Li has long been identified in the inner circle as being reform-minded and "too liberal" in his foreign-policy views. For a report on his assumption of the post of party secretary in the Foreign Ministry, see "China's Foreign Policy Staff Moves," *Far Eastern Economic Review*, March 2001, p. 8; interviews in Beijing.

24. See note 1.

——— 6 ———

The Role of *Mishu*s in the Chinese Political System

Change and Continuity

James C. Mulvenon and Michael S. Chase

Introduction

The works of Ken Lieberthal, Mike Lampton, Lucian Pye, Li Wei, Cheng Li, and other Sinologists have highlighted the critical role of the *mishu* in Chinese politics.[1] These writings draw from a burgeoning Chinese literature on *mishuxue*, or *mishu* studies.[2] Overall, the English-language analysis of this literature, particularly the writings of Lucian Pye and Li Wei, provide a remarkably comprehensive and well-informed view of the *mishu* phenomenon, discussing the types of *mishu*s and their functions, leader-*mishu* relations, and sources of *mishu* power. One topic that has received insufficient attention, however, is the set of important changes occurring in the *mishu* system, mainly as a result of the changing political, economic, military, and social landscape in reform-era China. This chapter will attempt to fill that gap, drawing upon interviews and previously unavailable primary source materials to discuss both continuity and change in the *mishu* system.

Important Enduring Trends in the *Mishu* System

Pye and Li are indeed correct when they describe the *mishu* as "ubiquitous," since it seems that they permeate every corner of the Chinese system. This ubiquity has two key dimensions: the first is organizational, manifest in the presence of *mishu*s in nearly all of China's political, economic, and military units, and the second is vocational, defined by the remarkably broad scope of the *mishu*'s role and influence.

The Roles of the *Mishu*

Despite many changes discussed in the next section, the traditional roles of the *mishu* have continued to be relevant to the reform era. As Li and Pye relate, *mishu*s continue to serve their leader as adviser, ghostwriter, personal representative, policy coordinator, office administrator, personal manager, servant, and bodyguard.[3] They manage calendars, attend meetings or conferences, handle a leader's personal affairs, supervise projects, issue instructions, filter correspondence and requests for audiences, conduct investigations, draft papers, speeches, and briefings, compile transcripts, coordinate policies, and deal with all aspects of documents work, including document handling, official seals, and security.

Within the bureaucracy, *mishu*s therefore continue to act as "intellectual entrepreneurs," marketing ideas to other *mishu*s, often in the form of consensus-building documents, which are critically important vehicles for building consensus within the complex structure of China's "fragmented authoritarianism."[4] In this way, *mishu*s buttress the collective nature of decision making. *Mishu*s also serve as policy formulators and coordinators for leaders. With their own leader, they must "figure out the leader's intentions" (*linghui lingdao yitu*). Once the leader's position is known, the *mishu* conducts business on behalf of his *shouzhang*, with the *shouzhang*s rarely meeting with one another. *Mishu*s handle "communication and coordination" between leaders, and even smooth over personal disputes or policy rifts.

As a result of the multifaceted role of the *mishu*, leaders become dependent on them, and vice versa. The result is a mutually interdependent patron-client tie. Leaders rarely scapegoat their *mishu*s, and *mishu*s do not conspire in *mishu* cliques, since neither has an incentive to upset the current system. Indeed, *mishu*s are often treated as though they were the *shouzhang*, receiving many of the same perquisites and acts of deference. In the media, for example, *mishu*s are usually referred to as "those who work alongside the leader" (*shenbian gongzuo renyuan*). Eventually, it is common for *mishu*s to become leaders themselves. Indeed, serving as a *mishu* is the most common path to political power. According to interviews, a high percentage of current and past leaders began their careers as *mishu*s, as there seems to be a "lack of any clear separation in the career paths of the *mishu*s and the principal political actors."[5] For leaders, the main purpose of promoting former secretaries is to create a network of supporters who will serve as a base for their former principal's promotion to most senior levels. While serving as *mishu*s, individuals also learn many essential skills necessary for leadership, including familiarity with the system, an ability to deftly manage personal relations, and the value of discretion.

The *Mishu* and Organization

In China, secretarial departments are also an ubiquitous feature of the bureaucratic landscape. As one source puts it, "from the center to the provinces, localities, and counties, party organs at all levels and large and medium-scale enterprises and work units all contain secretarial departments (*mishu bumen*)."[6] The primary responsibility of offices (*bangongting/shi*) and secretarial departments (*mishuting/ju/chu/ke*) is "to serve the leaders of the organization to which they belong and assist them in carrying out all aspects of their work."[7]

Published sources on secretarial work reveal a great deal of information about the organization of secretarial departments at the central, provincial, city, and county levels.[8] In Party Central organizations and State Council organizations the system is said to be one of "division of management" (*fenli zhi*). At this level, the general office (*bangongting*) is an organization that is equal in rank to a ministry or commission (*xiangdangyu buwei yiji de jigou*). Beneath this there are a variety of bureau-level organizations (*juji jigou*), such as the secretarial bureau (*mishuju*), confidential bureau (*jiyaoju*), correspondence bureau (*xinfangju*), guards bureau (*jingweiju*), and organization affairs management bureau (*jiguan shiwu guanliju*). Departments (*chu*) occupy a place on the bureaucratic ranking ladder one step below the bureaus (*ju*).[9] In contrast to Party Central and State Council organizations, the Standing Committee of the National People's Congress (*quanguo renda changweihui*) and Standing Committee of the Chinese People's Political Consultative Conference (*quanguo zhengxie changweihui*) are said to employ a system of "comprehensive management" (*zonglizhi*). In this system of organization, the office (*bangongting*), under the direction of a secretary general (*mishuzhang*), is tasked with the "comprehensive management of daily work." As in the division of management system, there are a number of bureaus (*ju*), departments (*chu*), and offices (*shi*) below the general office (*bangongting*).[10]

Similarly, organizations at the provincial, city, and county levels adopt either the division of management or comprehensive management systems to organize their subordinate units. Party organs generally use the division of management system. They normally have an office (*bangongting/shi*), which is equivalent in rank to a department, commission, or bureau (*bu, wei, jupingxing*). In Party organs at these levels, secretarial departments or sections (*mishuchu/ke*), confidential departments or sections (*jiyaochu/ke*), documents and archives departments or sections (*wendangchu/ke*), and administrative departments or sections (*xingzhengchu/ke*) are all subordinate to the general office (*bangongting/shi*). In some organizations, there is also a specialized documents section (*wenshu ke*) within the office (*bangongshi*) or secretarial department (*mishuchu*).[11] At the lowest levels, party and government organizations some-times lack the dedicated departments or units that specialize in handling doc-uments and secretarial work and perform those functions within organizations at higher levels. In these "grassroots" organizations and low-level units, a few individuals are assigned to deal with the necessary secretarial and documents work.[12] In keeping with the organizational pattern established at the central government level, People's Congresses and Political Consultative Conferences at local levels also employ the comprehensive management system, in which all of the departments and sections responsible for day-to-day work are sub-ordinate to the secretary general. The system of organization and bureaucratic division of responsibility is somewhat flexible, allowing party and government units at local levels to create new units under the control of their general offices "in order to adapt to the developments and suit the requirements of modern secretarial work." In some places, according to a published source on secre-tarial work, new units such as "information departments" (*xinxichu*) and "re-search departments" (*diaoyanchu*) have been established to help local officials cope with a broad range of evolving challenges.[13]

The scope of *mishu* penetration of the bureaucracy is illustrated, for ex-ample, by an examination of the role of *mishu* organizations in the document drafting process. Secretarial units are among the most important organizations involved in the drafting and handling of official documents. According to a recently published book on secretarial work, handling official documents is one of the most important elements of the day-to-day professional work of secretarial departments.[14] Indeed, according to this source, "handling docu-ments is the most fundamental task in the work of secretarial departments," and it is also the task that accounts for the greatest proportion of their overall workload.[15] However, it would be a mistake to assume that secretarial units have sole responsibility for drafting documents. As one source notes, "people often think general offices handle all of the documents work, but professional departments (*yewu bumen*) and functional departments (*zhineng bumen*) are often involved in drafting, handling, and filing documents as well."[16] Indeed, a variety of sources indicate that secretarial departments often work together with other specialized units within an organization to draft documents. Some organizations choose to centralize responsibility for documents work in the office (*bangongting*), while others elect to divide up the responsibilities among their office and professional departments (*yewu bumen*). "Every organization decides how to organize its documents and secretarial work based upon its actual situation and work requirements," according to a publication on the document system.[17] For example, while secretaries clearly play an important role in the documents process, they are not usually professional writers, so they function more as coordinators, according to one source.[18] Yet secretaries, action officers from functional departments, and general office staff often work alongside professional writers and researchers.

The relationships among secretarial departments and other units that deal with documents work, their counterparts at higher administrative levels, and local leaders are multifaceted. These relationships consist of both direct interaction with the leaders that the secretarial departments work under and comparatively indirect interaction with their organizational counterparts at higher levels within the bureaucratic system. Vertical bureaucratic relationships between secretarial departments and other organizations that deal with documents at various levels within the system are usually relatively weak. As one source explains, there is no direct "leadership system" structuring the relations between higher- and lower-level organizations that deal with documents and secretarial work. On the contrary, for secretarial departments and general offices, the leaders they serve are by far their most important bureaucratic superiors. Although these horizontal relationships are of primary importance for secretarial departments and offices, it is worth noting that vertical relationships with their counterparts at higher levels are not insignificant. Specifically, the office departments (*bangong bumen*) of higher-level organizations can exercise "professional guidance" (*yewu zhidao*) over the document and secretarial work (*wenshu gongzuo*) of lower-level organizations, according to a source on documents work.[19]

In addition to their roles in document drafting and handling, their role in managing the flow of incoming information for their leaders means that secretarial departments must also perform a variety of tasks related to secrecy work (*baomi gongzuo*), including protecting classified documents and handling secrecy work at classified party and government meetings.[20] Secretarial organizations thus constitute an "important link" in the protection of Party and state secrets, according to one published source. This source emphasizes to aspiring secretarial personnel the importance of devoting attention to secrecy and security—and underscores the fact that in many organizations secretarial departments have extraordinarily broad access to sensitive information and documents—by stating that secretarial departments are in effect the "harbors" (*tuntugang*) through which official documents pass on their way into or out of the organization and the "point of confluence" for the veritable rivers of classified documents and paperwork that flow throughout the Chinese bureaucratic system. "Most Party and state secrets are reflected in all kinds of official documents," the editors note, and for that reason "establishing a sound secretarial work system helps to plug the loopholes through which secrets can leak, thus preventing harm from coming to state security and effectively protecting Party and state secrets."[21] While it is evident that secretarial departments are tasked with handling a variety of secrecy and security functions, it is not clear from published sources how this work is divided among secretarial departments, secrecy organizations, and other units with responsibilities for security work and safeguarding classified information.

Key Changes in *Mishu* Work in the Reform Era

*Mishu*s have been forced to adapt to the many tectonic political, military, social, and economic changes underway in the country since the late 1970s. In the wake of the Cultural Revolution, the Party Center needed to rebuild the *mishu* system after ten years of chaos and turmoil. According to the official literature, the first task for the leadership was to "normalize" (*zhengchanghua*) and "systemize" (*xitonghua*) the *mishu* system, rapidly organizing and revamping the personnel system.[22] After the cadre system was rehabilitated, the process of economic reform reshaped the character of the bureaucracy, including the *mishu* class. Key trends in the reform era are the need for greater technocratic competence and professional training, the introduction of modern office automation, new types of document and archive responsibilities, the need for greater public outreach and gauging of public opinion, and the changing nature of the leadership and *mishu* promotion patterns into the leadership.

Technocratic Competence

As Li and Pye assert, the qualifications in the past for becoming a *mishu* were "political reliability, good general education, good writing skills, obedience, and competence to wage class struggle."[23] Since the late 1970s, the technocratic professionalism of *mishu*s has increased, given the greater technical complexity of government affairs under economic reform. Now, depending on their work, *mishu*s must be familiar with geography, economics, finance, education, astronomy, medicine, or mathematics, in contrast to the earlier emphasis on politics, literature, national and Party history, and Marxism–Leninism–Mao Zedong Thought.[24] The external manifestation of this new technocratic emphasis is the rise of *mishu*s engaging in formal "policy research" (*zhengce yanjiu*). While *mishu*s have historically conducted investigations (*diaocha*) on behalf of their principals, this new data collection and analysis trend marks a break with the past, because it is more institutionalized and less personal.

At the same time, *mishu*s are still encouraged to be "generalists," with a broad and replaceable set of skills, but the content of that generalism has changed, thanks to the technocratic challenges of managing government affairs in an increasingly global economic and political environment. While the vistas for *mishu* work have broadened, the breadth of expertise in the political leadership, by contrast, has narrowed. A Mao or a Deng could claim wide-ranging experience in the military, economic, and political arenas, while the current leaders generally have experience in only one or two arenas. As a result, specialized military secretaries fill the knowledge gap for their bosses. For example, Jiang Zemin's lack of military experience forced him to rely on a military secretary, Jia Ting'an, to deal with issues related to the armed forces.

Professional Training

One of the most important changes in the *mishu* system has been the rise of a formal training system, subsumed under the rubric of what is known as *mishuxue*, or *"mishu* science." Classes on this subject are now offered in more than 150 Chinese universities.[25] The field also sports at least ten professional journals, which senior leaders and *mishu*s contribute to on a regular basis. The most important of these is entitled *Mishu gongzuo*, published by the Central Committee's *Mishu* Bureau.

Introduction of Office Automation

The Chinese political system is still dominated by paper documents and the all-important chop, but the information revolution has made some identifiable inroads into the life of the *mishu*. Traditionally, the *mishu*'s instruments were "a pen, a sheet of paper, and a telephone."[26] The modern office environment, however, presents the *mishu* with new "challenges," forcing the *mishu* to "adapt to requirements of the times."[27] Specifically, the introduction of computers, cell phones, beepers, and fax machines has significantly altered government bureaucratic work. Since the 1990s, Party, state, and government bureaucracies have made some efforts to take advantage of the opportunities for increased efficiency and productivity presented by the communications and information technology revolution. In a more general sense, according to another published source, modern communications methods are invaluable because they "make communications between government agencies and units easy and quick. It is a piece of a cake to send voice, data, texts, and images from an office to a nearby or distant place. Things that used to require tens of hours or even several days now can be done in several minutes or seconds. Advanced communications technology has become an indispensable pillar of technology for modern office automation."[28]

Limited evidence from a variety of sources shows that many parts of China's bureaucratic apparatus are indeed using computers and electronic communications networks for these reasons, and *mishu*s are no exception.[29] Based on such fragmentary information, however, it is extremely difficult to present an overall assessment of the extent to which Party, government, and military offices have become computerized and networked in recent years, and even more difficult to assess the extent to which the official document system itself relies on computers and information technology. Nevertheless, while there is little reason to believe that Beijing is rushing toward a "paperless office" or striving to radically alter the traditional document system by creating a virtual replacement, it is clear that computers are becoming an increasingly indispensable part of the bureaucratic office environment in China, and this places a much greater onus on the *mishu* to be a competent user of these new technologies.

New Types of Document and Archive Work

*Mishu*s are the critical players in the Chinese document system, and these responsibilities have widened in the reform period. One source asserts that *mishu* offices at every level have increased their documents work, including the drafting, revision, publishing, transmitting, and handling of documents. *Mishu*s do not generally serve on the drafting teams themselves, since they are not usually professional writers. Drafting teams are instead drawn from Party and government research offices (*shiwei yanjiushi* and *shifu yanjiushi*), though they do not do their own research. The research itself is largely provided by think tanks and other research institutes in the system. There is predictable competition between the drafting teams and the researchers.[30] The current leaders do not write as much as their predecessors did, so *mishu*s have had to pick up the slack.

*Mishu*s at the county level and above also have added duties of collecting, arranging, and managing materials for storage in archives (*dang'anguan*), Party history data collection offices (*dangshi ziliao zhengji shi*), and local records offices (*difang zhibian shi*). Moreover, *mishu*s at economic units not only have strengthened their history and personnel archives, but also have started to attach importance to and establish new types of archives related to science and technology (*keji dang'an*), economics (*jingji dang'an*), and pedagogy (*jiaoxue dang'an*).

Public Outreach and Relations with Non-Party Elements

Modern *mishu*s are expected to provide their leaders with new types of information, particularly inputs from increasingly critical sources like public opinion and the business community. Public opinion, which manifests itself today in a dizzying array of call-in radio shows, Internet chatrooms, letters to the editor, books, and magazines, is watched closely by the leadership as a barometer of satisfaction with government policies, and the leaders' *mishu*s are charged with monitoring these developments. Concretely, this task is often subsumed under the growing amount of so-called correspondence work (*xinfang gongzuo*), although this term in Chinese has a much wider meaning than its English equivalent. According to one source, the increasing number of correspondence-related offices and personnel perform important work that helps the leadership understand "public sentiment and opinion" (*minqing sheyi*), deal with the "rehabilitation and redress of mistaken policies or injustices" (*pingfan yuanjia cuoan*), "combat economic crimes" (*daji jingji fanzui*), "check unhealthy tendencies" (*shouzheng buzheng zhifeng*), "defend policies, laws, and discipline" (*weihu zhengce faji*), and "protect the people's interests" (*baozhang remin quanli*).[31] This *mishu* role is likely to become more important over time, as the Chinese leadership experiments with limited pluralism and incorporates more public opinion into government policymaking.

*Mishu*s are also an important conduit to China's entrepreneurs and business leaders, many of whom do not have legitimate intraparty channels to the leadership. While top leaders do meet with some important business leaders, mainly foreign, they cannot meet with all businessmen or others seeking influence, so the *mishu* sometimes acts as a plausibly deniable cutout. As the Chinese Communist Party implements Jiang Zemin's concept of the "Three Represents" (*san ge daibiao*), part of which involves the recruitment of members of the commercial class into the Party, this *mishu* role may decline in importance over time.

Mishu*s and the New Generation of Leaders*

Particularly in the 1970s and 1980s, *mishu*s played a key role in helping China's increasingly gerontocratic leaders stay active in the policy game. As the Fourth Generation of leaders emerges at the Sixteenth Party Congress in 2002, however, these younger leaders will not need *mishu*s to perform this function. Instead, these generally more technocratic and professional politicians will require *mishu*s to also possess many of the same characteristics. In this way, some *mishu*s will continue their transformation into technical policy advisers, capable of offering informed advice on a variety of specialized topics, especially economics and finance.

*Mishus-cum-Politicians. Mishu*s historically have been able to turn their proximity to power into official power and position, but they have never been able to stray far from their area of expertise. Chen Boda, for example, was never able to exercise influence outside of the Party work arena. The current generation of *mishu*s, however, is increasingly able to move across policy arenas, which is an important break from past constraints.[32] This is another reflection of the technocratization of the *mishu* class.

Conclusion

The *mishu* is as important to the Chinese political system today as he was in the Mao or Deng era, but the dramatic changes in the policy environment have forced significant changes in the background, skills, and roles of the *mishu* corps. Specifically, *mishu*s in the reform era must acquire greater technocratic competence and professional training, be comfortable with the introduction of modern office automation, handle new types of document and archive responsibilities, perform greater outreach to gauge public opinion, adapt to the changing nature of the Fourth Generation leadership and thereby alter their own patterns of promotion into the leadership. There is a significant amount of evidence to suggest that these trends are already well underway.

As a result, one must conclude that the *mishu* is a highly adaptive political form. Indeed, as the Chinese political system continues to evolve, the *mishu* will likely continue to play a central role, perhaps even facilitating the expected growing pluralism within China's single-party state by providing new channels for wider public opinion to reach the country's unelected leadership. It would therefore be a mistake to link the *mishu* system with authoritarianism, and thereby conclude that democratization would bring it to an end. Indeed, the Taiwan experience tells us that *mishu*s can play an equally powerful role within a democratic system, suggesting that the *mishu* system has more to do with Chinese culture than ideology or structure. If so, we should expect the *mishu* to occupy a permanent, unique, and profound position in the Chinese political universe.

Notes

1. Wei Li and Lucian Pye, "The Ubiquitous Role of the *Mishu* in Chinese Politics," *China Quarterly* no. 132 (December 1992): 913–36. It is difficult to translate the term "*mishu*" into English. The term "secretary" is far too narrow and limiting, and even "special assistant" does not convey the breadth of the *mishu*'s responsibilities.

2. Some notable examples include *Mishuxue* (Mishu studies) (Beijing: Zhongguo shangye chubanshe, 1993); Deng Naixing and Zeng Zhaole, ed., *Mishu yu xiezuo* (Mishus and writing) (Guangzhou: Jinan daxue chubanshe, 2001); Zhu Zhuanzhi and Ye Ming, ed., *Mishu lilun yu shiwu* (Mishu theory and practice) (Hangzhou: Zhejiang daxue chubanshe, 1995); Hou Rui, *Zenyang dang bangongshi zhuren* (How to work as director of a mishu office) (Beijing: Dang'an chubanshe, 1990); Ou Yangzhou, ed., *Xiandai mishuxue: yuanli yu shiwu* (Modern mishu studies: principles and practice)

(Changsha: Zhongnan daxue chubanshe, 2000); Yi Chengjie et al., *Zhengwu jieqia yu lingdao huodong anpai* (How to receive official visitors and arrange leaders' activities) (Beijing: Dang'an chubanshe, 1990); Wang Qiangong et al., *Shiyong mishu gongzuo shouce* (A practical handbook for mishu work) (Beijing: Guangming ribao chubanshe, 1987); Ning Maochang, ed., *Mishuxue* (Mishu studies) (Qingdao: Shandong daxue chubanshe, 1996); Qi Peiwen et al., *Zenyang danghao lingdaoren mishu* (How to be a good personal mishu) (Beijing: Dang'an chubanshe, 1990); Chen Heyi, *Mishuxue* (Mishu studies) (Hunan: Jiangnan University Publishing House, 1997); Chen Xianhua, *Mishu gongzuo lun* (On mishu work) (Chengdu: Sichuan University Publishing House, May 1996); *Shiyong mishu quanshu* (Practical mishu handbook) (Xi'an: Shanxi Normal University Publishing House, May 1999); *Junshi mishu xue* (Military mishu studies) (Beijing: Haichao chubanshe, 1992); Xu Ruizin et al., *Zhongguo xiandai mishu gongzuo jichu* (The essentials of the contemporary mishu profession) (Beijing: Gaodeng jiaoyu chubanshe, 1989); Zheng Xinghan, *Dangzheng jiguan mishu gongzuo gaishu* (An outline of mishu work in party and state organs) (Beijing: Dang'an chubanshe, 1989); *Zhonggong mishu gongzuo jianshi, 1921–49* (Chinese Communist Party mishu work, 1921–49) (Shenyang, Liaoning: Liaoning renmin chubanshe, 1992); and Lu Yufang, ed., *Mishuxue gailun* (A discussion of mishu studies) (Shanghai: Fudan daxue chubanshe, 2001).

3. Li and Pye, "The Ubiquitous Role of the *Mishu*," pp. 918–25.

4. Kenneth G. Lieberthal and David M. Lampton, eds., *Bureaucracy, Politics, and Decision Making in Post-Mao China*, (Berkeley: University of California Press, 1992), pp. 6–12. Lieberthal and Lampton define "fragmented authoritarianism" as the fragmentation of bureaucratic authority over resource distribution, policymaking, and policy implementation at levels below the apex of the political system that has characterized Chinese politics during the economic reform and opening period. In "fragmented authoritarianism," institutional structure and decentralization of control over resources create a system in which reaching a decision on a particular issue often requires several governmental bodies to bargain or negotiate with each other because none of the organizations with a stake in the problem has the power to issue binding orders to the other involved parties.

5. Li and Pye, "The Ubiquitous Role of the *Mishu*," p. 914.

6. Ning Maochang, ed. *Mishuxue* (1996), p. 28. There are some exceptions to this rule. "Basic-level and relatively small-scale units usually do not have their own secretarial departments," the editor notes, "but they still have an appropriate number of secretarial personnel."

7. *Wenshuxue* (Document studies) (Beijing: Archives Publishing House, 1993), p. 115. This source notes that "generally speaking, there are two kinds of units within organizations: professional (*yewu*) or functional (*zhineng*) departments, and office departments (*bangong bumen*)." The mission of the latter is to assist the leaders of the organization.

8. *Mishuxue* (Mishu studies) (Beijing: Zhongguo shangye chubanshe, 1993).

9. Ibid., p. 89.

10. Ibid. The substantive differences in terms of formal organizational structure or bureaucratic process that differentiate the two types of systems are not clearly explained in this volume.

11. Ibid.

12. *Wenshuxue* (1993), p. 116. The information this source provides is basically

consistent with the above description, indicating that in a typical organization, the secretarial department (*mishuchu/shi*), correspondence department (*xinfangchu/shi*), confidential room (*jiyaoshi*), typing room (*dazishi*), sending and receiving room (*shoufashi*), and so on are all established under the general office (*bangongting/shi*).

13. *Mishuxue* (1993), p. 89

14. Deng Naixing and Zeng Zhaole, *Mishu yu xiezuo*, p. 131.

15. Ibid., p. 131.

16. Ibid., p. 116.

17. Ibid., p. 117.

18. Interview.

19. *Wenshuxue* (1993), p. 116.

20. Zhu Zhuanzhi and Ye Ming, *Mishu lilun yu shiwu*, pp. 252–54.

21. Deng Naixing and Zeng Zhaole, *Mishu yu xiezuo*, pp. 132, 146–48. The editors of this volume observe that "secretarial departments bear an especially important responsibility" in terms of secrecy work. This is because they draft and handle numerous classified documents, and at meetings "they are often called upon to handle classified information, even top-secret information." Furthermore, the editors note that because secretaries work so closely with their principals, many other aspects of their jobs also require a high degree of confidentiality. Since secretarial personnel have extensive access to classified information, secretarial departments and secretaries have become an important target for foreign intelligence services. According to the editors: "secretarial personnel, and even their relatives, friends, and old acquaintances, are often the target of people who are fishing for information."

22. Lu Yufang, *Mishuxue gailun*, pp. 31–32.

23. Zheng Xinghan, *Dangzheng jiguan mishu*, p. 159.

24. Qi Peiwen, *Zenyang danghao lingduoren mishu*, pp. 216–29.

25. Zheng Xinghan, *Dangzheng jiguan mishu*, p. 62.

26. Zhu Zhuanzhi and Ye Ming, *Mishu lilun yu shiwu*, p. 282.

27. Ibid.

28. *Baomi zhishi duben* (Secrecy Knowledge Reader).

29. Interviews, January 2001 and November 2001.

30. Interview with a high-ranking *mishu*, September 28, 2000.

31. Lu Yufang, *Mishuxue gailun*, p. 32.

32. Interview with a high-ranking *mishu*, September 28, 2000.

Where Do Correct Ideas Come From?

The Party School, Key Think Tanks, and the Intellectuals

Joseph Fewsmith

One broaches the subject of think tanks with a degree of wariness. One fears that a discussion of think tanks will lead to the belief that there is a magic bullet to understanding China—that if only we can identify who is whispering in the prince's ear, we will understand where Chinese politics is going. Certainly, as in any political system, what is being whispered in the prince's ear is important. The trouble is, first, that there are lots of things being whispered in the prince's ear from lots of different people and groups, and second, that who the prince decides to listen to changes from one point in time to another, depending on shifting political forces, the prince's understanding of the economic situation or other domestic needs, the changing international environment, the whim of the prince, or perhaps even the quality of the last bit of policy advice someone whispered. And, of course, the "prince" is not the only decision maker. Particularly in the post-Deng era, decision making is more complicated than convincing a single individual. At least on most decisions, there appears to be considerably more consultation and bureaucratic input to decision making than in the past. This does not mean that decisions are made by consensus, but it usually means that issues have been vetted and that the leader knows what the possible problems are, where the opposition lies, and how much opposition there is.

Another caveat when thinking about decision making and think tanks is that the constellation of people and organs giving policy advice varies over time. Some organizations appear to have greater ability to exert influence out of institutional design. But even such structural arrangements do not guarantee steady influence. This has certainly been the case in China. Moreover, the influence exerted by one person or one organization is very often based on informal relations. Again, this is not unique to China; American presidents have their kitchen cabinets. But there may be an even greater reliance on informal relations in China, if only because the institutional arrangements tend to be more fluid. That fluidity is partly determined by the personality and needs of the top leadership and partly by the development of reform.

If one goes back to the mid- and late 1970s, one of the most important think tanks was the Political Study Office (*Zhengzhi yanjiu shi*). This was an office Deng Xiaoping established in the State Council in 1975 in order to compete in the ideological arena with the Gang of Four. Members of the office included Hu Qiaomu, Wu Lengxi, Hu Sheng, Xiong Fu, Yu Guangyuan, and Deng Liqun. This office helped draft the so-called three poisonous weeds— "Twenty Articles on Industry," "Outline Report on the Work of the Academy of Sciences," and "On the General Program of the Work for the Whole Party and Country"—for which Deng was later criticized.[1]

When Deng was purged, the Political Study Office was not closed formally, though its staffers stayed away from the office. Following the arrest of the Gang of Four, however, as the political atmosphere became more favorable to Deng, members of the office began to return and reestablish their contacts. This was one of the channels through which Deng kept in touch with political goings-on in that period prior to his return to office.[2]

It will be noticed that members of this office went on to become important members of the ideological establishment after Deng's return to power. Hu Qiaomu became the first president of the newly established Chinese Academy of Social Sciences (CASS), joined the Politburo, and had overall responsibility for ideology. Hu Sheng succeeded Hu as president of CASS, and Deng Liqun and Yu Guangyuan became vice presidents of CASS. Xiong Fu became the very conservative editor of *Red Flag*, and Wu Lengxi became minister of Radio and Television. So the Political Study Office was not only an important think tank in its own right, but also generated the leaders of other think tanks and bureaucratic organs. It should also be noted that being together in one think tank did not guarantee unanimity of opinion. Yu Guangyuan became one of the most liberal thinkers in Dengist China, while Hu Qiaomu, Deng Liqun, Xiong Fu, and Wu Lengxi became some of the most conservative. It is unwise to assume that people who work together agree with each other.

The Political Study Office exemplified the characteristics of an establishment think tank (though who precisely was the "establishment" was in dispute in this period) in that its staffers were all certified members of the political establishment (Hu Qiaomu had served as Mao Zedong's secretary, and Deng Liqun had served as Liu Shaoqi's secretary) and they worked to support Deng Xiaoping. It was also an ideological think tank in the sense that their job was both to identify broad policy directions and then to justify those policy directions in ideological terms. Ideology was crucial. A great deal of attention was paid to justifying policy innovations in ideological terms. This can be seen in the critical report that Hu Qiaomu gave to the State Council in July 1978, "Act in Accordance with Economic Laws, Step up the Four Modernizations."[3] Although one can assume that the policy direction came first in people's thinking and the ideological justifications came second, it is also important to recognize that ideology was a real constraint on what could or could not be done in policy terms. Even if the bounds of ideology have expanded considerably in the twenty years since then, the attention to ideological justification remains an important part of the decision-making process.

Another example of an establishment think tank is the Central Party School, which played a key role in working out the ideological parameters of the Dengist period. The Central Party School plays an important role as the training ground of cadres who are already in important positions and who are being considered for promotion to yet higher positions. Although the Party School runs many training programs, its most important one is no doubt the year-long program it runs for up-and-coming cadres. This is basically a mid-career training program. Cadres get to listen to high-level officials discuss problems and policy options, they get to meet other up-and-coming cadres (networking), and no doubt the best and brightest are noted by the leadership of the Party School.

Because of this role, the Central Party School has always played an important role in articulating interpretations of Marxism-Leninism. After all, one needs to be able to teach Party history and current policy directions as consistent with the ideological line. This makes the Central Party School the most important think tank in ideological terms, and leadership over the Party School is always important.

The role of the Central Party School in the drafting of the famous article "Practice Is the Sole Criterion of Truth" is well known and need not be repeated here. Suffice it to say, the Party School faced an important issue in trying to define the party line and being able to teach it to its students. It was precisely this issue of how one determines what is "right" or "wrong" ("truth") that led people at the school to think about the criteria for judging policy. It was also important that Hu Yaobang, a very open-minded official, was in effective control of the Party School. It was Hu who approved the text of the article and first ran it in the Party School's internal journal *Lilun dongtai* (Theoretical Trends), a journal that Hu had established to take up the thorniest ideological issues of the day.[4]

It might also be said that the Central Party School played a role in the more conservative theoretical trend that emerged in the early 1980s. Hu Yaobang left the Party School when he became general secretary of the Party, and Wang Zhen took over the running of the Party School. Some of the more liberal-minded theorists, most notably Ruan Ming, were forced to leave, while others trimmed their sails accordingly.[5]

The 1980s are also known for their less orthodox think tanks. The prototype of these groups was the Agricultural Development Group, established by Chen Yizi. Whereas the Central Party School was the preeminent permanent establishment think tank and the Political Study Office was equally establishment albeit more ad hoc, the Agricultural Development Group was something new on the scene. Many of those Chen gathered together were former Red Guards who had been disbursed to the countryside during the Cultural Revolution. Mao had told them to learn from the peasants, and they did—but not always what Mao hoped they would learn. Having labored at the grassroots level, they understood the many failings of the commune system. With the passing of Mao and the reestablishment of the university examination system, these people were able to return to the cities (mostly Beijing in this case) and test into some of the leading universities in China (mostly Beijing University and People's University). Perhaps these people can be described as practical idealists. They no longer had ideological faith in Maoism—the Cultural Revolution had shattered that—but they still had enough idealism to believe that they could do something for China. But they were very practical. They understood how the ideological fervor of the Mao era had damaged the fabric and economic viability of rural China, and they were determined to find alternatives that were politically viable and economically rational.[6]

It was this group that began doing systematic rural surveys that reported on the success of the household responsibility system. Going down to the grassroots to investigate the real situation was nothing new; Mao had long advocated doing such research (though in practice he discouraged honest reporting). What was new about what this group was doing was their unofficial standing, at least until 1981. They were what we might call a voluntary association or a nongovernmental group. They were not exactly a lobbying group because much of their effectiveness depended on their close relations with top officials, which indicated that they were not an exemplar of "civil society." But they were not part of the establishment either. Even after their incorporation into CASS, they still acted independently—doing pretty much what they wanted.

The other aspect that was new about this group was their determination to carry out systematic investigations and to write reports that reflected both the real situation on the ground and a freedom from ideological cant. Indeed, it was this group that first introduced the term "think tank" into Chinese.[7] They aspired to do independent research, letting the chips fall where they may. That, of course, is difficult to do in China (and elsewhere!), and they became very closely identified with Premier Zhao Ziyang, as did their later offshoot, the Institute for Economic Structural Reform (tigaisuo).

What is important about these groups is that they provided new and different perspectives from those provided by the bureaucracies. Every bureaucracy in China has its own research institute. Often they are staffed by people who have worked in that particular sector for a long time, and they have resources, including access to data, that these semi-independent think tanks could not compete with. But this was a stage of reform in which broad ideas about how to reform and about policy direction were more important than reams of data about conditions in one or another sector of the economy. So these think tanks were able to bring a new type of knowledge to the table, and thus have an impact not only on policy but, perhaps more importantly, on the way people thought about problems.

The four think tanks most closely associated with Zhao Ziyang were closed following Tiananmen, and the relationship between the government and intellectuals was tense for some period of time. Official think tanks of various sorts—the Development Research Institute of the State Council, CASS, the Central Party School, and so forth—remained open, and they continued to play a role, albeit a diminished one. Many of those associated with the closed think tanks went abroad—some to study and a few to stay in exile. Because of their importance, economists, some of whom were affiliated with another government think tank, the State Council Development Research Center, continued to play a role in shaping government thinking about policy, particularly as the immediate impact of Tiananmen faded.

It is, however, important to note that the single most important event in that period—Deng's trip to the south of China—appears to have had no connection to any think tank. Deng maintained his own office, but precisely how that office worked and what advice it solicited is hidden deep in the "black box" obscuring elite politics. Deng's determination to head south and condemn the "left" appears to have been a deeply political decision—Deng did not like the ideological and policy direction China had been following since Tiananmen— rather than a carefully thought out development strategy for which expert advice needed to be sought.

It is more in the mid-1990s, when some of the policy consequences of Deng's trip became apparent and as Jiang Zemin moved to take effective control of the polity, when think tanks, or at least thinkers, reemerge as important. Nevertheless, it should be noted that by this time there was a substantial difference in the relationship between the government and intellectuals. First, with generational succession, many of the top leaders were themselves well educated and comfortable discussing ideas with intellectuals (or at least reading their ideas). This tendency is exemplified by Jiang Zemin's bringing Wang Huning, who headed the Department of International Politics at Fudan University, to Beijing, where he became head of the Political Section of the Chinese Communist Party's (CCP's) Policy Research Office.[8] It is difficult to imagine Deng Xiaoping having such a close relationship with an intellectual adviser. In other words, from a political perspective, there was an increasing legitimacy to intellectual input and an increasing attention to the technical details of policy formation.

Second, the problematique had changed considerably. In the 1980s, the question was often whether to reform or not. Although the distinction between "reformers" and "conservatives" does not capture the complexity of decision making in the 1980s, it does suggest that the issues on the table were those of broad policy direction. As suggested above, this was something that the think tanks of the 1980s were good at thinking about. By the 1990s, however, the situation is much more complex. Although the "conservative-reformer" dichotomy still had some meaning, it was much diminished. "Reformers" were doing things that "conservatives" had advocated in the 1980s. A case in point is tax reform. In the 1980s, conservatives had worried about the loss of fiscal control the central government experienced and lobbied endlessly for increasing the central government's tax revenues. But in their recommendations, the increase in tax revenues was always associated with strengthening the role of economic planning. In the 1990s, Premier Zhu Rongji worried about the decline in central revenues as well—something he began to reverse with his tax reform of 1994—however, Zhu was not interested in strengthening the plan but in strengthening the use of macroeconomic tools to control an increasingly market-oriented economy. In broader terms, the problems of the 1990s were much less about whether to reform than they were about how to reform. The details became important. How does one carry out housing reform? How does one build an adequate social security system? How does one prevent corruption? At least for most people, there was less talk of "isms" and more talk of "problems."

At the same time that the problems facing government became more technical, the government's own capacity to deal with problems was increasing. In part, this was simply a matter of following the learning curve. Bright young technocrats recruited in the 1980s had accumulated enough experience and had risen to sufficiently high positions that they could think both creatively and carefully about difficult problems. The government was much less one in which bureaucrats defended the turf of the various ministries and much more of a technocracy that dealt with specific problems. This appears to be particularly true as the State Trade and Economic Commission increased its clout in government circles.

In part, this growing governmental expertise came as a result of recruiting into the government experts who had served in think tanks in the 1980s. This is particularly true on the economic side where Zhu Rongji has promoted a number of economists he has known to important policy positions. As Barry Naughton has written, Zhu Rongji specifically recruited Lou Jiwei, previously an economist at the Rural Development Center (RDC), to be vice minister of finance (after having been tempered in several positions, including vice governor of Guizhou) to supervise tax reform. Similarly, a number of agricultural specialists, including Chen Xiwen and Du Ying, who worked with the Rural Development Research Institute in the 1980s, have taken up senior positions in the Development Research Center (DRC) and the Ministry of Agriculture where they have had a significant impact on policy.[9] Another such person is Guo Shuqing, previously an economist with the DRC who, like Lou Jiwei, served as vice governor of Guizhou, and has recently been promoted to vice governor of the Bank of China.

The technocratization of government made think tanks—at least the sort of think tanks that were associated with Zhao Ziyang in the 1980s—less important even as it made expertise more important. Thus, individuals with expertise, whether in government or out, probably have greater access than they did in the 1980s. In general, this expertise resides in individuals rather than in think tanks.

Third, as the nature of government has evolved, so has the nature of the intellectual community. The term "intellectual" used to be a much less problematic term. Intellectuals recognized who was, and who was not, an intellectual; there was a sense of community if not of amicability. Intellectuals were generalists. They were rooted in the old scholarly tradition of thinking about the big questions and offering morally rooted advice. Qu Yuan lived in the souls of intellectuals. By the 1990s, Qu Yuan was dead, or nearly so. Some intellectuals had gone on to become technocrats, either in government or in the various universities. Others had turned their backs on intellectual pretensions and had leaped into the sea of the commercial economy; respected writers found themselves writing for television. Others retreated into the university towers to pursue pure scholarship. In short, by the late 1990s, the intellectual community was far more fragmented; it increasingly resembled its counterparts elsewhere in the world.[10]

In broad terms, compared with the 1980s, the Chinese government in the 1990s had greater expertise, individuals with expertise had greater influence, the intellectual community in general was more distant from government, and the sort of think tank associated with Zhao Ziyang—in the state but not of the state—was less important. However, as society has become more diverse and complex, a variety of private think tanks have sprung up, and increasingly are playing an important role, sometimes at the national level but frequently at the local level.

The Economic Research Center at Beijing University, run by Lin Yifu, is one of the best examples of an independent think tank. Lin has recruited some of the best economists in China, and they raise funds through grants and consulting—something that was not possible in the 1980s. Another independent think tank is Mao Yushi's Unirule Institute, which relies on consulting for its funds but carries out both basic and policy-relevant research. The influence of such think tanks derives primarily from their expertise and the reputations of their researchers rather than any relationship either with individual political leaders or structural access to decision making.

Another interesting semi-independent think tank is Hu Angang's National Conditions Research Group, formerly of the Chinese Academy of Sciences (CAS) and now based at Qinghua University. Hu came to the attention of Deng Xiaoping when a book he had contributed to, *Survival and Development*, was forwarded to Deng by his daughter, Deng Nan, who worked at CAS. Since then his research group at Qinghua University has had little difficulty securing research funds. But rather than write quietly for government patrons, Hu has sought a public role, thus exemplifying one other aspect of contemporary think tank people—frequently playing the role of public intellectual, trying to persuade large audiences rather than just a handful of policymakers. Indeed, Hu is quite frank about his efforts to coordinate the publishing of his ideas in narrowly circulated internal publications, in more widely circulated internal publications, and in widely circulated open publications.

Hu is an interesting example of a think tank person because much of his most influential research has been carried out collaboratively with Wang Shaoguang, formerly of Yale University and now at Hong Kong University. In this sense, China's "think tanks," like Chinese intellectual discourse in general, have become internationalized; they draw their ideas and even their research partners from outside China's borders, something inconceivable in the 1980s.

Hu's movement to Qinghua University is interesting because it exemplifies the movement away from government auspices (even if the recruitment of people like Lou Jiwei and Guo Shuqing into the government marks the flow of people in the other direction). Although this chapter does not focus on international relations think tanks, the movement of high-profile foreign policy analysts such as Yan Xuetong and Chu Shulong from the China Institute of Contemporary International Relations to Qinghua University similarly suggests that universities are—finally—being seen as repositories of policy expertise.

Another independent think tank is the World and China Institute run by Li Fan. Unlike the economic think tanks, Li's group has focused on more political questions, including the organization of government at the local level. In 1997, Li was very much involved in organizing the first township-level election, held in Buyun township in Sichuan Province. There are also groups like the Legal Assistance Center at Wuhan University, that might be considered a think tank regarding legal issues, but is also a nongovernmental organization assisting those with legal problems (often involving the government). As these and other groups show, China's vibrant society is generating groups that straddle the state/society divide; as with the economy, there is an ongoing privatization of expertise.

Finally, let us consider government think tanks. As mentioned above, virtually all government administrative organs maintain some kind of research capacity. In most cases, these seem to feed data to organization heads, rather than engage in innovative research that could lead to new policies. Some, however, are notable for doing just that. The best-known example in this regard is the Bureau of Basic-Level Governance Construction in the Ministry of Civil Affairs' Rural Division. Over a period of years, this bureau, first under the leadership of Wang Zhenyao, studied the problems of rural governance and supported the organization of village elections. Over a period of a dozen or more years, this bureau has provided critical research and policy advice in addressing the critical problems in the countryside.[11]

Recently, much attention has been focused on the topic of political reform not only because of its urgency but especially because the CCP has been discussing this subject at a high level. It is important to point out that most of this sort of discussion occurs in the black box that surrounds elite politics, but some general statements can be ventured.

One interesting example is the book *China Investigation Report*, which was written by the organization departments of various provinces and edited by the Central Organization Department. This book reported in considerable detail on the negative trends, particularly those that protest government actions either peacefully or violently, many of which are known to the outside, but are rarely admitted in official publications. The book created a much greater stir abroad, because of the publicity given to it by the *New York Times*, than it did in China, where it is virtually unknown, because it was withdrawn from circulation immediately after it was reported. This book appears to have been one product of a much wider effort made by the CCP and the State Council to collect data about conditions in China, interpret those data, and draw out their implications for the political system in preparation for the Sixteenth Party Congress.[12]

We do not normally think of the Organization Department as a think tank, but obviously the Organization Department maintains a considerable investigative capacity, which it uses to address the issues of party building. This is one capacity that those who think that the party is likely to collapse underestimate. Events may overtake the organizational capabilities of the party, but the party obviously has no intention of being surprised by events. It is constantly researching and adapting to change, which suggests that it may be more resilient than some think.

A second interesting example appears to be more an instance of intragovernment freelancing than of a government think tank. A research report, dated January 2001, on political reform was circulated on the Internet under the name of Pan Yue, deputy director of the State Council Economic Restructuring Office and son-in-law of General Liu Huaqing. Reportedly, Pan had recruited a number of liberal intellectuals to think about political reform, and this report was the summary of a larger effort. There was considerable irony in Pan's sponsorship of this research; in the early 1990s, Pan had been closely connected with neoconservative thinking then popular in some circles. There is much speculation as to whether Pan was undertaking this research on his own or whether it was part of a larger effort to consider political reform; reportedly Pan's efforts have been rejected by the leadership, but comparison between his report and ideas circulating in party journals suggests either that his ideas have wide support or that others have derived very similar ideas independently. More recently, National People's Congress head Li Peng has criticized Pan.[13]

In any event, the appearance of this report again cautions us to be careful about how we think about think tanks. Although Pan works at an office tasked with thinking about reform, there is no reason to think that the Economic Restructuring Office's mandate stretches to political reform. The point is that proposals can pop up from almost anywhere on the political landscape and that personal relationships and reputations are probably more important than organizations in bringing ideas to the attention of leaders.

Another example of think tank activity we know more from the "output" than the "input" is the "Three Represents" (that the party represents the fundamental interests of the broad mass of the people, that it represents the advanced productive forces, and that it represents advanced culture). This ideological innovation first surfaced in February 2000 and has been bruited with increasing force ever since. The Three Represents appear to have emerged from the joint efforts of the Political Research Office of the Central Committee and the Central Party School. One thing I think we can say about the Three Represents is that a great deal of thinking went into their formulation. Part of this effort was directed at understanding the lessons of the collapse of socialism in the former Soviet Union and Eastern Europe. Another part of the effort was directed at trying to understand the implications of the social and economic changes China was experiencing, including the emergence of high-tech, the spread of globalization, and the growth of the private sector. Yet another part was directed at thinking through how the changes the Party thought it needed to make could be justified in ideological terms. Just as with the inauguration of reform, maintaining ideological justification is an important part of the reform process.

Jiang Zemin's July 1 speech appears to have come out of the same broad process. Discussions that led into the speech have been taking place for perhaps two years and have included people at the provincial and subprovincial level as well as those in Beijing. Again, this cautions us as to how we think about think tanks. Although the party theoreticians, whether at the Central Party School, the Policy Research Office, or elsewhere, may shape the product, the effort in this case was obviously much broader than can be encompassed by the term "think tank." There has been much speculation in recent months about the role of people at the Central Party School, their discussions with the Social Democrats in Germany, their relationship with Vice President (and soon to be General Secretary) Hu Jintao, and whether a breakthrough in political reform may emerge from these discussions and this relationship.

Unless more information becomes available, it seems wise to handle this speculation cautiously. First, there is no question that people at the Central Party School and elsewhere have spent a lot of time thinking about the failures of the Communist Party of the Soviet Union and other socialist parties and what sort of changes the CCP needs to make in order to retain power. They have certainly considered the experiences of social democrats, and there are no doubt people who would like to rename the CCP the Chinese Social Democratic Party, as some believe will eventually happen. The idea of a "whole people's party" (*quanmindang*), that is, one that is representative of all social classes and interests (as opposed to the class nature of a communist party) has attracted a lot of attention. But there is a difference between talking about such ideas and adopting them. As just noted, there has been a very extensive effort to think about ideological and political reform, but that does not mean that the farthest-reaching ideas will carry the day. Many people are consulted and the outcome is likely to approximate a consensus (which does not mean that everyone is happy).

Second, the tradition of the CCP has been to change while maintaining continuities with the past. When Deng launched his reforms, he did not jettison Mao (indeed, he criticized those who wanted the History Resolution to pass a harsher judgment on Mao). Instead, Deng returned to Mao's famous article "On Practice," and built his interpretation of Mao Zedong Thought around the criterion of practice. It is useful to remember that the Chinese have always been critical of Khrushchev's wholesale denunciation of Stalin. And they remembered that lesson when they turned away from Mao. My belief is that the CCP will again follow this approach, reinterpreting CCP tradition and Marxist-Leninist ideology in ways that will support the policy direction that they want to move in but will stop well short of changing the name of the Chinese Communist Party.

Third, it seems evident from the commentary available so far that the CCP will approach political reform cautiously. This does not mean that it will not be important. The main theme of Jiang Zemin's July 1 speech, in my opinion, is that the Party wants to change itself from a "revolutionary party" (*geming-dang*) to a "ruling party" (*zhizhengdang*). This terminology is rather awkward, considering that the CCP has been in power for fifty years, but it is meant to convey a change from a party that is above the law (indeed, a system in which there is little law), in which power is highly concentrated in individual cadres, and which is based on a model of mobilization, to one that operates within the framework of the law, one in which decisions on both promotions and policy are made in accordance with procedures, and one in which the relationship between the Party and society is regularized. It is intended to be a party of administration rather than a party of mobilization. Whether such changes are feasible is another matter; these are the terms in which Party ideologues are currently thinking. The idea of a "whole people's party" is explicitly refuted.[14]

In conclusion, in thinking about the role of intellectuals and think tanks in contemporary China, I think one needs to take into account the changing nature of the Chinese political system, the changing nature of Chinese society and the problems that poses for governance, and the changing nature of the intellectual community. Unfortunately, there is no magic bullet. You cannot study one individual or one institution and understand where China is going. Individuals and think tanks such as the Central Party School are important, but the discussions that go on are wide-ranging, both within the central government and inclusive of lower levels, so that the outcome reflects a broader consensus than the opinion of one or two think tanks or leaders. In this sense, the contrast between the drafting of the article "Practice Is the Sole Criterion of Truth" and the drafting of Jiang Zemin's July 1 speech (our knowledge of which remains sketchy) is instructive. I expect this more complex, quasi-institutionalized policymaking process to continue. Hu Jintao may accelerate the pace of change, but it will be done within a framework that draws its ideas from a broad range of institutions and individuals and within a context that takes the complexity of Chinese society into account. Political reform of various sorts will take place, but the likelihood of a radical breakthrough—democratization—strikes me as small.

Notes

1. Tang Zongji and Zheng Qian, ed., *Shinianhou de pingshuo* (An evaluation ten years later) (Beijing: Zhonggong dangshi ziliao chubanshe, 1987), p. 123; and Deng

Liqun, "Guowuyuan zhengzhi yanjiushi gongzuo he yundong de jiben zongjie" (A basic summary of the work and movements of the State Council Political Study Office), in Deng Liqun, *Deng Liqun wenji* (Collected works of Deng Liqun) (Beijing: Dangdai Zhongguo chubanshe, 1998), vol. 1 pp. 40–49.

2. This relationship is covered in my book, *Dilemmas of Reform: Political Conflict and Economic Debate* (Armonk, NY: M.E. Sharpe, 1994).

3. Hu Qiaomu, "Act in Accordance with Economic Laws, Step Up the Four Modernizations," *Xinhua*, October 5, 1978, trans. FBIS, October 11, 1978, pp. E1–22.

4. Michael Schoenhals, "The 1978 Truth Controversy," in *China Quarterly*, no. 126 (June 1991): 243–68.

5. Ruan Ming, *Deng Xiaoping diguo* (The empire of Deng Xiaoping) (Taipei: Shih-pao ch'u-pan kung-ssu, 1991).

6. Fewsmith, *Dilemmas of Reform*, pp. 34–41.

7. Deng Yingtao et al., "Lun zhanlue yanjiu" (On strategic research), in *Nongcun, jingji, shehui* (Villages, economy, and society), vol. 1, ed. Chinese Rural Development Group, pp. 261–86.

8. Gao Xin, *Jiang Zemin de muliao* (Jiang Zemin's counselors) (Hong Kong: Mingjing chubanshe, 1997).

9. Barry Naughton, "Economic Think Tanks in China: Their Role in the 1990s," in Murray Scot Tanner, *China's Think Tanks: Windows on a Changing China* (n.p., 2000), pp. 59–71.

10. Joseph Fewsmith, *China Since Tiananmen: The Politics of Transition* (New York: Cambridge University Press, 2001).

11. Shi Tianjian, "Village Committee Elections in China: Institutional Tactics for Democracy," *World Politics* 51, no. 3 (April 1997): 385–412.

12. Lianjiang Li and Kevin O'Brien, "The Struggle over Village Elections," in *The Paradox of Post-Mao Reforms*, ed. Merle Goldman and Roderick MacFarquhar (Cambridge, MA: Harvard University Press, 1999), pp. 129–44; and Tianjian Shi, "Village Committee Elections in China."

13. "Pan Yue Encircled by Conservatives for Calling For Political Reform—Li Peng Reportedly Orders Pan's Dismissal, Barring Pan from Entering 16th CPC Central Committee," *Ching chi jih pao* (Hong Kong), January 8, 2002, p. A17.

14. Joseph Fewsmith, "Rethinking the Role of the CCP: Party Commentators on Jiang Zemin's July 1 Speech," *China Leadership Monitor*, no. 2 (January 2002).

IV

Challenges to Governance and Reform

8

From the July 1 Speech to the Sixteenth Party Congress

Ideology, Party Construction, and Leadership Transition

Guoguang Wu

On July 1, 2001, the eightieth anniversary of the Chinese Communist Party (CCP), the Party General Secretary Jiang Zemin delivered a speech that later proved controversial. In the speech Jiang stated that private entrepreneurs could be qualified to join his Party, the self-claimed vanguard political organization of the working class.[1] A bold move in the eyes of international media,[2] this was another step in Jiang's ongoing effort to revitalize the Party's official ideology and to redefine the nature of this biggest political party in the world.[3] The major framework Jiang has proposed for this revitalization and redefinition is the "Three Represents" (*Sange Daibiao*). The "Three Represents" suggests that the CCP represents the requirements of China's advanced productive force, the orientation of the development of the country's advanced culture, and the fundamental interests of the overwhelming majority of the Chinese people.[4] It has been argued that this contrasts with the traditional definition of the Party exclusively as the political representative of the working class.[5] To recruit capitalists into the Party is one concrete measure under this framework of party-building and reform.

Some, both domestically and abroad, cheered this embrace of capitalism, while others, mainly within the Party, have been less pleased—as has been revealed by several open letters signed by about a dozen veteran Chinese communists.[6] None, however, deny that the delivery of this speech is an important move in Jiang's efforts to build up his own theory, which is leading to a profound transition in Chinese communism. Also, few doubt that, through this speech, Jiang and the leadership with him as the "core" are trying to delineate the major themes of the Sixteenth National Party Congress and to use this "Three Represents" theory to revise the platform of the Chinese Communist

Party. Thus, the following questions arise: What do the July 1 speech and the "Three Represents" theory indicate about the future of the CCP and the prospects for the Party's reform? Do the July 1 speech and the Leftist criticism of Jiang offer a preview of debates that will surround the Sixteenth Party Congress? What political implications do Jiang's "revisionist" efforts at ideological rebuilding and Party construction—or the challenges these efforts might encounter—have for the regime and the country?

Addressing these questions, this chapter offers interpretations of Jiang's July 1 speech at three levels, by regarding the efforts as, respectively but not mutually exclusively, (1) the responses of the CCP to the involvement of China in economic globalization, (2) the program to rejoin the CCP with the new social structures that have been greatly restratified during socioeconomic transition, and (3) Jiang's personal strategy to manage the leadership transition that is expected to happen at the Sixteenth Party Congress. At the same time, the discussion will emphasize the criticism raised by the Leftists, and discuss why the criticism arose, why the criticism failed (or at least appears to have failed), and what it implies for the political developments taking place around the Sixteenth Party Congress.

Strengthening the Party, Responding to Globalization: The Speech in an International Perspective

As China has become more involved in the world political economy,[7] the CCP has correspondingly become more sensitive to the changes in the international system than it was before the reform era.[8] Thus, to understand a decision made by the CCP, one cannot ignore its international background as well as other factors in shaping the decision. Chinese leaders, particularly Jiang and Premier Zhu Rongji, have recently, and indeed constantly, shown a strong concern for the challenges facing China as a result of the country's increased involvement in the global economy, especially the possible shock to the country brought by China's joining the World Trade Organization (WTO).[9] Analytically, such shocks have at least two dimensions: economic and political. How to deal with these shocks has preoccupied the leadership's agenda since 2001, the very year when China finally completed its long journey of negotiation and gained entry into the WTO. The economic impacts of such participation may be both positive and negative, but the political aftermath is seemingly more a challenge than a benefit to the Chinese regime. As reported by a Hong Kong–based pro-Beijing magazine, the Chinese leadership has realized that the WTO challenges include a challenge to "the CCP's way of ruling the country and the government's way of operating." The sixth session of the Fifteenth Central Committee that was held in September 2001 as a follow-up action to Jiang's July speech was thus an example of the Party preparing to meet this challenge.[10] According to Yang Jingyu, the ministerial-level director of the Legality Office of the State Council, joining the WTO will be, more than any other potential events in the country, a test of the Chinese government.[11] An even more frank statement comes from a policy adviser of Jiang Zemin: "The biggest shock to us from joining the WTO targets our government, and our government has for a long time been under one-party leadership. Thus, what is behind the shock is actually the ways of ruling and the leadership of our Party."[12]

According to this line of reasoning, Jiang's new program of Party member recruitment could have two implications that would help the CCP strengthen both its economic and political bases of power in the face of increasing Chinese involvement in the world system and the invasion of foreign capital in the Chinese economy. First, the eligibility recently given to private entrepreneurs to join the CCP will clear the way for Chinese capitalists to begin to enjoy political privilege, and, eventually, political power under the CCP regime. This, no doubt, will further stimulate the growth of national capital. More important, this will stimulate the growth of the CCP's political power and the newly developed national capitalists' business power. This will increase the capability of the CCP regime to control the spread of international business influence in China. Many in China's current regime feel that, despite the obvious benefits international investment brings to the Chinese economy, foreign involvement in China brings with it some negative effects for the current regime and its corresponding institutions. According to Li Junru, who is well known for his "liberal" inclination among Jiang's advisers, "the open-door causes our Party to be challenged, more directly than before, by hostile Western forces through their 'Westernizing' (xihua) and 'splitting-up' (fenhua) strategies and their ideologies." Lee comments that the "Three Represents" theory and related policies, as a result of Jiang and the leadership's "deep pondering and thoughtful envision" (shenmou yuanlu), can offer the Party a guarantee to meet the challenge.[13] In a very important speech delivered at the opening ceremony of the fall term of the Central Party School, Hu Jintao, the designated heir to Jiang Zemin, repeated those sentences to stress, "we are faced by the new tests that deep international changes have caused."[14] In this context, it is understandable to see the CCP use "national" things, either economic and cultural factors or a material force such as national capital, against Westernization, and, furthermore, attempt to use the "combination" of domestic power, both political and economic, against what they see as the Western "splitting-up" plot.

A principal drafter of Jiang's July 1 speech, Zheng Bijian, who is currently the executive vice president of the Central Party School, has made this nationalistic point very clear when introducing the study of Jiang's speech at the school. He stressed that the CCP's communism is "inseparably consistent with patriotism," which is a feature and an advantage of the Party. He refers to three historic events critical to the Party—the founding of the CCP in the 1920s, the anti-Japanese war in the 1930s–40s, and the collapse of communism in the Soviet Union and Eastern Europe in the 1990s—to show how nationalism supported the CCP's birth, success, and survival.[15] According to Zheng, being the vanguard of the Chinese people and the Chinese nation, as Jiang described in his July 1 speech, is not contradictory to the CCP's nature as the vanguard of the Chinese working class. Rather, as history has shown, nationalism is a powerful energy that the Party can use and has used to gain important ground in its class mission. In other words, the CCP, as a political party arguably capable of learning from its own experience, should always adapt itself to changing situations and utilize the social force of nationalism for its own advantages.

By the same token, the second implication of the Party's new recruitment strategy directly points to foreign-owned enterprises, where the CCP now plans to establish its grassroots organizations, including the recruitment of managerial and technical staff into the Party. Under the slogan of "broadening the Party's political coverage" (*kuoda Dang de zhengzhi fugai mian*), the CCP has, since the late 1990s, made progress in Party construction through the so-called "new economic organizations," namely, private enterprises, and, in particular, foreign-owned enterprises.[16] Such progress is achieved even overseas, as exemplified in the establishment of twenty-five Party branches in Chinese-owned companies abroad affiliated with the Shanghai foreign trade bureau.[17] According to insider information, China's leadership has recently reached consensuses on several issues related to meeting the challenges and opportunities posed by China's joining of the WTO and the "post–September 11 decline of the United States' power to restrain China." One of them is that, before and after the Sixteenth Party Congress, the CCP should expand its coverage and presence into new fields that have emerged in the marketizing transition and that would emerge as the country participates in the WTO. This means developing Party organizations in private enterprises.[18]

Jiang's speech further opens the way for the CCP's expansion into private enterprise, as a recent open celebration commemorating the establishment of a Party branch in a Taiwanese-owned enterprise based in Shenzhen has indicated.[19] One may argue that it is not necessary to allow entrepreneurs to join the Party in order to achieve this goal. After all, the CCP can depend on the ordinary, or blue-collar, workers in those enterprises, as traditional Marxism has required. However, under contemporary enterprise structures, this is obviously not enough to enhance the Party's power. In terms of internal stratification of a manufacturing enterprise, labor has few channels to influence decision making at its enterprise, particularly in the current Chinese context where—due to the CCP regime's fear of a possible repeat of the collapse of

Polish communism—labor movements and independent trade unions are practically prohibited in both foreign-owned and Chinese-owned enterprises.[20] If the CCP wants to maintain substantial influence in a private enterprise, it has to reach the levels of managers. Therefore, the CCP needs to recruit the non–working class members, the entrepreneurs. Furthermore, many foreign-owned enterprises are structured so that "white-collar," workers, or, in Jiang's words, "entrepreneurs and technical personnel" in "scientific and technical enterprises" and "managerial and technical staff" in "foreign-funded enterprises," make up an overwhelming majority, if not the whole, of personnel. Only as the CCP opens the door to such groups of people can it really "broaden political coverage" in those growing industries and expanding sectors.

In sum, with the "Three Represents" theory in general and the new policy of Party recruitment in particular, the CCP is developing a strategy for strengthening its own political position with China's anticipated full participation in the capitalist global economy. Partially because of nationalistic pressure within from both the ruling elite and below,[21] and partially due to their rationality as national leaders, Jiang Zemin and his comrades have to play a Janus-faced strategy in setting up China's international agenda. On the one hand, they push China hard to join the world economy, and, at the individual level, they link their own political and family-business interests to the enhanced economic connections between China and the outside capitalist world. On the other hand, they are equally, if not more, concerned about how to maintain their Party's monopoly on political power in the face of the rise of plural society—a development that is both domestically and internationally driven—which requires the Party to broaden its reach into the domain of the capitalist economy, building up "battle castles" (*zhandou baolei*) under the noses of, and even among, capitalists. In this sense, both liberal and Leftist interpretations of Jiang's speech are somehow naïve in asserting that the CCP under Jiang's leadership is embracing capitalists. They have both at least simplified the complex situation the CCP faces and the sophisticated strategy it is adopting to deal with this situation. It is perhaps correct to see an embracing of capitalists in Jiang's speech, but it is also correct to say that it is, politically, a bear's embrace in order to nourish itself, and, internationally, a move to join with national capitalists (read as, in the eyes of the CCP, the rich under the leadership of the Party) against foreign capitalists (read as, anticommunism and potentially an anti-China force).

Elite Circulation vs. Structural Reform: Options for the Party's Future

According to Jiang and his associates, Party construction is a major theme that the "Three Represents" theory addresses. It is said that the "Three Represents" theory is a response to the fundamental questions of Party construction, that is, what kind of a Party the CCP should be and how this Party should be constructed.[22] The ideal, suggested by Jiang's speech, seems to be a situation in which the Party opens the door to private entrepreneurs and other social influential groups but, at the same time, keeps the Party closely connected with its traditional class bases. As Jiang explicitly stresses, the Party "must constantly consolidate the class foundation" and meanwhile "expand its popular support and increase its social influence." For the latter purpose, Jiang suggests that the Party also recruit members from among "entrepreneurs and technical personnel employed by scientific and technological enterprises of the nonpublic sector, managerial and technical staff employed by foreign-funded enterprises, the self-employed, private entrepreneurs, employees in intermediaries, and freelance professionals." He argues this will not change the character and the nature of the Party as long as the Party upholds the advanced worldview of Marxism-Leninism.

Is Jiang right? Can the CCP really "represent" both capitalists and the working class? Will the addition of private entrepreneurs to the Party cause the nature of the CCP to be changed, as some expect, to a social democratic party? Or will the CCP transform the new rich, as declared and designed by Jiang and his comrades, into another strong pillar of the one-party dictatorship? Does Jiang's emphasis on Party construction indicate some follow-up programs for political reform, or is it a signal that the CCP will continuously resist democratization?

To answer such questions, one may find some lessons in historical experience. In actuality, the CCP has never been a party composed mainly of the working class, and it has already made several shifts of its "class foundations" without changing its structural position in Chinese politics. As Jiang himself points out in the speech, the CCP originally was a political party largely composed of members from the peasantry, rather than from the working class. Jiang argues that this did not negatively affect the nature of the Party as the vanguard organization of the working class. Actually, workers made up 10.9 percent of the total 130,194 members of the CCP in 1928, while peasants made up 76.7 percent, the overwhelming majority. This ratio declined even further, as workers in the Party dropped to 7 percent in 1929, 5.5 percent in 1930, and 1.6 percent in 1931.[23] After 1949, when the CCP took power, it strove to increase the percentage of members with working-class backgrounds,[24] but, as the relative size of the working class in agricultural China was limited, such a percentage has never been high. Even today, industrial workers make up only 20 percent of China's population and the pecentage of industrial workers within the Party is not much higher than it is within the general population.[25] In particular, members with working-class backgrounds have almost always been absent from the Party's leadership during various historic periods.[26]

There was a shift in Party recruitment policy in the early years of reform under Deng Xiaoping, when the CCP emphatically recruited new blood from intellectuals by redefining intellectuals as a part of the working class. This has brought about the rise of technocrats in the CCP power elite,[27] which certainly helped the Party to accomplish its tasks in modernizing the Chinese economy. But, so far, it has not much changed the structural position of the Party in Chinese politics for monopolizing state power.[28]

We may conclude from this brief historical review that changes in the composition of Party membership in terms of their class backgrounds did help as the CCP first emerged in an agricultural society and later survived historical transformations. If one assumes that the CCP enjoys exclusive privilege in ruling China, and, therefore, it is a major—if not the sole—group of political elite, we may regard such changes in Party member composition as a sort of "elite circulation," using Pareto's term.[29] This is neither a revolutionary circulation with a change in basic political institutions nor a change in state-society relations, but a circulation within the CCP political framework. It is akin to a person using new blood to renew life in an old body, and, certainly, an old brain, although the new blood might have certain impacts on the biological functioning of life.

Now it seems that Jiang's new policy in Party recruitment will bring the CCP another internal circulation of the elite, and, therefore, it is expected to help the Party survive during the transition from the closed state-planned economy to an open, market-oriented society. First of all, as argued by Jiang and Party theoreticians, it will enhance the CCP's social connections and broaden its political influence within a Chinese society that has been profoundly transformed during the course of reforms that began two decades ago. Since both the ideological attractiveness and political legitimacy that the Party enjoyed in the prereform era have now diminished to a point where the leadership senses a danger of losing control of society, as some Party theoreticians have realized in discussing Jiang's speech, the Party is faced with an urgent challenge to exercise the "function of political integration."[30] This integration needs to occur through some substantive measures based on the political middle ground between going back to traditional ideology and carrying out political institutional reforms that many in the leadership regard as radical options that would cause social instability in the country. To redefine ideology thus becomes a realistic and politically safe method for the current leadership to adapt the regime to socioeconomic change while, at the same time, maintaining and even strengthening the traditional political framework in which regime legitimacy relies on the functioning of the official ideology. This story differs from the one about the new bottle of old wine: The old bottle here is much more critical in keeping Chinese society, which, under the reforms, is becoming new wine, both integrated and controllable.

In particular, the new recruitment program will help the Party to effectively build up a new linkage between the mainstream of the Party, that is, those who are the most powerful under authoritarianism, and the new rich, who have recently emerged in marketization. This unholy alliance will embody the main resources of power in China, and thus could be unbeatable in the face of the potential unrest of the have-nots. Being the political representative of such an alliance, those who comprise the powerful in the current situation, if not the CCP as a whole, will no doubt enhance its capability to survive in any possible political transition that might one day arise.

Yet the occurrence of Leftist criticism of Jiang's speech has indicated that such a plan for integrating Chinese society around the CCP could be problematic, because first it might cause the Party itself to split, as the critics have warned. At a minimum, such severe criticism means that the gap between the Party's so-called "class foundation," arguably represented by the Leftists in this case, and "mass foundation," stressed by the Party's mainstream leaders, could be enlarged by Jiang's new policy on Party recruitment. In the most severe situation, the CCP could become a victim of internal political disintegration, rather than the cement of social integration as desired by Jiang Zemin. To deal with this situation, Jiang and his associates responded with both sticks and carrots. First, Jiang moved quickly and resolutely to silence Leftist criticism by scolding key signers of open letters and closing their journals.[31] This head-on blow seems to have successfully stopped a further assembly of potential critiques of Jiang, thus further consolidating his authority in the realm of ideology. At the same time, a propaganda campaign has been launched, and some measures for theory building based on Jiang's speech have followed. Lecture delegations composed of high-ranking Party officials were sent to the provinces to help local cadres understand Jiang's speech. This is the first time such a move has been made since the Cultural Revolution ended in 1976. The press, sponsored by the Party, is crowded with "reflections on studying Jiang's important speech," in which local cadres and Party School professors have found Jiang's speech powerfully convincing and brilliant in developing Marxism. Some of them maintain that the present division among the owner, the manager, and the laborer is becoming increasingly blurred, and more and more people will have multi-identities that cross all three.[32] Furthermore, it is said that the working class under socialism should not be the "proletariat," and that today it is not right to identify the working class with the have-nots in terms of property, nor to judge their political progressiveness according to their possession of more or less property.[33] According to this line of reasoning, should the CCP one day choose to revise their definitions, the new rich could be defined as part of the working class. This would follow the pattern that the Party used to redefine intellectuals as a part of the working class in the early 1980s.

On the other hand, there are also some clues intimating that, at the level of Party elites, Jiang and his mainstream force in the CCP are trying to remedy the gap between their procapitalist move and the requirements of fundamental Maoists, and, in terms of state-society relations, the gap between their power-money alliance and the poor who are suffering significantly from the capitalization of China without democratization. It is reported that Jiang Zemin and Zhu Rongji have recently warmed their relations with Deng Liqun, an undisputed leader of the CCP fundamentalist wing, as Jiang postponed promoting his right-handman, Zeng Qinghong, to the Politburo when Deng expressed his discontent with Zeng's work.[34] Meanwhile, at the Sixth Plenary of the Fifteenth Central Committee, held in September 2001, Jiang emphasized that the Party should help poor people and fight official corruption,[35] two prominent issues cited frequently by Leftists in their criticism and causing the spread of ordinary citizens' discontent with the regime.

But neither in Jiang's July 1 speech nor the Sixth Plenary is there a sign to indicate political institutional reform—something regarded by non-Leftist critiques of the regime, many mid-level and grassroots Party-state officials, and ordinary people as an effective solution to the critical issues perplexing China, including governmental corruption. Although some analysts expect that the new Party recruitment policy and the recent emphasis on Party construction will help to stimulate political reform in China, I am suspicious of this expectation. As I have shown in my previous discussion, in its eighty-year history, the CCP has experienced several "internal circulations" of members in terms of their class backgrounds, yet none of those events resulted in any structural changes to the Party. By "structural," I mean both the Party's position in monopolizing political power to govern the nation and its internal hierarchy as a Leninist organization. For all intents and purposes, such an elite circulation within the current political framework is more an alternative than a stimulator of structural reform. This will likely remain true in the short term around the Sixteenth Party Congress. No doubt administrative reform and some legal reform will follow as China joins the WTO, and, in the long term, once it contains a large number of "capitalists," the CCP could eventually find itself under pluralistic pressure for political reform. But all the conclusions we have reached above indicate that it is too early, under either the current leadership or the next generation leadership, to seriously discuss any possibility of carrying out substantive structural reforms of the Chinese political system. Despite Jiang Zemin's and Zhu Rongji's attempts to show enthusiasm for democracy and gradual political reform when they have met Western visitors, their actions indicate a very different view. As we have seen, Jiang did not tolerate any criticism even from Maoists, who have political advantages in Chinese politics in comparison with liberals. This was true despite the fact that their open letters intentionally legitimized their criticism of both Marxism and the Party constitution. The letters ironically turned to "democratic procedures" to blame Jiang's "personal worship," but Jiang answered them with further violation of the Party and state constitutions that guarantee Party members and citizens a right to criticize the leaders. In defending his power, Jiang did whatever it took to silence his high-ranking CCP critics. With this track record, how can one expect Jiang and his colleagues in the Politburo to give political liberty and even democracy to the Chinese people?

Ideology and Jiang's Individual Strategy for Leadership Transition

Considerations of national autonomy in the face of international interdependence and of regime legitimacy in the face of challenges from a pluralizing society, as we have discussed above, are not sufficient for a full understanding of Jiang's motivations for the July 1 speech. When examining a politician's rationale for making a decision, at some point, one must examine personal motivations. In this case, in taking the ideological and policy initiative to include capitalists in the Party, Jiang took a political risk that could result in his own personal loss. As this chapter shows, some Leftist open letters have gone so far as to call directly for Jiang's confession and describe him as another Hua Guofeng, the heir to Mao Zedong who was criticized by Deng Xiaoping and his old revolutionary comrades for encouraging a personal cult of himself and thus was forced to step down in the early 1980s.[36] Given that the leadership transition expected to occur at the Sixteenth Party Congress is approaching, this move was especially sensitive and meaningful.

So, what incentives stimulated the shrewd politician, Jiang Zemin, to take these initiatives? My interpretation is that this move is part of the overall strategy for Jiang Zemin and his men to manage the tough issue of the leadership transition from the so-called Third Generation to the Fourth, through what I will refer to as "ideology-advantage strategy." Basically, this round of the leadership transition is more constrained by institutional factors than others that have taken place. According to previously established norms and consensus, Jiang is thus under great pressure to retire at the Sixteenth Party Congress, at the age of 76. On the other hand, with the concept of politics as a struggle to win all, Jiang has worked during the past twelve years to become powerful enough to utilize the weaknesses of Chinese institutions and other resources to his advantage in the power game.[37] Actually, Li Peng, number two in the current leadership, also strongly intends to remain in power, which greatly complicates the leadership transition issue. Li Peng in particular feels unsafe if retreating from power, because he is accused of being responsible for the June 4 Tiananmen massacre and family corruption. Rumor says he is recommending his associate Luo Gan, a Politburo member in charge of legal affairs, to the Politburo Standing Committee specializing on affairs of Party discipline and state legality. But, even if successful, Li Peng would have several reasons to remain anxious. Luo Gan would be a junior member on the Standing Committee in comparison with Li Peng's own senior rank (in terms of seniority, Li has sat on the Standing Committee even longer than Jiang Zemin). And, if sufficiently pressured, Luo could betray Li. In terms of both political capability and resolve, Luo will thus certainly not be as strong as Li himself in the case of a struggle to defend the interests of Li and his family. Even now, as a member of the top decision-making body in Chinese politics, Li Peng still sometimes feels uncomfortable with potentially explosive issues like family corruption and June 4. It seems unlikely that retirement, and the resulting diminishment of power, will bring him more peace of mind on these issues.

Li Peng's desire to retain some formal political influence could prove to be troubling for Jiang Zemin. First, this will hinder the planned power transition to the next generation of leaders. Jiang would be blamed if the transition is postponed, and his relationship with the Fourth Generation would be in trouble. Second, this will give Li prominence in the leadership paralleling that of Jiang himself, an outcome that Jiang would most certainly find distasteful. The third, and most important, impact of Li's seeking to remain in power is to greatly reduce Jiang's autonomy in making the decision either to keep at least one official position, say, the chairmanship of the Central Military Commission (CMC), namely, half-retirement (*bantui*) or to totally retire from any Party-state position (*quantui*). Because Li would be seeking to match (*panbi*) Jiang, for the moment, Jiang is seemingly under pressure to give up the "bantui" option and to commit to "quantui." Jiang has made great efforts to force Li to totally retire, including improving his relationship with Zhu Rongji, the premier openly committed to retirement. But so far, unlike Zhu, and, to some degree, Jiang himself, Li still has not committed to any retirement plans. It seems that Jiang needs more political resources to support his dominant status during this leadership transition.

Another axis concerning the power transition, one more important than that between Jiang and Li, is the axis between generations, particularly between Jiang and his designated successor, Hu Jintao. Assuming Jiang wants to keep his paramount position of power and will work to maintain it through any means after the Sixteenth Party Congress, at least three factors will make

Jiang's position uncertain once Hu takes office. First, Hu is not Jiang's choice as heir; he was chosen by Deng Xiaoping and his old revolutionary comrades. In this sense, Jiang's personal connections with Hu are fundamentally problematic—at least they are not as close as the relationships of previous leaders with successors, such as between Deng and either Hu Yaobang, Zhao Ziyang, or Jiang Zemin himself. Second, Jiang's power base in, and thus legitimacy to govern the Party-state, particularly the military, is basically rooted in his institutional positions as Party chief, state president, and highest commander of the military, in contrast to Deng Xiaoping, who could be the paramount leader without any official title due to his unchallengeable power base in the communist system that was established through long-time experience in the revolution, war, and statecraft. Unlike Deng who did not rely on his formal titles to put him in charge, Jiang apparently will have difficulty using Deng's model for his future political influence once he retires. As institutional resources begin to be excluded, Jiang will need something else to grant him Deng-like informal power.

Third, the two factors above will put Jiang in an awkward post–Sixteenth Party Congress position even if he is able to stay as chairman of the CMC, as many have speculated. Because Hu would be number one, at least nominally, at that time, he will have the discretion to seek advice from his former political patrons, such as Song Ping, rather than from Jiang. It is actually very difficult to utilize the CMC to intervene in daily governance in the atmosphere of today's Chinese politics where there is no crisis of war or martial law. In such circumstances, the CMC chairmanship could represent a hollow title rather than a back-seat driver, as in Deng Xiaoping's case. This means that even if Jiang is to retire only partially, it will also greatly reduce his institutional power resources.

These factors together may leave Jiang in search of some other powerful resources. In communist Chinese politics, ideology is a rich resource that could help Jiang greatly in dealing with the difficulties discussed above. He may develop some other institutional and personnel resources for remedying his handicapped political future, such as promoting his loyalists like Zeng Qinghong to more critical positions and creating a new institution of governance under his own chairmanship, like the once-proposed State Security Council, but these actions will definitely open new battlefields in which Jiang has no absolute advantage in winning. The ideological domain is a battlefield, as has been proved by the occurrence of tough criticism from the Left, but Jiang has strong reasons to choose this spot to dig up his political potential. First, in the Chinese communist system, ideology states norms and makes rules, as Schurmann's classic account has explained.[38] This means that an accomplishment in this domain will make Jiang *the* rule-maker, rather than *a* decision-maker. The rule-maker can be above the institutions that govern current political opera-tions, but a decision-maker, no matter how strong this person is in comparison with other decision-makers, has to follow the rules. As we indicated earlier, what Jiang urgently needs is something to lift himself beyond the institutional constraints. Or, to follow Fewsmith's analysis, Jiang can utilize "old Party norms," read as ideology here, to overcome the difficulties of the "new legal rational norms."[39]

Second, the legacy of ideology is much more durable than any personnel or institutional linkages, and such durability is obviously critical for an old man who is retiring. It is widely expected that Jiang Zemin will become the next CCP leader whose thought is recognized by the Party constitution as the guiding principles of the Party, joining the ranks of Mao Zedong and Deng Xiaoping. Actually, the current Party leadership has reportedly already reached a consensus in October 2001 for listing the "Three Represents" theory with Marxism–Leninism–Mao Zedong Thought, and Deng Xiaoping Theory as their successor and development under new social circumstances.[40] It seems likely that the coming Party Congress will endorse this consensus, which will put Jiang Zemin on a divine level in the ideological temple of Chinese communism for teaching generations to come.

Third, such a legacy is even more politically reliable than other methods of exerting influence to control the next generation. Jiang sees the recognition of his "thought" or "theory" as the general guideline of the Party to be a valuable asset. Some of Jiang's associates are working hard to get the Party to officially recognize that Jiang has contributed more to the CCP politically and to Marx-ism ideologically than Deng and is second only to Mao.[41] The "Three Rep-resents" theory is their major basis for such rhetoric. Should Jiang Zemin Theory be written in the Party constitution at the coming Party Congress, Jiang himself would be the only living authority that could explain his theory, that is, the rules the Party has to follow in the future. In this sense, Jiang would indeed surpass Deng and be second only to Mao in terms of political influence. Deng Xiaoping Theory gained this ideological status only after Deng died and could no longer speak out on policy issues or contradict interpretations of his ideological writings. Jiang's theoretical constructs on the other hand, would gain this status at the Sixteenth Party Congress, when Jiang is *only* 76 years old. In future years, it is hard to imagine there will be no possible adjustments of Jiang's current policy by the new leadership and even disputes between the new leadership and Jiang. The recognition of Jiang's theory by the Party con-stitution could result in a more Maoist-style government. Should the new lead-ership have any differences with Jiang on how to interpret realities, policies, or anything else relevant either to governing China or power distribution, who, according to the Party constitution, would be more authoritative in having the final word? Certainly it would be Jiang rather than any Fourth Generation leader including Hu Jintao, just as Mao was always right either in policy disputes or power contention with Liu Shaoqi and Deng Xiaoping before the Cultural Revolution or with Lin Biao in the late 1970s. This was because Mao Zedong Thought had already been given the authority to decide which was right in Chinese politics.[42] In today's Chinese politics and in the future, what is right and what is wrong? Now Jiang Zemin's speech will set the criterion.

Finally, under the Chinese communist system, ideology is a kind of resource that not every leader has the capacity to utilize. Only those super-leaders who have already spent a long time in building their leading status have this capacity, while other leaders have to follow. Mao Zedong could not utilize ideological weapons in 1935 as he struggled to seize the real power to command the military during the Long March. It took him ten years to consolidate his undisputable position at the Seventh Party Congress in Yan'an. As we have mentioned, Deng could not do this when he was alive—his power was always somewhat in check at the hands of his old revolutionary comrades, such as Chen Yun, during the 1980s and even the early 1990s. In current Chinese politics, it is impossible for other members of the Third Generation leadership to touch the ideological domain, nor will the Fourth Generation leadership be able to establish any ideological framework under its name in the near future. If Jiang's "Three Represents" are adopted into the Party constitution, in terms of Communist ideology, Jiang Zemin will hold the mandate of heaven.

By making a break in ideology building, Jiang Zemin is successfully transforming his current institutional advantage into an ideological one, a vantage point from which he will not only be able to make rules for other leaders and for the operation of institutions but he will also, in the years to come, be in a position to judge which rules and leaders are politically correct. In terms of the leadership transition, Jiang will become the kingmaker as he retires as king. This ideological resource, under the Chinese communist political system, is easily transferred back to the institutional and personnel domains. For example, the central and local leaders are currently competing in paying tribute to Jiang's contribution to Marxism, just because they know that in doing so their performance will please Jiang, and thus have an important effect on their political careers, which come to a turning point on the eve of a Party Congress when the composition of all decision-making bodies will be reshuffled.

Thus, it is impossible for Jiang to give an inch in the ideological domain to Leftists, or anyone else, even though he can appease them in other ways. Actually, Leftist criticism also occurred in the shadow of the leadership transition around the two axes discussed above. Li Peng is widely regarded by the high leadership as the spokesman of the CCP traditional wing, and, during Hu Jintao's early political career, he was intimately linked with some veteran revolutionaries who are thought to have been behind Deng Liqun and his Leftist comrades. Jiang's victory in the first round of this debate will largely depend on his skillful manipulation of relationships among current top leaders as well as agenda setting in decision-making bodies. In the near future, provided he is continuously successful in doing this, Leftists could conceivably launch another wave of attack against Jiang, but it is unlikely that they would be able to defeat him.

Concluding Remarks

This chapter has examined the political implications of Jiang Zemin's new effort to rebuild an ideology for the CCP, as reflected generally in the "Three Represents" theory and particularly in the new policy of recruiting capitalists to the Party, which was revealed in Jiang's July 1 speech. Also, the chapter has emphatically addressed how Jiang's move to allow entrepreneurs into the Party and the subsequent criticism this decision has received have interacted to influence both the political direction and the power transition at the coming Sixteenth National Party Congress. Linking such efforts to the broader socioeconomic transitions that China is experiencing, this chapter examines Jiang Zemin's (and the CCP's) motivations for formulating this policy on three levels. The first level refers to China's increasing involvement in the world political economy, primarily indicated by China's participation in the World Trade Organization. On this level, the CCP decided to allow entrepreneurs into the Party in order to strengthen its grassroots organizations in capitalist domains, promote its political, spiritual, and economic linkages with national capital, and thus maintain its legitimacy in monopolizing political power while embracing the opportunities offered by capitalist globalization for stimulating Chinese economic growth. The second level deals with the Party's political bases within Chinese society. Chinese society has experienced profound changes in terms of both status stratification and class structures, and, thus, challenges the CCP, on the one hand, to serve as the vanguard of the working class while, at the same time, to deal with an urgent need to broaden its roots in the newly accumulated wealth. Those new efforts have formed a political program of elite circulation aimed at transforming the Party's social bases, as an alternative to structural political reform that could destroy the Party's monopoly on state power. Finally, this move can also be viewed as Jiang Zemin's individual strategy for ensuring his position in the power struggle he will face during the buildup to the transition from the Third Generation to the Fourth Generation of leadership. The criticism of Jiang by fundamentalist Maoists is also partially a reflection of this struggle. As Jiang moves substantially to mobilize ideological resources to secure his post–Sixteenth Party Congress position as the paramount leader, he risks fighting with the old guard of traditional communist ideology. As the Maoist challenge is having difficulty gaining support from the current leadership, its momentum for this criticism seems to have waned since its first strike. Meanwhile, Jiang is emerging to establish his popedom while retiring from the kingship.

Notes

The author thanks David M. Finkelstein, Rear Admiral Michael McDevitt, and Carol Lee Hamrin for their comments on a previous version of this chapter. Thanks also go to Maryanne Kivlehan for her help. The author, of course, takes sole responsibility for the content of the chapter.

1. For the official English translation of Jiang Zemin's speech at the eightieth anniversary of the Chinese Communist Party, see *China Daily*, July 2, 2001, pp. 4–6.

2. For such media reports and comments in the English world, see, for example, John Pomfret, "China Allows Its Capitalists to Join Party," *Washington Post*, July 2, 2001, p. A1; Craig S. Smith, "China's Leader Urges Opening Communist Party to Capitalists," *New York Times*, July 2, 2001, p. A9; and Thomas L. Friedman, "Introducing the China Ruling Party," *New York Times*, August 11, 2001, p. A15.

3. For an account of such efforts, see, for instance, Wu Guoguang, "The Return of Ideology? Struggling to Organize Politics during Socioeconomic Transitions," in *The Nanxun Legacy and China's Development in the Post-Deng Era*, ed. John Wong and Zheng Yongnian (Singapore: Singapore University Press, 2001), pp. 221–46.

4. Jiang's July 1 speech. Also, *Jiang Zemin lun sange daibiao* (Jiang Zemin on "Three Represents") (Beijing: People's Press, 2001).

5. *The Constitution of the Chinese Communist Party*, various editions.

6. For reports about Leftist criticism of Jiang's speech, see, for instance, Richard McGregor, "Jiang Draws Flak from Old Guard," *Financial Times*, August 16, 2001, p. 6; Anthony Kuhn, "Jiang's Bid to Bring Capitalists into Communist Fold Roils Cadres," *Los Angeles Times*, August 15, 2001, p. A3; Mark O'Neill, "Showdown of Ideologies," *South China Morning Post*, August 15, 2001, p. 14.

7. For fine accounts of this change, see, for example, Nicholas R. Lardy, *China in the World Economy* (Washington, DC: Institute for International Economics, 1994); Yoichi Funabashi, Michel Oksenberg, and Heinrich Weiss, *An Emerging China in a World of Interdependence: A Report to the Trilateral Commission* (New York: Trilateral Commission, 1994); and Elisabeth Economy and Michel Oksenberg, ed., *China Joins the World: Progress and Prospects* (New York: Council on Foreign Relations Press, 1999).

8. For China's responses in policymaking behavior to its increasing involvement in the world political economy, see, for instance, Thomas G. Moore and Dixia Yang, "Empowered and Restrained: Chinese Foreign Policy in the Age of Economic Interdependence," in *The Making of Chinese Foreign and Security Policy in the Era of Reform, 1978–2000*, ed. David M. Lampton (Stanford: Stanford University Press, 2001), pp. 191–229.

9. Ren Huiwen, "Zhonggong gaoceng danxin rushi chongji wending" (The CCP leadership worries that participation in the WTO would shake stability), *Hong Kong*

Economic Journal, November 16, 2001, p. 28; Tang Wencheng, "Jiang Zhu wei shiliuda he ru shimao weiyu choumou" (Jiang and Zhu preparing for the Sixteenth Party Congress and China's joining of the WTO), *Mirror*, no. 290 (September 2001): 18–20.

10. Tang Wencheng, "Jiang and Zhu," p. 19.

11. Yang Jingyu, "Rushi yu zhengfu guizhi" (Joining the WTO and governmental institutions), *Zhonggong zhongyang dangxiao baogao xuan* (The Central Party School's selection of reports), no. 9 (2001): 14–18.

12. Interview of Li Junru (a vice president of the Central Party School) by Liang Liping, "Yi gaige de jingshen jiaqiang zhizhengdang jianshe" (Strengthening construction of the ruling party with the spirit of reform), *Zhongguo dangzheng ganbu luntan* (The National Forum for Party-State Officials), September 2001, p. 7.

13. Ibid.

14. Hu Jintao, "Shenru xuexi zhengque linghui quanmianguanche Jiang Zemin tongzhi Qiyi zhongyao jianghua jingshen" (Thoroughly study, correctly understand, and comprehensively implement the spirit of Comrade Jiang Zemin's important July first speech), *Zhonggong zhongyang dangxiao beogao xuan*, no. 13 (2001): 1–13.

15. Zheng Bijian, "Xin shiji Zhongguo gongchandang quanmian jiaqiang zishen jianshe de Makesi zhuyi xin juexing" (The new awakening of Marxism in the new century as the CCP comprehensively strengthens its own construction), *Zhonggong zhongyang dangxiao baogao xuan*, no. 13 (2001): 14–32.

16. See, for example, Zhonggong Shanghai shiwei dangxiao ketizu (The Project Group of the Shanghai Party School), "Xin jingji zuzhi dangjian gongzuo de xianzhuang yu qianzhan" (The current situation and prospects of party construction under new economic organization), *Dangjian yanjiu neican* (Internal references for studies of party construction), no. 6 (2001): 11–13; Chen Zhenhong, "Kuoda fei gongyouzhi jingji zuzhi he shehui tuanti zhong dangjian gongzuo fugaimian" (Broadening the coverage of party construction work in non-public-owned economic and social organizations), *Dangjian yanjiu neican*, no. 4 (2001): 8–9.

17. Wu Dexing, "Jiji tansuo jiaqiang jingwai qiye dangjian gongzuo de youxiao banfa" (Actively searching for effective ways to strengthen party construction in enterprises abroad), *Dangjian yanjiu neican*, no. 8 (2001): 15–17.

18. Ren Huiwen, "Zhonggong gaoceng zuijin xingcheng liutiao gongshi" (The Chinese high leadership has recently built up six-point consensuses), *Hong Kong Economic Journal*, November 9, 2001, p. 12.

19. *Shenzhen tequ bao*, the organ of the Shenzhen Munipal CCP Committee, reported this information. See *Ming Pao Daily*, December 20, 2001, p. B15. It was also disclosed that eight-three more party branches were established in Shenzhen's private enterprises since Jiang's July 1 speech.

20. For a comprehensive study of the collapse of communism in Poland, see, Bartlomiej Kaminski, *The Collapse of State Socialism: The Case of Poland* (Princeton: Princeton University Press, 1991).

21. For such nationalism, see, for example, Yongnian Zheng, *Discovering Chinese Nationalism in China: Modernization, Identity, and International Relations* (Cambridge: Cambridge University Press, 1999).

22. For example, see Hu Jintao, "Shenru xuexi"; Zheng Bijian, Xin shiji Zhongguo"; Li Junru (the interview by Liang Liping); and Cai Xia, "Lishi jingyan yu shidai jingshen de jiejing" (The distillation of historical experience and spirit of the time), *Zhongguo dangzheng ganbu luntan*, no. 8 (2001): 6.

23. Suo Yanwen, "Guanyu dang de jieji jichu yu qunzhong jichu wenti" (On the issues of the class foundation and the mass foundation of the party), *Dangjian yanjiu neican*, no. 9 (2001): 2.

24. Interview of Xing Bensi, a leading party theoretician and a former vice president of the Central Party School, by Zhao Huizhu, "Sixiang luxian he xinshiqi dang de jianshe" (Thought line and party construction in the new era), *Zhongguo dangzheng ganbu luntan*, no. 8 (2001): 5.

25. Suo Yanwen, "Guanyu dang de jieji," p. 3. Interestingly enough, the author does not offer the current percentage of workers who are party members, which one may regard as a sign that this percentage is not high enough to claim that the Party is a working class party. Even in the *People's Republic of China Yearbook 2000*, this percentage is absent from the data concerning the CCP, where it states only that, among 61 million members, 30.17 million, or 48.8 percent of the total, are workers, farmers, herdsmen or fishermen (Beijing: Foreign Language Press, 2001, p. 157). Due to the obvious fact that the population of the latter three categories listed here is much greater than the first category, we can believe the percentage of workers who are party members is not much higher than the workers' percentage in the total Chinese population.

26. Chen Yun was said to be a rare exception because he had been an intern worker in Shanghai before he joined the CCP.

27. Li Cheng and Lynn White, "Elite Transformation and Modern Change in Mainland China and Taiwan: Empirical Data and the Theory of Technocracy," *China Quarterly*, no. 121 (March 1990): 1–35; Hong Yung Lee, *From Revolutionary Cadres to Party Technocrats in Socialist China* (Berkeley: University of California Press, 1991); David Shambaugh, "The CCP's Fifteenth Congress: Technocrats in Command," *Issues and Studies* 34, no. 1 (January 1998): 1–37.

28. For such an attempt to restructure the position of the Party in state politics and its failure, see a historic record in Wu Guoguang, *Zhao Ziyang yu zhengzhi gaige* (Political reform under Zhao Ziyang) (Hong Kong: Pacific Century Press, 1997).

29. Vilfredo Pareto, *The Mind and Society* (London: Jonathan Cape, 1935), 4 vols. For contemporary discussions and comments of Pareto's theory, see, for example, T.B. Bottomore, *Elites and Society* (London: Penguin Books, 1964), and Suzanne Keller, *Beyond the Ruling Class: Strategic Elites in Modern Society* (New Brunswick, NJ: Transaction, 1963/1991).

30. Wang Changjiang, "Weishenme yao qiangdiao dang yao tongshi chengwei Zhongguo renmin he Zhonghua minzu de xianfengdui?" (Why it is stressed that the party should meanwhile be the vanguard of the people and the nation of China?), *Zhongguo dangzheng ganbu luntan*, no. 8 (2001): 17.

31. Erik Eckholm, "Chinese Censors Shut Down Marxist Journal Critical of Jiang," *New York Times*, August 16, 2001, p. A13; Mark O'Neill, "Party Closes Leftist Journal That Opposed Jiang," *South China Morning Post*, August 14, 2001, p. 1

32. Ibid.

33. Zhang Zhiming, "Panduan renmen zhengzhi shang xianjin yu luohou de biaozhun yinggai shi shenme?" (What should be the criterion to tell the progressiveness in politics from the backwardness?) *Banyue tan* (Half-month forum), no. 18 (2001): 10–13.

34. Ren Huiwen, "Zhonggong gaoceng danxin."

35. Ren Huiwen, "Zhonggong gaoceng zuijin."

36. For the history of this period, see, for example, Richard Baum, *Burying Mao: Chinese Politics in the Age of Deng Xiaoping* (Princeton: Princeton University Press, 1994); and Roderick MacFarquhar, "The Succession to Mao and the End of Maoism,

1969–82," in *The Politics of China: The Eras of Mao and Deng*, 2d. ed., ed. Mac-Farquhar (New York: Cambridge University Press, 1997), pp. 248–339.

37. Joseph Fewsmith's analysis of conflicting political impulses in Chinese politics is helpful here. See his "Elite Politics," in *The Paradox of China's Post-Mao Reform*, ed. Merle Goldman and Roderick MacFarquhar (Cambridge, MA: Harvard University Press, 1999), pp. 47–75.

38. Franz Schurmann, *Ideology and Organization in Communist China* (Berkeley: University of California Press, 1968), enlarged edition, p. 38.

39. Fewsmith, "Elite Politics," p. 73.

40. Ren Huiwen, "Zhonggong yaoqiu yi diaocha yanjiu ying shiliuda" (The CCP required [cadres] to make investigations and studies for preparing the Sixteenth Party Congress), *Xinbao*, January 18, 2002.

41. A closed-door talk at the Chinese University of Hong Kong given by a visiting scholar from Shanghai who is said to be close to Jiang's camp, October 2001. Some other personal information resources confirmed this information. A pro-Beijing Hong Kong magazine also recently confirmed this information, saying "Jiang Zemin, after Mao Zedong, is testified by facts as another outstanding leader of the CCP who has been in office for a long time since the Party took power." Here it does not even mention Deng Xiaoping but ranks Jiang directly with Mao. Cited from Tang Wencheng, "Zhongnanhai xin jucuo baozhang minying jingji, Shiliuda jiang kuoda minzhu tiaozheng renshi" (Zhongnanhai [took] new measures to protect the private economy, and the Sixteenth Party Congress will enhance democracy and adjust personnel), *Jingbao yuekan*, no. 1 (2002): 29.

42. For a comprehensive history of the Cultural Revolution, particularly in terms of the internal struggles of the CCP leadership leading to the origins of the event, see Roderick MacFarquhar, *The Origins of the Cultural Revolution* (New York: Columbia University Press, 1974–97), 3 vols.

9

Economics as the Central Task

Do Entrepreneurs Matter?

Bruce J. Dickson

Jiang Zemin made a stunning proposal in his speech celebrating the eightieth anniversary of the Chinese Communist Party (CCP) on July 1, 2001. As general secretary of the CCP, he recommended that private entrepreneurs be allowed to join the CCP, ending a ban he himself had advocated in August 1989 immediately following the suppression of the Tiananmen demonstrations. This turn of events implicitly recognized how much had changed in China since 1989, and how anachronistic the ban had become. He claimed that entrepreneurs were among the new social strata making significant contributions to the country's development and modernization, and, therefore, deserved a place in the ruling party. Because promoting economic growth had been the CCP's central task for more than two decades, this might seem like a logical and uncontroversial proposal. The rapidly expanding private sector of the economy was the source of most new jobs and economic growth and absolutely necessary to the achievement of the Party's goals. From the perspective of the Party's orthodox leaders, however, Jiang's proposal was quite controversial indeed. How could a party created to champion the interests of workers and peasants admit capitalists, long excoriated as exploiters of the laboring masses? Was there a place for China's new bourgeoisie alongside the proletariat?

Jiang's seemingly innocuous proposal made front-page news in the United States, where it was described as heralding yet another step away from communist rule. At the same time, orthodox Party leaders in China unleashed a torrent of criticism against both the proposal and Jiang himself. They claimed Jiang, who was not only the leader of the CCP but also president of China and the "core of the Third Generation of leaders," had violated Party discipline by making the recommendation without first gaining the approval of the Party's decision-making bodies, especially the Politburo and its Standing Committee. They claimed the proposal itself violated both the Party constitution and its traditional principles. If the CCP did not retract the proposal and rebuke Jiang's inappropriate behavior, they warned, his proposal would lead to the end of the CCP.

Why did this proposal gain so much attention, both favorable and inflammatory? Most observers, whether inside or outside China, expect that continued economic reform will ultimately lead to political change in China. Advocates of change are in favor of promoting economic reforms in order to indirectly achieve other political goals. They hope that marketization, privatization, and the integration of China into the international community will raise standards of living and promote the development of a civil society, which will in turn create pressures for democratization. Conversely, those who want to preserve the CCP's power in China and to avoid the uncertainty that democratization would likely create want to limit the scope of the private economy in general and the presence of private entrepreneurs in the Party in particular. In other words, both sides in this debate are in general agreement about the political implications of economic and social change in China arising from the reform and opening policies. They disagree, however, on whether those implications represent their best hopes and dreams or their worst nightmare.

This chapter focuses on interrelated questions about the rise of private entrepreneurs in China. What is the Party doing to accommodate this newly emerging group of economic elites, and how likely to succeed is the Party's strategy for adaptation? Relatedly, what are the prospects for political change arising from the growing numbers of private entrepreneurs, many of whom are closely linked to the State in various ways? On the one hand, the CCP has adopted a two-pronged strategy toward the private entrepreneurs. First, it has created a variety of business associations to which most entrepreneurs belong. These associations are designed to be an institutional link between the State and the private sector, allowing for an interchange of ideas between government and business, but also allowing local government and Party officials to wield some degree of leadership and influence over the private sector. Second, it has promoted the growing numbers of "red capitalists," private entrepreneurs who are also Party members. Some of these red capitalists are former officials who have left their posts and "plunged into the sea" (xiahai) of the private economy. Others were co-opted into the Party as a consequence of their business success. Although the recruitment of entrepreneurs was officially banned in 1989, at least some local Party committees ignored or circumvented the ban, recognizing that as private entrepreneurs grew in numbers, economic significance, and social prestige, local political elites needed to reach out to them to prevent them from creating a potential opposition that would rally popular support and threaten the regime.

That is the crux of the matter: Are entrepreneurs likely to be partners with the State, promoting regime goals of economic growth and political stability, or will they ultimately contribute to the undermining of China's remaining communist institutions? The empirical evidence so far suggests we may get affirmative responses to both questions: Most entrepreneurs seek to be more closely integrated with the State, rather than form an autonomous opposition to it. Furthermore, they do not exhibit the kinds of political beliefs that make them natural allies with democracy advocates. However, the emergence of "red capitalists" in China does signal a fundamental challenge to continued Party rule in China's still nominally communist system. More than twenty years of economic reform have brought profound changes to the Party's authority and relations between the State and society. China's red capitalists are one of the most tangible and intriguing aspects of the changes underway in China.

Red Capitalists: Symbol of a Changing China

The emergence of red capitalists in China is a perfect metaphor for the entire reform era. Red capitalists symbolize the competing and seemingly contradictory nature of contemporary China: the existence of a free-wheeling economy alongside Leninist political institutions. China's leaders have wrestled with how to allow the free flow of information, labor, capital, and goods and services necessary for economic development without losing their hold on political power. Red capitalists therefore represent the merger of economic and political power in China.

So far, China's private entrepreneurs have not asserted themselves as an organized or coherent interest group. Government-business relations in China, as in much of East Asia but in sharp contrast to many Western countries, is more cooperative than antagonistic.[1] Indeed, private entrepreneurs have been among the primary beneficiaries of economic reform in China and have little reason to challenge the regime's policy priorities. Nevertheless, private entrepreneurs, and red capitalists in particular, have been the focus of ongoing debate within the CCP. Leftist leaders in the CCP are concerned that the ultimate political interests of the Party and private entrepreneurs are incompatible, and that the growing influence of entrepreneurs in the Party threaten its traditional norms, orientation, and relationships with other social groups. They contend that the ban on entrepreneurs in the Party should be maintained and that their influence on policy matters be minimized. In contrast, other Party officials and scholars argue that private entrepreneurs should not be punished for taking advantage of the economic opportunities made available by the Party's *gaige yu kaifang* (reform and opening to the outside world) policies. They contend that since the Party is basing its claim to legitimacy on its ability to raise living standards, successful entrepreneurs should be applauded as role models, not castigated as class enemies as they were in the Maoist era. More ominously, they warn that if the CCP does not reach out to the private entrepreneurs, they could potentially form an organized opposition to the State. From this perspective, the closer integration of government and business is meant to preempt a challenge to the Party's authority. Leftists reject this logic and argue that this integration will weaken the Party and ultimately lead to its demise, rather than promote its successful adaptation.

Whether private entrepreneurs will prove to be partners with the state or agents of political change remains uncertain, and, therefore, Party policy toward them represents something of a gamble. With Jiang Zemin's speech advocating the admission of entrepreneurs into the Party, the CCP seems to be betting that it can adapt to the changing economic and social environment its reforms are bringing about and thereby prolong its right to rule.

The CCP's Strategy of Adaptation

As the CCP moved away from the planned economy and class struggle policies that characterized the Maoist era, it began to rely less on coercion and propaganda to control society and developed links with other organizations, both new ones that it sanctioned and old ones it revived, such as united front organizations, labor unions, or professional associations. Links between the Party and these organizations allowed the articulation of interests emerging in the course of economic reform and also allowed the Party to remain as the arbiter of competing interests. Throughout the reform era, the Party created a wide array of economic and social organizations in order to provide channels for interest articulation, facilitate the exchange of information between the State and key groups in society, replace the State's direct and total control over the economy and society with at least partial social regulation, and screen out unwanted groups. In these ways, the State's recognition of social organizations allowed it to incorporate interests and viewpoints it found acceptable and to exclude and, in some cases repress, those it found unacceptable or threatening.[2]

The "Regulations on the Registrations and Management of Social Organizations," issued in draft form in 1989 and finalized in 1998, established and formalized this corporatist strategy of the CCP. Neither the State nor the social organizations in China explicitly use corporatist terminology to describe their relationships, but the regulations contain many of the familiar elements of corporatism. For example, every organization must register with the government and have a State unit as its sponsor, which in turn is responsible for its daily affairs. This responsibility may include providing officers and financial support to the organization. Social organizations enjoy a representational monopoly, at least at their level. In any jurisdiction, each profession, activity, or interest can be represented by only one organization. When more than one such organization exists, the State requires them to merge or to disband. Some local social organizations belong to peak organizations, but others have limited horizontal or vertical links to other similar organizations. In practice, however, this representational monopoly is one of the weaker aspects of the corporatist strategy in China. For instance, the rapidly proliferating software industry has a growing multiplicity of organizations, many with overlapping memberships and areas of interest and activity. And while these various organizations representing software companies must all continue to have a state sponsor, they use this embeddedness in the State to work on behalf of their members, rather than be subject to the State's control.[3]

This implicitly corporatist strategy contrasts with the expectations of a civil society, which is normally characterized as consisting of various political, economic, and social organizations that are distinctly autonomous from the State, and in many cases antagonistic to it, particularly in nondemocratic societies.[4] While confrontations between an authoritarian State and a dissident civil society are quite common, and, in many cases, have contributed to the democratization process, not all elements of civil society are hostile to the State. Yanqi Tong makes a useful distinction between a civil society organized to regulate the supply of goods and services (a "non-critical realm" that does not pose a direct challenge to the regime, and may even be welcomed by it) and a political society designed to "influence state decisions or to obtain a share of state power" (a "critical realm" that does threaten the regime's monopoly on power and therefore becomes the target of repression). The success of the critical realm depends on the existence and support of the non-critical realm. They are complementary, though not equal, and "the development of non-critical and critical realms often represent different stages in the emergence of an autonomous civil society and, in the process, of political change."[5] The CCP is pinning its hopes for survival on the success of its corporatist strategy to link itself with the "non-critical realm" represented by private entrepreneurs. The following sections will assess the role of business associations, both their ability to provide Party leadership over the private sector and their ability to represent the interest of the entrepreneurs who belong to them, and the political activities of entrepreneurs.

The Influence of Business Associations

As the private sector began to grow during the reform era, the state sanctioned a variety of business associations to maintain organizational links with private entrepreneurs. Like the mass organizations of the Maoist era, one task of these associations was to maintain control over their members. The heads of the associations were typically local Party and government officials with jurisdiction over the economy, and association offices were often in Party and government office buildings. Unlike other mass organizations, however, the business associations had greater potential to actually represent the interests and viewpoints of their members instead of simply serving as a transmission belt for official policy. Entrepreneurs had the economic resources and business savvy to work the system to their benefit. Margaret Pearson described this dichotomy as the "Janus face" of business associations: they simultaneously represent the State and the businessmen themselves.[6] This may seem contradictory in nature, but, as will be seen below, both local Party and government officials and private entrepreneurs accept this dual role of business associations.

China has three large business associations for different types of entrepreneurs, as well as a variety of industry-specific associations. The Self-Employed Laborers' Association (SELA) is aimed at small-scale operations with small numbers of workers and low sales volumes. As a consequence of this, previous research has found SELA to have the least amount of prestige and influence.[7] The Private Entrepreneurs' Association (PEA) encompasses slightly larger enterprises, and the Industrial and Commercial Federation (ICF) includes the largest and most prestigious enterprises, and is typically seen as having the greatest clout. Although SELA and PEA are products of the post-Mao era, the ICF has its origins in the United Front strategy of the early 1950s, when capitalists were included in the policy deliberations of the State. Its status is equivalent to one of the eight so-called democratic parties. Each of the business associations is headquartered in Beijing with local branches throughout China.

How effective are these business associations in representing their nominal members, and how influential are they on policy matters? To answer these questions, I conducted a survey and interview project targeting the owners and operators of large- and medium-scale private enterprises (those with reported annual sales of over 1 million RMB) and the local party and government officials with whom they interact. In all, eight counties were selected as survey sites: two each in Zhejiang, Shandong, Hebei, and Hunan. The sites were selected to include a mix of areas with varying levels of economic development and privatization. The survey was conducted in three counties in fall 1997, and the other five counties in spring 1999.[8] The following analysis is based on data collected from this survey.

Most of the private entrepreneurs in this study belonged to one or more business associations, and the distribution of membership varied significantly among the eight counties studied. Among the respondents in this survey, SELA members are concentrated in the poorer counties, PEA members are concentrated in the more developed counties, and ICF members are evenly split between poor and developed counties. When private entrepreneurs belonged to more than one business association, they were asked which one they most closely identified with, and the analysis below is based on this distinction.

One role of the business associations is to represent the interests of their members, and the vast majority of businessmen in my survey believe that they in fact do so (see Table 9.1). Moreover, most believe that their business association shares their personal views. Cadres have similar views on these two questions. Most businessmen also reported they have used their business association to try to resolve their problems and that the associations were generally helpful in solving those problems (see Table 9.2). These problems most commonly related to economic and financial matters (such as getting loans on time and payment of taxes), disputes between businesses, or general problems, such as getting permits or having goods inspected for export. The fact that the business associations proved to be so helpful indicates strong confidence that they can act on behalf of their members, specifically by intervening to resolve their business problems. Developing a reputation for "delivering the goods" is the best way for business associations to demonstrate their value to private entrepreneurs, and to elicit greater support from them.

These findings might seem to suggest that the business associations enjoy a fair amount of autonomy from the State, a primary criterion of a civil society, and therefore indicate that private entrepreneurs are poised to serve as agents of change. However, representing the views of their members is only one of the responsibilities of business associations. They are also intended to represent the State, and the survey data show that the associations are performing this role as well. As seen in Table 9.3, a slight majority of businessmen also believe the associations represent the government's position.

Variations among the responses of businessmen on these questions are worth teasing out. Given findings by previous studies, we would expect to find that private entrepreneurs belonging to the SELA would be more likely to agree that their business association represented the interests of the government over their own, and that private entrepreneurs in less-developed areas would have the same viewpoint. This is because SELA members typically are small-scale vendors with few economic resources and little political clout. However, neither of these predictions is supported by the survey data. Less than half of SELA members believed their business association represented the government; in contrast over three-quarters of them believed SELA represented the

Table 9.1

Views Toward Business Associations

1. Business associations are able to represent the interests of their members.

Business association	Strongly agree	Agree	Disagree	Strongly disagree
Self-Employed Laborers' Association	24.3	55.9	15.3	4.5
Private Entrepreneurs' Association	33.3	55.9	10.8	0.0
Industrial and Commercial Federation	30.1	55.3	12.6	1.9
Other	38.1	52.4	4.8	4.8
None	22.5	54.1	18.0	5.4
All entrepreneurs	28.3	54.2	14.1	3.4
Officials	27.0	50.9	17.6	4.5

2. Under most circumstances, the business association and I share the same viewpoint on the affairs of enterprises.

Business association	Strongly agree	Agree	Disagree	Strongly disagree
Self-Employed Laborers' Association	22.9	56.0	17.4	3.7
Private Entrepreneurs' Association	25.2	62.1	11.7	1.0
Industrial and Commercial Federation	23.8	61.4	14.9	0.0
Other	28.6	66.7	4.8	0.0
None	14.0	61.7	18.7	5.6
All entrepreneurs	21.5	60.4	15.7	2.4

interests of its members and their personal views. A bare majority of ICF members believed the ICF—the largest and generally regarded as the most influential business association—represented the government. The PEA and other local business associations had the highest percentage of members who believed their associations represented the government's perspective. In short,

Table 9.2

Business Associations and the Government's Views

Q: On most matters, the business association represents the government's views.

Business association	Strongly agree	Agree	Disagree	Strongly disagree
Self-Employed Laborers' Association	24.1	23.2	35.2	17.6
Private Entrepreneurs' Association	30.7	31.7	30.7	6.9
Industrial and Commercial Federation	15.2	37.4	38.4	9.1
Other	28.6	33.3	38.1	0.0
None	8.5	47.2	33.0	11.3
All entrepreneurs	20.5	34.3	33.7	11.5
Officials	11.0	51.4	29.4	8.3

Table 9.3

The Helpfulness of Business Associations to Their Members

1. When you encounter problems, have you ever gone through your business association to solve them?

Business association	Yes	No
Self-Employed Laborers' Association	58.49	41.51
Private Entrepreneurs' Association	69.61	30.39
Industrial and Commercial Federation	44.9	55.1
Other	57.89	42.11
None	32.2	67.8
All entrepreneurs	51.02	48.98

2. How helpful was the business association in solving your problem?

Business association	Very helpful	A little helpful	Not very helpful	Not helpful at all
Self-Employed Laborers' Association	30.65	56.45	9.68	3.23
Private Entrepreneurs' Association	34.33	53.73	11.94	0
Industrial and Commercial Federation	26.19	66.67	4.76	2.38
Other	20	80	0	0
None	10.26	69.23	12.82	7.69
All entrepreneurs	26.82	60.91	9.55	2.73

3. If you encounter a problem again, will you ask the business association to help you solve it?

Business association	Yes	No
Self-Employed Laborers' Association	84.76	15.24
Private Entrepreneurs' Association	85.86	14.14
Industrial and Commercial Federation	79.17	20.83
Other	88.24	11.76
None	68.47	31.53
All entrepreneurs	79.67	20.33

there was no simple linear relationship between the reputations for independence and influence of a business association and the views of its members regarding whether it represented the views of the government.

The economic context was more important in determining the businessmen's views of their associations. Those in the four counties with prosperous economies and high levels of privatization were much more likely to agree that their business association represented the government's viewpoint: 71.9 percent as opposed to only 41.6 percent in the four less prosperous counties.

In contrast, the views of local Party and government officials did *not* vary according to the level of economic development. Whether through better socialization, better knowledge, or a different perspective on the roles of government and businessmen, officials consistently shared similar views on whether business associations represented the government's perspective.

Another measure of the potential strength of business associations is their ability to influence policy. This can be a sensitive issue, because the CCP has traditionally been resistant to letting organized groups outside the State participate in the policy process, unless the Party itself invites them. The businessmen and officials in this survey were asked about whether business associations could influence the local implementation of policy (not the more contentious issue of whether they could influence the policy decision itself), and the two groups expressed markedly different views. Over two-thirds—68.4 percent—of businessmen claimed their associations *can* influence policy implementation, but three-quarters—74.9 percent—of officials believe that business associations *cannot* influence policy (see Table 9.4). This sharp difference of opinion between entrepreneurs and officials points to one potential area for future conflict. If businessmen believe their associations can influence policy, they may be more likely to try to do so; and if they believe they can influence the implementation of policy, it is a small step to try to influence the decision-making process itself.

Of course, not all private entrepreneurs believe their business associations can influence policy implementation. Here again, the level of development is an important factor in explaining differences of opinion among entrepreneurs. In the less-developed areas, roughly three-quarters of private entrepreneurs believe the business associations can influence policy implementation. This optimism holds true for all business associations, and even among businessmen who do not belong to an association. In the more-developed counties, however, private entrepreneurs are less optimistic—and perhaps more realistic—about the ability of their business associations to influence policy. Even in these developed areas, however, a clear majority—61.2 percent—of private entrepreneurs believe business associations can be influential. Moreover, the more clout a business association is reputed to have, the more likely are its members to believe associations can influence policy implementation. On this question, the SELA ranks lowest and the ICF highest. Ironically, businessmen who do not belong to any association are the most likely to claim that associations can be influential.

Taken together, these survey data suggest that businessmen view business associations as able to represent their views, solve their problems, and influence the local implementation of policy. The business associations are seen as legitimate by both businessmen and officials, and therefore may increase the

Table 9.4

The Policy Influence of Business Associations

Q: The business association can influence the local implementation of policies.

Business association	Strongly agree	Agree	Disagree	Strongly disagree
Self-Employed Laborers' Association	27.3	43.6	20.9	8.2
Private Entrepreneurs' Association	25.0	40.0	25.0	10.0
Industrial and Commercial Federation	17.4	49.0	23.5	10.2
Other	23.8	38.1	33.3	4.8
None	15.1	55.7	22.6	6.6
All entrepreneurs	21.5	46.8	23.3	8.4
Officials	5.5	19.6	48.0	26.9

potential for these organizations to engage in collective action on behalf of their members. Although business associations were initially created by the State, and are still primarily staffed and overseen by Party and government officials, they may come to represent the interests of their members as much as—if not more than—the interests of the State. As this development occurs, the prospects for a civil society will be enhanced. However, the analysis here also reveals a contrary trend: in the more-developed areas, the views of private entrepreneurs regarding the roles of business associations are converging with the views of officials and deviating from the views of entrepreneurs in less-developed areas. In addition, entrepreneurs in developed areas have lower expectations for the ability of business associations to influence policy implementation. These findings suggest increased embeddedness, not greater autonomy, and may make entrepreneurs less likely to challenge the State and also less likely to promote political change, at least under existing conditions.

Political Participation by Private Entrepreneurs

Private entrepreneurs are active in the political system in a variety of ways. Some are members of the CCP, whether before or after going into business;

some serve as delegates in local people's congresses and political consultative congresses; and some have won election at the grassroots level to the posts of village chief or village council. In these and other ways, private entrepreneurs have been combining their economic resources with political influence, which is one of the main concerns of orthodox Party leaders.

The cooptation of private entrepreneurs into the Party is not a new trend. The State Industrial and Commercial Administrative and Management Bureau reported in 1988 that 15 percent of owners of private firms were already Party members.[9] In Wenzhou, one of the pioneers in economic reform and privatization, 31.7 percent of private (*siying*) entrepreneurs were Party members, according to a 1989 survey; of these, over half were former state cadres (i.e., *xiahai* entrepreneurs), a finding consistent with my survey almost ten years later.[10] Other surveys from the mid-1990s also showed that 15–20 percent of private entrepreneurs belonged to the CCP.[11]

Of the entrepreneurs included in my survey, 40.4 percent identified themselves as Party members, which is much higher than the national average. Approximately two-thirds of these red capitalists had joined the Party before going into business (what I refer to as *xiahai* entrepreneurs). The remainder, slightly more than one-third, had been recruited into the Party as a result of their business success (what I refer to as coopted entrepreneurs). Because my survey targeted relatively large-scale enterprises, rather than a random sample of all private enterprises, it is not surprising that the proportion of Party members among the entrepreneurs is so large. Among smaller-scale enterprises, it is likely that the proportion of red capitalists would be smaller.[12] In my sample, there is a positive relationship between a firm's number of workers and gross annual revenue and the likelihood that its owner is a Party member. In addition, the higher the prestige of a business association, the more likely its members are to be Party members, either as coopted or *xiahai* entrepreneurs (see Table 9.5). The Party's cooptation strategy clearly favors the most influential and prestigious entrepreneurs.

Many of the other entrepreneurs who are not already Party members would like to join the CCP. More than one-quarter (26.7 percent) of the entrepreneurs in my sample said they wanted to join the Party, and about half of them had applied.[13] Not only were these entrepreneurs willing to join the Party, but local Party officials were seeking them out. About one-quarter of the non-CCP entrepreneurs reported that they had been asked by local Party officials to join the Party; of these, about two-thirds said they wanted to join the Party. If we recall that only 5 percent of the general population are Party members, the fact that 40 percent of large- and medium-scale entrepreneurs are already Party members, and that an additional 25 percent of the other respondents want to join the Party and have even been recruited by local Party officials, is truly astounding. It shows how closely the Party and the private sector are entwined:

Table 9.5

Membership Among Private Entrepreneurs

Business association	Coopted entrepreneurs	*Xiahai* entrepreneurs	Non-CCP entrepreneurs
Self-Employed Laborers' Association	9.9	17.1	73.0
Private Entrepreneurs' Association	14.8	23.2	62.0
Industrial and Commercial Federation	16.8	34.7	48.5
Other	19.1	38.1	42.9
None	12.0	22.7	65.3
All entrepreneurs	13.4	24.6	62.0

Two-thirds of the entrepreneurs in this survey were either already Party members or wanted to be. There is no question that the number of red capitalists in China could grow even larger. The formal ban on recruiting private entrepreneurs into the Party restricted the numbers and perhaps the types of private entrepreneurs that could join the Party, despite the numerous examples of cooptation. Although the ban was ignored or circumvented in some areas, it had to be done quietly and on a limited scale. In other communities, Party officials clearly abided by the ban. Now that Jiang Zemin has proposed recruiting entrepreneurs into the Party, it is likely that an even greater share of entrepreneurs will join the CCP. Compared to the general population, private entrepreneurs are already overrepresented in the Party and that preferential treatment is likely to grow once the ban is lifted.

Although the CCP has successfully targeted entrepreneurs for recruitment, it has been less successful with traditional Party building practices in the private sector. Less than one-quarter of the private entrepreneurs included in my survey reported that their workers had been recruited into the Party in recent years, and only 18.4 percent said there was a Party organization in their enterprise.[14] The Party's co-optation strategy is a partial substitute for its traditional Party building practices—it is now targeting elites instead of its traditional focus on workers and peasants—but the weakness of Party building in the rapidly growing private sector makes it difficult for the Party to monitor much less control what goes on there. The strategy to encourage Party members to go into private business and to co-opt other successful entrepreneurs is a partial substitute for the deeper penetration of the State into society that characterized the Maoist era and is a trademark of all Leninist parties. Whether this emphasis on co-optation at the expense of traditional Party building will allow the Party to adapt or simply contribute to its decay remains to be seen.

Private entrepreneurs are assuming other political roles besides membership in the CCP. A few private entrepreneurs serve, or have served, as members of local people's congresses and political consultative congresses. According to a report on the development of the private sector, over 5,400 entrepreneurs belonged to people's congresses at the county level or higher, and over 8,500 belonged to political consultative congresses at the county level or higher.[15] Among the private entrepreneurs in this sample, fifty-five (11.3 percent) either have served or are serving in local people's congresses, and twenty-three (4.8 percent) in local political consultative congresses.[16] The vast majority of them are Party members (77.8 percent of private entrepreneurs in people's congresses and 60.9 of those in consultative congresses). The CCP obviously carefully screens those who participate in these congresses; for all those, including private entrepreneurs, who want to be politically active in formal institutions, Party membership has definite advantages. Given the largely symbolic role of these bodies, however, the presence of entrepreneurs in them does not guarantee that businessmen are able to use these honorary appointments to shape policy, although it does reflect the regime's recognition and support of them as a distinct and important group.

Private entrepreneurs also participate in village-level elections in an apparent effort to combine their economic power with some degree of overt political power. According to anecdotal evidence from around China, examples of private entrepreneurs running for village chief or for village councils have become commonplace. Among the respondents in my sample, eighty-one private entrepreneurs (16.1 percent) had been candidates in village elections. To make the point clearer, private entrepreneurs had run for village chief or village council in twenty of the twenty-five townships and towns that were part of this survey, and the level of development did not affect the frequency of their participation. The vast majority of these candidates—72.5 percent—were red capitalists. Moreover, co-opted entrepreneurs had the highest level of participation in village elections among all respondents: 40.6 percent of co-opted entrepreneurs had been candidates in their villages' elections, as opposed to only 22.8 percent of *xiahai* entrepreneurs, and 7.6 percent of nonmembers. These findings suggest a potential benefit for the CCP from its strategy to co-opt private entrepreneurs. As noted above, one of its key goals is to keep all political participation under its control and not allow independent political actors to create a potential opposition. It follows, therefore, that it prefers that private entrepreneurs who run for local office be Party members. Co-opting entrepreneurs, especially those with political ambitions, may prevent non-CCP entrepreneurs from controlling elected offices in the villages, which would further threaten Party influence at the grassroots level.

If private entrepreneurs continue to run in and win village elections, and, furthermore, if the Party decides to allow competitive elections at higher levels of the political system, as recent indications suggest it might, the CCP may be faced with an awkward dilemma. Even though the success of entrepreneurs in village elections has proved controversial within the Party, the CCP may not be able to refuse their candidacy or disavow their elections if they demonstrate they have the local popular support needed to win elections, especially if they are already Party members. But their desire to run for local office by itself is not a direct challenge to Party rule: Most of the respondents who had been candidates were already Party members. In addition, more than two-thirds said a candidate who wins an election should join the Party if not already a member. This reinforces the viewpoint that entrepreneurs seek to be integrated into the State, not autonomous from it. In short, red capitalists may require the Party to adapt to accommodate their increased political participation but they do not necessarily pose a threat to it.

Conclusion

The dramatic rise and expansion of the private sector has been one of the most distinctive aspects of China's post-Mao reforms. Along with this growth has come the increased integration of the State and private sector, symbolized by the large numbers of red capitalists among private entrepreneurs. Although China's private entrepreneurs and their business associations may constitute a key part of the emerging civil society in China, they are not playing the role that many adherents of the civil society paradigm expect. Rather than seeking autonomy to enhance their power and wield influence over the State, they seek to be more closely integrated into the political system as it exists. They do not pose an inherent threat to the CCP, and indeed the CCP is reaching out to them, both in the creation of business associations and the co-optation of successful entrepreneurs.

China's red capitalists are unlikely to be advocates of democratization or supporters of democratic activists. In that regard, the actions of Wan Runnan, a founder of the Stone Group, during the Tiananmen protests seems more the exception than the rule. Other businessmen report less enthusiasm for democratization, fearing the potential instability it may generate.[17] But the CCP is mindful of the fact that the defection of the middle class and business interests has made a significant contribution to democratization in other countries.

Therefore, it seeks a closer relationship with the private sector, as seen in Jiang's "Three Represents" formula, even it if does not fit comfortably with Party traditions. Although China's red capitalists may be potential king-makers, for the present they seem more interested in good governance than in democracy per se. In that regard, they have much in common with other segments of society.

Notes

This chapter is adapted from my book, *Red Capitalists in China: The Party, Private Entrepreneurs, and the Prospects for Political Change* (Cambridge: Cambridge University Press, 2003).

1. For example, see Jean C. Oi, "Fiscal Reforms and the Economic Foundations of Local State Corporatism," *World Politics* 45, no. 1 (October 1992): 99–126; Andrew G. Walder, "Local Governments as Industrial Firms: An Organizational Analysis of China's Transitional Economy," *American Journal of Sociology* 101, no. 2 (September 1995): 263–301; Jonathan Unger and Anita Chan, "Corporatism in China: A Developmental State in an East Asian Context," in *China after Socialism: In the Footsteps of Eastern Europe or East Asia*, ed. Barrett L. McCormick and Jonathan Unger (Armonk, NY: M.E. Sharpe, 1996); Margaret M. Pearson, *China's New Business Elite: The Political Consequences of Economic Reform* (Berkeley: University of California Press, 1997). For comparative perspectives, see Peter Evans, *Embedded Autonomy: States and Industrial Transformation* (Princeton: Princeton University Press, 1995), and Karl J. Fields, *Enterprise and the State in Korea and Taiwan* (Ithaca: Cornell University Press, 1995).

2. See Gordon White, Jude Howell, and Shang Xiaoyuan, *In Search of Civil Society: Market Reform and Social Change in Contemporary China* (Oxford: Oxford University Press, 1996).

3. Scott Kennedy, *In the Company of Markets: The Transformation of China's Political Economy*, Ph.D. dissertation, George Washington University, 2001, ch. 4.

4. Kenneth W. Foster, "Associations in the Embrace of an Authoritarian State: State Domination of Society?" *Studies in Comparative International Development* 35, no. 4 (Winter 2001): 84–109; Michael W. Foley and Bob Edwards, "The Paradox of Civil Society," *Journal of Democracy* 7, no. 3 (1996): 38–52.

5. Yanqi Tong, "State, Society, and Political Change in China and Hungary," *Comparative Politics* 26, no. 3 (April 1994): 334. Gordon White and his collaborators make a similar point regarding the separate but potentially reinforcing market and political dynamics of China's emerging civil society; see White, Howell, and Shang, *In Search of Civil Society*, especially pp. 7–10.

6. Margaret M. Pearson, "The Janus Face of Business Associations in China," *Australian Journal of Chinese Affairs*, no. 31 (January 1994): 25–46.

7. Christopher Earle Nevitt, "Private Business Associations in China: Evidence of Civil Society or Local State Power," *China Journal*, no. 36 (July 1996): 25–45; Jonathan Unger, "'Bridges': Private Business, the Chinese Government and the Rise of New Associations," *China Quarterly*, no. 147 (September 1996): 795–819.

8. Entrepreneurs were selected from three townships and towns where the private economy was relatively developed for that particular county. The name-lists of rela-

tively large-scale enterprises provided by the Industry and Commerce Bureau were used to create a sampling pool with the first 100 names from the lists of two townships/ towns and the first 150 names of the list of a third township/town. Using a random start, fixed interval system, a sample of twenty enterprises was chosen from the first two townships/towns, and a sample of thirty from the other. In each county, specific officials were targeted: seventeen county-level Party and government cadres, including the Party and government leaders and those in charge of the relevant political, economic, and united front departments; six township and town (*xiangzhen*) cadres from the places of the enterprises in the sample; and six village level cadres. This is not a random sample of China's population, and was not intended to be. The respondents represent the economic and political elites in their communities. In all, 524 private entrepreneurs and 230 local Party and government officials participated in the survey.

9. Reported in *Jingji cankao*, November 4, 1988, and in FBIS, December 7, 1988, p. 36.

10. Kristen Parris, "Local Initiative and National Reform: The Wenzhou Model of Development," *China Quarterly*, no. 134 (June 1993): 259, 261.

11. The sampling designs of these surveys make their results suspect. According to a survey of 1,171 private firms in eighty-three counties spread across twelve provinces and provincial level cities, 13.1 percent of private entrepreneurs belonged to the CCP in 1993, 17.1 percent in 1995, and 16.6 percent in 1996. However, local officials were apparently allowed to handpick the people they interviewed as part of these surveys, rather than select a more representative sample. See *Zhongguo siying jingji nianjian, 1996* (China's Private Economy Yearbook, 1996) (Beijing: Zhongguo gongshang lianhe chubanshe, 1996), p. 162, and *Zhongguo siying qiye fazhan baogao (1978–1998)* (Report on the Development of China's Private Enterprises [1978–1998]) (Beijing: Shehui kexue wenxian chubanshe, 1999), p. 164.

12. According to a nationwide representative sample organized by Andrew Walder, 2.6 percent of those classified as *getihu* (individual businesses) and 14.8 percent of private entrepreneurs were Party members. I would like to thank him for sharing his data with me.

13. This corresponds to an earlier report that 24.1 percent of private entrepreneurs not already in the CCP wanted to join; see *Report on the Development of China's Private Enterprises (1978–1998)*, p. 164.

14. This fits with reports in the Chinese media of the Party's weak organizational presence in the private sector. See Dickson, *Red Capitalists in China*, ch. 2.

15. See *Report on the Development of China's Private Enterprises (1978–1998)*, p. 109.

16. A 1997 survey of private entrepreneurs found that 6.4 percent were members of people's congresses at various levels, and 12.7 were members of political consultative congresses at various levels. See *Report on the Development of China's Private Enterprises (1978–1998)*, p. 164.

17. Pearson, "The Janus Face of Business Associations in China"; David L. Wank, "Private Business, Bureaucracy, and Political Alliance in a Chinese City," *Australian Journal of Chinese Affairs*, no. 33 (January 1995): 55–71.

10

Social Dynamics and New Generation Politics

Carol Lee Hamrin

In the past decade, the rapid development of the market economy has produced new socioeconomic groups whose rights and interests are not understood or protected by the existing system. Central leaders have had to use indirect methods of assessing changing public expectations from a growing plurality of social strata.[1] As society continues to outgrow the Leninist bureaucratic structures intended to contain and control it, central authorities are uncertain how to cope with the new constraints on their authority created by commercialization and cultural impact from the outside.

China's leaders in the 1990s addressed the challenge with Band-Aids—marginal readjustments to shore up the existing social and political structures for co-opting and controlling society. The focus on internal Party reform at the Sixteenth Chinese Communist Party (CCP) Congress is viewed as a substitute for systemic structural change. Yet, in the attempt to strengthen State authority, leaders have found that capacity building keeps lagging behind the pace of social change and the use of State coercive capacity often is self-defeating. State dominance over society inhibits rather than enhances economic innovation, public morality, personal search for significance, and good international relations, all of which are needed to allow China's emergence as a great nation. The next generation of leaders will be under pressure to restructure and transform the key power relationships: Party-State, central-local, civil-military, and also State-society. This is imperative for sustaining economic growth and social order and for keeping China competitive in the global game. In the 1990s, the growth of the market injected competition into the State-monopoly economic sector and a consequent need for restructuring, so this decade will see growing competition in the State-dominated nonprofit sector and a need for social restructuring through new social policies.

Market Leninism: Problems in State-Society Relations

To fully understand current trends and options requires a closer look at the traditional Party mechanisms for co-opting and controlling social groups outside the political elite.[2] At the Politburo and Secretariat levels, select Party leaders coordinate the little-known "united front and mass work" sector. The United Front Department (UFD) of the Central Committee, and its subordinate bureaus at each level, determine policy and leading personnel for noncommunist groups: prominent nonparty intellectuals; capitalists; religious and ethnic minorities; and overseas Chinese (including those in Hong Kong, Taiwan, and Macao as well as those who have returned to China). It is important to note that personnel in this department, as in other powerful Party departments (organization and propaganda), are recruited heavily from the children of current and former leaders based on criteria weighted toward "red" over "expert." There is little overseas exposure and experience for staff in this highly secretive arena. Thus, the united front sector tends to be highly conservative in shaping social policies.

Implementation of united front work is carried out indirectly through specialized government organs (such as the Religious Affairs Bureau) and monopoly "nongovernmental" organizations assigned to each group. Examples include professional associations such as the National Association of Commerce and Industry, the All China Federation of Returned Overseas Chinese, and the five authorized "patriotic" religious organizations. The leaders of such groups form the approved social elite of China. Ostensibly, they serve as "representatives" of their "constituencies" in the people's political consultative system, but in fact the conferences are hollow shell organizations staffed and operated directly out of the UFD. The UFD perceives itself as the sole, legitimate voice representing the political interests of the "nonparty clan." All noncommunist organizations, including the eight "democratic" parties left over from the 1940s and all religious institutions, have Communist Party members on staff near the apex. Those leaders of social organizations willing to cooperate with this arrangement are rewarded with political status and material perquisites, and given monopoly control over assets in their sector. "Mass work" is organized in similar but more straightforward fashion through overtly Party-run organizations, since there is no reason to hide Party leadership over youth, women, and labor affairs. The Communist Youth League, Women's Federation, and Trade Union Federation have the same bureaucratic status as the UFD. One anomaly in this system is the absence of a comparable farmers' association, despite periodic suggestions that one be created. The Civil Affairs Ministry/bureau oversees grassroots rural village committees as well as urban resident committees, which are "mass" organs supervised by Party cadres.

In the past two decades, there have been adjustments to this system in an effort to keep up with rapid social change. With the focus of all work on economic development, noncommunist professionals have been asked to consult on economic and social policy documents, and a number of government-organized state nongovernmental organizations (GONGOs) have been spawned to fulfill new functions such as charity, relief and development work, environmental or legal aid work. Examples include the leading institutions in China's budding Third Sector: the China Charities Federation organized and staffed by the Ministry of Civil Affairs, the Amity Foundation affiliated with the (Protestant) China Christian Council, and the China Youth Development Foundation affiliated with the Youth League. Increasingly, these organizations find themselves competing for public support and foreign funds with spontaneous and autonomous grassroots organizations—from clans to religious charities.[3]

Urban Residents' Committees

As the Party in the 1990s sought to keep its hold over a diversifying society, it encountered growing headaches. One headache has been the urban residents' committees (*jumin weiyuanhui*), which had become largely defunct or disrespected as intrusive control mechanisms by the late 1980s. In a few areas, including Shanghai, these were revitalized in the 1990s as neighborhood service centers with better-educated staff, larger budgets, and new functions to meet new needs—such as job provision, brokerage of nanny or handyman services and collection of charitable donations. Still, social change continues to threaten the committees with obsolescence; new housing area residents and the middle class in general are using new private (profit and nonprofit) sources for housing and services.[4]

Religious Groups

The multiple efforts over the years to entice or force unregistered Protestant groups to associate with the authorized monopoly system (run jointly by the Three-Self Patriotic Movement [TSPM] and the China Christian Council) provides another example of failure. Members of the autonomous groups actually form a majority (roughly estimated at 45–70 million compared with 15–40 million in the registered churches).[5] Younger, better-educated leaders of both registered and autonomous groups are beginning to claim their rights and cultivate foreign support. In 1998, a coalition of house church networks published a statement of orthodox faith and a manifesto insisting that the government acknowledge that the official church was merely one minority denomination, and adopt international definitions and norms in dealing with "cults." In 2001, another house church consortium "usurped" the role of the official church by announcing a list of five priorities for the church in China, including global missions and social outreach to migrant workers. Yet another group, the South China Church, found itself banned as a cult after sending out an open call for "Bible-believing Christians" to attend an international conference in China.[6] Meanwhile, many local registered church leaders and seminarians boycotted or ignored a "theological reconstruction campaign" intended to weed out evangelicals who refused to downplay "divisive" issues of faith commitment and evangelism in favor of teaching universal social ethics. One provincial TSPM leader warned that the unpopular campaign was the "death knell" for the organization.[7]

Third Sector Regulations

The Party-State is especially lenient regarding charitable relief and development activity but is quite heavy-handed in controlling activities by religious groups, educated professionals, labor, youth, and women. Yet, there are important commonalities to the onerous organizational controls, which motivate efforts to bypass rather than abide by the "law":[8]

- There is a dual control system: government registration and functional affiliation. The Ministry of Civil Affairs and its subordinate units carry out general legal approval and oversight of most of the Third Sector with counterparts for special sectors such as the Ministry of National Minorities Affairs. Day-to-day line supervision is carried out by functional Party or government agencies with the assistance of official monopolies designated for each sector.
- Monopoly sponsors of affiliates have comprehensive duties for overseeing applications for registration, political and ideological work through formation of Party branches, finance and accounting, personnel management, policy research, and external relations. All is supposed to be provided without any fee, yet one major duty of monopoly social groups is to control all domestic assets and fund raising as well as foreign contacts and resources.
- Before registration, organizations must meet certain standards such as having a designated work place, certified professional staff, and a mini-

mum number of members. (Note the "catch 22": to meet some of these requirements before registration would mean recruiting members and performing activities that are technically legal only after registration.) Quotas and monopolies are used to limit scope and numbers; a new organization can register only if it will operate in a locality where there is not already an organization with the same or a similar function. National NGOs are strictly limited in number and autonomy; most new organizations must have no branches outside a limited locality or level, and must do no damage to Party leadership, socialism, public order, unity among nationalities, and so on.

With the downsizing of the central government, responsibility both for providing social services and maintaining social order has been delegated downward. Local governments, unable or unwilling to provide the full range of social services expected by the public, have begun to rely on private or foreign resources. This, in turn, weakens ties of dependency and control between the bureaucracy and grassroots communities. Much social activity is outside the State process and in the hands of nonstate decision makers with varying degrees of autonomy and legitimacy. In the process, a more equal symbiotic bargaining relationship between social groups and the State is emerging. In a path-breaking study of this dynamic, Tony Saich has pointed to the gap between rhetoric and reality wherein the State "appears to exert extensive formal control, but its capacity to realize this control is increasingly limited."[9]

The hard bargaining between the State and society will escalate over the next decade. Growing personal freedoms increase popular demands, educated citizens push the envelope in social organizing, and local governments become accommodating in exchange for gaining access to new local and foreign resources. Yet, the Party still wants to maintain tight constraints and monitoring over all organizational activity. This fundamental conflict of interest explains why abuses of human rights appear to be on the increase at the same time personal freedoms and de facto organizational independence are growing.

Succession Phase One: Attempts to Adjust the Conservative Program

To understand how China's social challenges relate to the political succession, it may be useful to think in terms of two phases. In the first current phase, through 2004, new leaders will have to attain and establish power through conformity to the requirements of current leaders and their status quo program. In the second phase, 2005–8, they will likely maintain power and build legitimacy only by abandoning that program in order to meet the demands of rising forces at home and abroad.

A Brief Turn Toward Liberal Solutions

Most actors in the political elite already know that the system must change fundamentally, but they are in a quandary as to how to proceed. The Fifteenth Party Congress in October 1997 and the National People's Congress (NPC) in 1998 authorized the expansion of social organizations and a renewed focus on political restructuring. As internal discussion focused on specific guidelines for such measures, there were hopeful signs that the leadership might authorize a major adaptation of the Leninist sociopolitical structure. These signals inspired a resurgence of liberal thought calling for institutional democratization. They also revived the discussion of policy concepts from the late 1980s. These included: the separation of the Party from government and State organizations, State control of the military, development of existing noncommunist parties, and the drafting of civil rights laws as well as regulations granting autonomy to social organizations. After a few brief months, however, leadership enthusiasm for this far-reaching reform agenda waned.

The Asian financial virus had spread to Russia, bringing about an economic collapse, and it also had contributed to an economic slowdown in China with resulting social unrest. Meanwhile, there surfaced widespread domestic and international support for the fledgling China Democratic Party; leaders of several large unregistered house church networks met to promote the national "unity movement"; and the Falungong spiritual movement experienced a surge of growth. All served as reminders that alternative voices outside the Party-State could emerge unexpectedly to articulate grievances and garner foreign support. No doubt fear of a political comeback by 1980s reformers played a part in giving Jiang Zemin cold feet on the eve of the tenth anniversary of June 4.

Return to Co-optation and Control

Top leaders turned to a more authoritarian option for regime adjustment to new realities, which focused on rebuilding the Party's capacity to control the state, military, and social organizations. Subsequent to the Falulngong demonstration at Zhongnanhai in April 1999, Jiang Zemin mandated a ban on "evil cults" and a freeze on registration of social organizations.[10] Beginning in January 2000, Jiang unveiled his "Three Represents" theory as the heart of a "Party building" campaign. The aim is to upgrade the CCP as an elitist, ruling

Party with sole authority to represent "advanced social forces, advanced culture, and the interests of the majority." Previously, the Party justified its monopoly on power by claiming it represented the vast majority of "workers." (Literally, the Chinese term for "proletariat," *wuchan jie*, means "propertyless," thus including farmers with workers.) Deng Xiaoping modified this by designating "intellectuals" as part of the working class, not an appendage of the bourgeoisie.

As Chinese society approaches an historic shift to a majority urban society with a growing middle class, major theoretical surgery was needed to pursue the same perennial goal—precluding the development of any competing political organizations. In a July 2001 speech on the Party's eightieth anniversary, Jiang made explicit the plan to allow Party membership for the new entrepreneurial-managerial class, with similar implications for other social elites. A strong emphasis on science and technology themes in ideology, education, and economic planning accompanied this step; all were justified as enhancing China's global competitiveness.[11]

The "Three Represents" slogan for party building has been accompanied by more frequent resort to political education campaigns. These foster personal loyalty to Jiang Zemin's theories and policies and justify highly politicized internal Party disciplinary campaigns against corruption, both of which have been used to promote Jiang loyalists in the succession process. In a study of rural Yunnan, Stig Thogersen has documented a return to social and cultural engineering at the grassroots level, whereby the Party once again is intruding into the sphere of privacy that had been built up around the family and household.[12] As he concludes for the rural cultural sphere, so in urban China as well, the State is trying to regain social and cultural territory it has lost.

A central committee directive in October 2001 launching a campaign for "citizen ethics building" is yet another effort to dictate public values from the top down.[13] The campaign, spurred by Jiang's call for "rule by law and rule by morality," reflects a new level of awareness by leaders of the practical and political costs of China's moral crisis. It also reveals a new sophistication in methods of mobilizing business, professions, and the nonprofit sector in this State-directed effort. Nonetheless, the Party's authority as moral arbiter in society remains fatally crippled by the continuing spread of corruption and abuse of authority at all levels despite perennial anticorruption campaigns. To dictate to citizens what Party members themselves fail to pursue is a nonstarter. Tellingly, the lengthy and detailed document on ethics failed even to mention the word religion, signaling an extraordinary sensitivity regarding this increasingly popular alternative source of ethical conduct and spiritual meaning.

Jiang Zemin's Party-building program reportedly has inspired comparative studies of political parties, including socialist democratic parties, as well as debates about the option of changing the name of the Chinese Communist Party.[14] The dark flipside of these seemingly positive trends is the reassertion of the Party's prerogative, as "representative of the majority," to determine the legitimacy of social groups and to exclude other voices from representing social interests. New slogans justify rebuilding Party cells in all economic and social organizations, not just Party or State institutions. How workable is this strategy? If entrepreneurs and managers are allowed to join or remain in the Party, will they be willing to organize Party cell groups in their private enterprises? Bruce Dickson's chapter in this volume suggests not, given low rates of Party recruitment of workers or setting up of Party cells in private enterprises. He concludes that new membership criteria for recruitment may not be a sign of new life for the Party, but an admission of defeat for the organization.[15] It would seem even more difficult to square the circle in the religious sector, where existing Party-run organizations are near collapse and the likelihood of a membership recruitment drive seems remote.

Corruption and Social Injustice as a Sign of System Failure

Widespread and rapidly growing corruption and abuse of coercive power is the inevitable result of trying to sustain the traditional Party co-optation strategy in a market economy. In the Mao era, there was also widespread abuse of monopoly power over state assets, but it took the form of special privileges that were largely hidden from public view. Today, privileged access to State assets results in monetary gains that become evident in more public displays of wealth. This trend is applicable to State-run nonprofit organizations as much as to State enterprises. One example is the running of the YMCA headquarters in Shanghai as a "family business" for decades, resulting in the disgrace of the now-retired president and court action against his son. Another is the venal reputation of a number of provincial State charity federations.[16]

As State-controlled noncommunist organizations have lost their effectiveness in co-opting or controlling their assigned social sectors, efforts to rebuild Party controls have increasingly required a heavy hand by the police. Among the most egregious examples of using coercion are:

- the destruction of "illegal" religious buildings in Wenzhou County in Zhejiang, which came to public attention in November–December 2000. Over 1,000 organizations reportedly were shut down and several hundred buildings razed or turned over to schools or other secular institutions,[17]
- the large-scale, nationwide, ongoing crackdown on unregistered Christian groups labeled "evil cults" (according to loose state definitions of heretical doctrine or criminal behavior),[18] and

- the "patriotic reeducation campaigns" involving armed force against "separatists" in Tibet and Xinjiang. After September 11, 2001, a Party directive reportedly intensified the annual "Strike Hard" campaign targeting separatists, cults, triads, and demonstrations by farmers or workers, as well as violent criminals, all now being lumped together as sources of "terrorism."[19]

Many local situations illustrate how corruption and coercion are two sides of the same coin. Sociologist Ding Xueliang has studied the systemic nature of this phenomenon, making the point that thoroughly punishing local abusers would leave localities without any government. He concludes that "Concrete social problems . . . routinely get covered up or distorted . . . into other forms of trouble. Once there is no way to cover up or suppress them anymore, the magnitude and acuteness of the accumulated and fermented social problems pose real political challenges to the government."[20] In the Wenzhou case above, one plausible explanation given for the crackdown was that local officials trying to cover up corruption through "taxes" on local temple tourism decided to close down all unregistered religious sites in a less-than-commendable show of equal treatment.[21] In Liaoning, house church members who left the local TSPM congregation due to corruption by its leadership were caught up in a police sweep motivated by high monetary rewards for arrests of cult groups. Lucky enough to hire a courageous lawyer, the group leader was still convicted and sentenced to two years of labor on the testimony of the local police chief, who argued before the local judge that "to be anti-government is the nature of cults; to oppose the TSPM is to be anti-government, so this group is a cult."[22]

While the policy goal of social stability is widely supported by the public, coercive implementation has sparked questioning within the intellectual elite. One prominent university president reflected, "If China allowed freedom for normal religions to grow, there would not have been space for the Falungong to gain such a following." Moreover, in all three cases above, what was intended to be secret repression ended up in the foreign media and sparked international outrage. One delegation of religious officials visiting the United States sought to whitewash the Wenzhou incident, claiming they had investigated and found that only buildings in violation of land-use laws were torn down. They were struck dumb when a member of the audience said, "Perhaps so, but I visited the site myself and read an official notice tacked to a demolition site stating its owners were banned as an 'illegal cult with illicit foreign ties.' "[23]

Phase Two: Transition to a Progressive Program

Current leaders, led by Jiang Zemin, are seeking to cement in place their conservative program for the long haul. They would like to project an image of unity and continuity through the political transition to new leaders and as China enters the uncharted waters of reforms related to its entry into the World Trade Organization (WTO), both of which make the regime vulnerable. Jiang also hopes to commit new leaders to his personal ideology and program, and to retain influence as its prime interpreter in the future. Examples of this effort include:

- the June 2001 Tibet work forum, which praised the policies of the 1990s and called for further assimilation of Tibet into the Chinese system. During the session, President Jiang emphasized the need to "strengthen" the administration of religious affairs, "vigorously adapt" Tibetan Buddhism to socialism, and "strike" criminal splittist activists. Hu Jintao followed up with a July visit to Tibet on the fiftieth anniversary of its "liberation," signaling that CCP leadership and socialism were Tibet's only option;[24]
- the national religious affairs work conference in December 2001, which also endorsed past tight control policies and authorized their continuation with minor modification. Insiders claim the required attendance by all Politburo Standing Committee members, with an address by Premier Zhu Rongji, was Jiang's attempt to commit full State resources to enforcing the Party's tough approach to unregistered groups. There was no attempt to consult widely within the religious community on the drafting of new national regulations to be unveiled following the session. Moderate suggestions for policies that would encourage the growth of religious groups to provide spiritual and moral leadership, as well as fulfill political and social service functions were turned down.[25]

It is unlikely, however, that current social and political arrangements are sustainable over the long term given the nature and pace of change in and around China. By the end of the 1990s, China was already experiencing greater income differentials than ever before in history, and these continue to increase more rapidly than elsewhere in the world.[26] This has engendered criticism that the Party now represents the interests of the wealthy and does not care for the poor. Social polarization may be China's greatest challenge in this decade, and requires remedies other than a "lockdown." Proactive leadership would be seeking alternatives. China's current leaders have worked hard through the 1990s to overcome the system's tendency to obstruct market institutions. It is up to the next generation to overcome the system's tendency to obstruct social innovation and the rule of law, both essential for sustainable economic growth.[27]

There is a quiet "dialogue" between government and populace with a shared focus on practical goals and utilitarian interests in the course of social and political reform. Both government and populace want peaceful evolution, not revolution. However, to keep alive this option of gradual change, new leaders will need to move beyond the Deng-Jiang program. International trends will continue to drive change as China seeks to compete globally. There is no clear procedural pathway from current policies to a new program, but the elements of a more progressive program fully responsive to both domestic and foreign expectations are fairly clear.

Healthy Development of the Third Sector

There is an "associational revolution" within the globalization process that is already having an impact in China. Governments everywhere are cutting back the welfare state, and the World Bank is seeking to empower community organizations in their development projects. The latest "intellectual fever" in Beijing is research and training in nonprofit theory and management, much of it in cooperation with international organizations.[28] Influential policy researchers have developed a compelling rationale for increasing autonomy for nonprofit and grassroots initiatives to redress social injustice.[29] NGO pioneers are learning from the vibrant nonprofit sectors in Hong Kong, Taiwan, and Singapore. At an international conference on poverty reeducation in Beijing in October 2001, NGO organizers offered to act as the "vanguard" in cooperation with international counterparts, as well as with Chinese government and business, in exploring new models for poverty alleviation.[30]

Reversing China's Brain Drain

Wooing educated Chinese employees has become a top priority for Chinese leaders and executives as they seek to keep from falling behind global frontrunners. Coastal city governments advertise for foreign experts (220,000 in China in 2000), and educated Chinese now in the United States and Asia are beginning to return at a higher rate. But China will be competing in a global shortage of top professionals over the next decade, and top-quality Chinese will come back to live in China in significant numbers only when they are convinced their rights, including those of belief and association, will be respected and protected. Just as Shanghai now advertises for foreign experts and People's Republic of China returnees with knowledge and experience in modern business management practices, so will savvy political leaders begin to woo those with Third Sector experience.

Accommodation of Cultural Pluralism

Peter Berger's list of four major global cultures are all visibly evident in China: Davos (business) culture; its twin McWorld (consumer) culture; Faculty Club (academic and NGO) culture; and evangelical/charismatic Protestant culture.[31] Meanwhile, elements of indigenous traditional culture—including elite Confucianism, local lineages, and folk religion—have been revitalized. It is important to note that all of these cultures have been conditioned by their transmission through overseas Chinese. Pop culture has been termed *Tai-Gang* (Taiwan–Hong Kong) culture. Even at the local level in remote areas, where television is widely available, there is now a complex mix of partially competing, partially cooperating cultural leaders. Fostering nonviolent cultural competition will require the State to give up its totalistic aspirations and to share moral authority.

Swift Accumulation of Social Capital

Chinese society is experiencing a confusion of competing value systems, at best, and a severe moral and spiritual crisis, at worst. The recent Party document on ethics-building speaks optimistically of combining values from Chinese tradition, the revolutionary tradition, and modern international experience. The operational public values, however, are suspicion and factionalism from the Party's "power struggle culture" combined with the greed and cronyism of the 1990s, which leaves China with the worst of both socialism and capitalism. Endemic cheating in the education system and fraud in consumer products and services have prompted heated public debate on the Internet about the lack of integrity and honesty.[32]

There is a notable lack of public virtues and habits that foster trust and cooperation. Development theorists, most prominently Francis Fukuyama, argue that these form "social capital" that is as important as financial capital for a healthy market economy. Development literature speaks of a "second wave of reforms" that produce the social and cultural development necessary for sustaining economic development.[33] However, the old-style method of Party-led political education campaigns and the goal of social conformity to State-defined values are more likely to add to the problem than to foster solutions. Fukuyama argues that government intervention to create social capital distorts the results in ways that actually inhibit economic development. Genuinely shared public morality and social creativity is most likely to arise not from top-down campaigns, but from truly voluntary community cooperation, as people experience self-direction and learn new civic concepts and skills.

A New Wave of Opening

China's new leaders must consider not only domestic change but also the pace of change on the outside. Globalization continues to rapidly transform China's neighbors and competitors, piling on the pressures of fierce competition. No one is standing still waiting for China to catch up. Thomas Friedman's study of globalization offered a list of criteria for "most likely to succeed" in the global sweepstakes. These include: getting wired; moving into services and high-tech industry; being a shaper (not just an adapter) of global institutions and norms; developing flexible management for fast response to change; attracting intellectual capital for maximum sharing and harvesting of knowledge (internal and external); developing a culture of openness, not secrecy; competing fairly in finding excellent management with strategic vision; developing a venture-capital mentality and a culture of reinventing old ways and institutions; developing strong alliances for cooperation through building trust and transparency; and building a positive "brand-name" identity (i.e., national reputation). Merely listing these criteria shows how far and fast China's new leaders must move.[34]

"Greater China" Integration

Current leaders reportedly are exploring the socialist models of France and Sweden for ideas to adapt in a still socialist China. These "statist" systems more closely fit the continental common law system enshrined in China's constitution (albeit not in practice). Yet, developments in the Chinese societies of Hong Kong, Taiwan, and Singapore, which have made the best economic showings in Asia, are based on U.S.-UK civil law norms and institutions. While Singapore offers a lone Asian example of successful authoritarianism, it, too, is likely to join the new Asian democracies once generational change occurs within the leadership. Taiwan's democratization and the looming 2007 date set for direct elections in Hong Kong provide a pragmatic rationale for mainland reforms that might close the institutional gap in noneconomic arenas. This would keep open the possibility of future unification or other creative means of formal affiliation.

Reinventing Governance

China's new leaders must push on beyond decentralization and downsizing to a reinvention of "governance" in which the State plays a limited and cooperative role relative to the business and nonprofit sectors. Already, there is an awareness that government goals can no longer be purely political but must reflect a stronger sense of public service. Discussing the changes that the WTO will require, Shanghai's mayor has stressed the need to change the functions of the government. Shenzhen's vice mayor has spoken of replacing the command-type government with a service-oriented government within three to five years.[35] Budding consumer and environmental movements reflect the public's quality of life concerns as well as practical governmental attention to obstacles hindering sustainable development. As the government's ability to solve problems and control events diminishes, it will become increasingly vulnerable to public opinion. To address the tidal wave of social change coming with a full-blown consumer revolution over the next ten years, pioneers in the various elites will have to undergo a fundamental paradigm shift. They must forge win-win-win alliances among government, business, and social organizations to create a new three-sector governance model.

Conclusion: Alternative Pathways

Recent sociological studies of the relationship between State and society in China, in the course of the onrushing consumer revolution, would suggest that new Chinese leaders will face some very difficult historic choices in social policy and political reform. Richard Madsen posits that, so far, the enjoyment of new freedoms in the consumer society has depended on the State's continued economic redistribution and enforcement of social stability through repression. Over the next decade, he predicts that to compete globally, the State will have to continue to reduce the real wages of the working class through layoffs, reduction of benefits, and repression of unrest. Yet, tolerance for this will diminish with rising public expectations for economic progress and social justice coupled with a growing critique of the moral and emotional anarchy of consumerism.[36]

A shift toward legal-electoral sources of legitimacy, and a new public morality fostering trust, tolerance, and cooperation among competing social groups will be necessary to provide a means of peaceful compromise in the event of crises.[37] The positive option is to curb elite corruption and expand channels for nonelite groups to shape policy choices, thus giving citizens a sense of "ownership" even in painful reforms. The negative option may well be facing real opposition, most likely a populist revolt, perhaps justified as part of a broader international antiglobalization backlash.

The legitimacy problem invites enterprising politicians to repudiate some or all of the elements of the Deng-Jiang program, perhaps blaming the Jiang–Li Peng–Zhu Rongji triumvirate rather than Deng Xiaoping for its limitations. This poses a danger to political stability as well as an opportunity for change as phase one of the succession moves into phase two. Competition between political factions and interest groups will heat up in 2005–6 in preparation for new appointments and policies to be unveiled at the next Party and People's congresses. China's elite and public both prefer a go-slow approach for the sake of stability, and the populace is highly risk-averse and psychologically unprepared for debate over grand issues. Nevertheless, events could come together at any time to prompt the fundamental questioning of national identity and political authority.

Appendix

Regulations, decrees or circulars affecting the Third Sector may number as many as fifty, but important ones include:

- Regulations for Management of Foundations (1988).
- Interim Provision for Administration of Foreign Chambers of Commerce (1989).
- Constitutional Provisions Mandating Villagers and Residents Committees (1993), followed by specific laws for the organization of each.
- Regulations Governing the Religious Activities of Foreign Nationals in China (1994) and Rules on Administration of Religious Activities of Foreign Nationals in China (2000).
- Regulations Governing Venues for Religious Activities (1994) and Regulations for Religious Activities (forthcoming).
- Regulations for the Registration and Management of Social Organizations (*shehui tuanti*) (1998). These are membership organizations.
- Provisional Regulations for the Registration and Administration of Private Noncommercial Institutions (*minban feiqiye danwei*) (1998). These are nonprofit service providers that can charge fees, but profits must revert to the organization.
- Provisional Regulations for the Registration and Administration of State-owned Noncommercial Institutions (*shiye feiqiye danwei*) (1998).
- Law on Donations to Public Welfare Undertakings (1999).
- Resolution of the National People's Congress Standing Committee Banning "Heretical Cult Organizations" (1999).

- Experimental Proposal on Improvement of the Social Security System (2000). This includes a clause on tax exemption for contributions to charitable nonprofits.
- Regulations for Registration and Management of Foreign Nonprofit Organizations (forthcoming).

Notes

1. "CASS Marks off Ten Social Strata in Chinese Society," *People's Daily Online*, December 17, 2001. See also Lu Xueyi, ed., *Dangdai Zhingguo Shehui Jiecheng Yanjiiu Baogao* (Research Report on Social Strata in Contemporary China), Shehui Kexue Wenxian Chubanshe (Social Sciences Documentation Publishers), January 2002. The Chinese Academy of Social Science (CASS) identified the following ten occupational strata: state and social administrators (2.1 percent), enterprise managers (1.5 percent), private business owners or entrepreneurs (0.6 percent), professional and technical personnel (5.1 percent), office staff (4.8 percent), self-employed business people (4.2 percent, admittedly a low estimate), industrial workers (22.6 percent), agricultural workers ("the largest," but declining), and the unemployed and semi-employed (3.1 percent and expanding).

2. Information on the united front system in the following paragraphs is from Tong Zhan, "The United Front Work System and the Nonparty Elite," in *Decision-making in Deng's China: Perspectives from Insiders*, ed. Carol Lee Hamrin and Suisheng Zhao (Armonk, NY: M.E. Sharpe, 1995), pp. 66–75.

3. China Development Brief staff, *250 Chinese NGOS: Civil Society in the Making* (Beijing: CDB, August 2001), introduction, pp. 9–19, discusses trends in this sector. Their website, www.chinadevelopmentbrief.com, continues to update lists of domestic and international NGOs operating in China. See also www.chinanpo.org, a site set up with Asia Foundation assistance and used by Chinese nongovernmental organizations (NGOs) for networking and announcements of activities.

4. Benjamin L. Read, "Research Note: Revitalizing the State's Urban 'Nerve Tips,'" *China Quarterly*, no. 163 (September 2000): 806–20, and Allen C. Choate, "Local Governance in China, Part II," Asia Foundation Working Paper Series no. 10 (November 1998).

5. Tony Carnes, "'New China: Same Old Tricks," *Christianity Today* 46, no. 3 (March 11, 2002): 38, citing estimates from *Operation World*.

6. Open Doors news release no. 21, www.assist-ministries.com, August 15, 2001.

7. Jason Kindopp, "Protestantism and Politics in Contemporary China: Social Control and Movement in a Single Party-state," draft dissertation, ch. 4: "The Official Church," cited with permission of the author.

8. See appendix for list of selected Third Sector regulations. Sources for information on Third Sector regulations include: China Development Brief staff, *250 NGOs*, appendix; www.asianphilantrophy.org, section on history and law; www.amity foundation.org. For information about regulations on religion in China see *Chinese Law and Government* 33, no. 2 (March/April 2000); 33, no. 3 (May/June 2000); and 33, no. 6 (November/December 2000).

9. Tony Saich, "Negotiating the State: The Development of Social Organizations in China," *China Quarterly*, no. 161 (March 2000): 124–41.

10. "Text of Chinese Parliament Resolution Banning 'Heretic Cults'," *Xinhuanet*, October 30, 1999; text of social organization regulations in China Development Brief staff, *250 Chinese NGOs*, appendix; Barnett F. Baron, "International Conference in Beijing Hails Emergence of Chinese NGOs," www.asiafoundation.org/news/news-high28.html. The latter discusses the controversy over the restrictive nature of October 1998 social organization regulations, as well as the July 1999 International Conference on NGOs in Beijing.

11. For documentation on Jiang Zemin's speech on the "Three Represents" theme and the subsequent campaign, see "Quarterly Chronicle and Documentation," *China Quarterly*, no. 163 (September 2000), pp. 884–85; Jiang Zemin, "Speech at the Meeting Celebrating the Eightieth Anniversary of the Founding of the CPC," July 1, 2001, *Xinhuanet*, July 12, 2001.

12. Stig Thogersen, "Report from the Field: Cultural Life and Cultural Control in Rural China: Where Is the Party?" *China Journal*, no. 44 (July 2000): 129–41. See p. 140 for a discussion of the "ten stars" award system.

13. Central Committee Circular, "Implementation Outline on Ethic Building for Citizens," *Xinhuanet*, October 24, 2001 (10,000 characters and eight parts).

14. Cheng Li, "China in 2000: A Year of Strategic Rethinking," *Asian Survey* 41 no. 1 (January/February 2001).

15. Bruce Dickson, "Economics as the Central Task: Do Entrepreneurs Matter?" this volume, pp. 186–203.

16. Two staff members of international foundations who have worked closely with the YMCA and the China Charity Foundation system, interviews with author, Beijing, November 2000.

17. May-fair Mei-hui Yang and Grace May, recounting results of field research, interviews with author, Washington, DC, November 14, 1997. By the 1990s, Wenzhou exhibited a remarkable societal vitality marked by open, public Buddhist, Catholic and Protestant activities. These activities occurred with the acceptance or even involvement of retired or active officials and the support of local business based on national- and international-scale trade. (Wenzhou communities can be found in major European and Chinese cities.) Pre-1949, Wenzhou had a high percentage of religious believers, in part the product of Christian missionary efforts. Thus, in the 1950s and 1960s, Wenzhou became a special national target in Mao's effort to eradicate religion. Throughout the late 1980s and 1990s, however, Wenzhou began to receive grudging leadership approval as a model market economy, despite sporadic attempts to suppress the revival of religion.

18. Committee for Investigation of Persecution of Religion in China (CIPRC), "Religion and National Security in China: Secret Documents from China's Security Sector," www.religiousfreedomforchina.org, February 11, 2002.

19. Vivien P.K. Chan, reports in *South China Morning Post*, November 14 and 20, 2001.

20. Ding Xueliang, "From Big Social Problems to Explosive Political Troubles?" paper presented at the international conference on the Challenges to China's Fourth Generation Leadership, National University of Singapore, November 8–9 2001, pp. 9–10, 20.

21. Beijing religious affairs expert, interview with author, Washington, DC, February 1998.

22. CIPRC, "Religion and National Security," appendix.

23. Personal attendance at a meeting with a China Christian Council delegation in Virginia, November 1997.

24. *Tibet Press Watch*, September 2001.

25. Beijing and Hong Kong religious affairs experts, interviews with author by telecommunication, August–December 2002. The day the conference ended following a hard-line speech by Jiang Zemin urging tighter Party control over religion, a much more moderate policy proposal was published by the deputy director of the State Commission for Economic Restructuring, Pan Yue, "CPC Theorist Pan Yue Says Marxist Religious Views Must Keep Abreast of the Times," *Shenzhen tequ bao*, December 16, 2001. This appears to have been part of a much larger research project on political reform cited in Joseph Fewsmith, this volume, pp. 152–64. National regulations still had not been publicized by mid-2002, perhaps reflecting internal debate.

26. Wang Shaoguang, "The Social and Political Implications of China's WTO Membership," *Journal of Contemporary China* 25 (September 2000), documents the unusually large regional gaps (seventeenth of seventeen countries in interregional inequality) as well as rural-urban disparities.

27. See Jeffrey Sachs, "Notes on a New Sociology of Economic Development," pp. 36–37, and Mariano Grondona, "A Cultural Typology of Economic Development," pp. 49–54, in *Culture Matters*, ed. Lawrence E. Harrison and Samuel P. Huntington (New York: Basic Books, 2000) for linkages among culture, system, and economic development.

28. Baron, "International Conference," discusses the profound impact of Lester Salamon's ongoing research at Johns Hopkins University and training programs being conducted by Qinghua University's new Center for the Study of NGOs. Author's interviews at the Center in November 2000 and June 2001 confirm the strong interest and rapid development of research and training.

29. Kang Xiaoguang, "China's Social Organizations in Transition," www.chinanpo. org, June 25, 2001. Kang and his colleagues at the Center for China Studies, writing in *Zhanlue yu Guanli* (*Strategy and Management*), June 1, 2002, explicitly warned that current trends in corruption and injustice would lead to political instability.

30. Conference Report, *Xinhuanet*, October 30, 2001.

31. Peter Berger, "Four Faces of Global Culture," *National Interest* (Fall 1997): 23–29.

32. Bruce Gilley, "People's Republic of Cheats," *Far Eastern Economic Review*, June 21, 2001, pp. 59–60.

33. Francis Fukuyama, "Social Capital and Civil Society," paper presented at the International Monetary Fund conference on Second Generation Reforms, *fukuyama.htm*, October 1, 1999. See also Partha Dasgupta and Ismail Serngeldin, eds., *Social Capital: a Multifaceted Perspective* (Washington, DC: The World Bank, 1999).

34. Thomas L. Friedman, *The Lexus and the Olive Tree* (New York: Random House Anchor Books, 2000), pp. 212–47.

35. Quoted in Willy Wo-Lap Lam, "China's WTO Membership—Now the Hard Part Begins," CNN on-line, November 13, 2001.

36. Richard Madsen, "Epilogue: The Second Liberation," in *The Consumer Revolution in Urban China*, ed. Deborah S. Davis (Berkeley: University of California Press, 2000), pp. 15–16.

37. Dingxin Zhao, "China's Prolonged Stability and Political Future: Same Political System, Different Policies and Methods," *Journal of Contemporary China* 10, no. 28 (August 2001): 427–44. Zhao has discussed "ideational" links between State and society as distinct from economic or political linkages. He describes alternative means of justifying State power and buttressing public perceptions of State legitimacy: by commonly accepted procedure (legal-electoral); by services the State provides (perfor-

mance); by promises for the future (ideological) or by hope placed on one leader's ability or personality (charismatic). Over the past two decades, China has shifted from the latter two types toward performance-based legitimacy. After showing how this has served to increase societal trust in government, he nonetheless makes the point that any regime basing its legitimacy on performance is intrinsically unstable because it provides limited opportunities for compromise in the event of major setbacks in performance.

——— 11 ———

The Absent-Minded Reform of China's Media

Anne Stevenson-Yang

Since 1998, the private media organizations that have thrived in the interstices of China's regulatory system have found it increasingly difficult to establish and preserve new media vehicles, even through the elaborate corporate structures they have established to preserve the appearance of government ownership. There was a long freeze on the issuance of new publishing licenses[1] and efforts to close down publications considered unsuitable.[2] Government content censors have applied a higher standard of ideological vigilance. Web sites have been forbidden to disseminate original news stories, and 17,000 Internet cafes were recently shut down.[3] Reporting on military affairs has been submitted to a new control regime.[4] A press law and various regulatory measures to allow a gradual opening of the media have been stalled,[5] and, recently, the State Administration of Radio, Film, and Television has required foreign broadcasters to broadcast from the "Sino Satellite" platform run by China Central Television (CCTV) in order to centralize government control over the signal and over content distribution. Such measures of media control are only becoming more stringent in what amounts to China's election year—the run-up to the Sixteenth Party Congress in the fall of 2002. As Propaganda Minister Ding Guangen told a meeting of Propaganda officials in Wuhan in early November, the work of next year's press, broadcasting, and film reform is to "elevate the level and create a new spirit of unity and beneficial atmosphere for the Sixteenth Party Congress."[6] The leadership wants to ensure that nothing is said to undermine the careful campaign to place a set of anointed successors in the top Politburo positions.

The political anxiety over the new independence of the press, however, indicates more a shift in the central government's regulatory strategy than an effort to reassert the kind of control that the government enjoyed before the beginning of economic reform in the 1980s. The days of total control over the media, as over the economy, are gone in modern China, but the Chinese Communist Party (CCP) agenda of shaping public opinion through the mass media remains intact. What regulatory policy of the past twenty years has shown is that, in order to achieve national unity and the economic growth upon which unity depends, the leadership is willing to relinquish its directorial rights over the theater of public debate just as it has relinquished direct command control of the economy. Instead, the CCP is controlling the media with a time-honored strategy of divide and conquer, ensuring that an envelope of insecurity surrounds each media organization, and that none grows large or strong enough to be immune to preemptive government action against it. From within the Chinese cultural outlook, this is an achievable agenda: traditionally, the Chinese government has shaped policy with the belief that factual and objective "information" on the economy and business can flow freely in order to provide maximum fuel to China's growing economy, while "subjective" and "spiritual" political and cultural information can be tightly restricted; the two will not encroach upon each other.

The First Reform Phase: Growth

Anyone buying newspapers from a hawker on the street in one of China's major cities today could be forgiven for seeing a media environment that looks a little like the yellow journalism wars between the Hearst and Pulitzer empires before the turn of the past century in the United States. Chinese tabloid headlines on a given day might feature an appeal by a child to find her long-lost parents, a story on the hammer-murder gang of muggers in Beijing, or an appeal by former Red Guards who want to meet their victims and ask for forgiveness before the victims grow old and die. Compare this with the press environment of the 1980s, in which daily newspapers were posted in glass cases on city thoroughfares to be read by passersby because the post office monopoly could not deliver them on time. The news consisted of lists of officials who had attended public events and encomiums to the happy diplomatic relationship between China and, say, Burundi on the occasion of the Burundi national leader's visit to Beijing. Of course, the official mouthpiece media, such as the *People's Daily*, preserve these traditional areas of focus, but most others do not.

China's media concerns have behaved more or less like other sectors of the economy in the liberalized atmosphere of the past two decades, multiplying in number and variety, turning managerial efforts toward consumers and financiers instead of supervising government agencies, and developing fragile, quasilegal new business structures to put a membrane between themselves and government control. The initiative that launched media reform was the 1978 political shift from "class struggle" to economic development, shuffling political control down from the central government. The first phase of media growth, in the early 1980s, was fomented by the gradual reduction of subsidies along with indications that, ultimately, media organizations would have to support themselves. At the period of highest growth in 1983–1986, a new newspaper appeared roughly every four days.[7] Since the opening of the reform period,[8] the number of China's newspapers has grown from 186[9] to about 1,800,[10] a little more than half the number at the peak of the growth period in the mid-1980s.[11] The number of magazines has risen from a few hundred to more than 7,000, TV stations from about 700 to around 9,000, including more than 5,000 cable networks, many of them privately run by state-owned companies or housing compounds.[12] Outdoor advertising has become a billion dollar business, and difficult-to-regulate Internet sites have done their part to chip away at the realm of information under direct government control. Publications operated with foreign cooperation or investment, using shaky, work-around structures to accommodate the ostensible illegality of any foreign involvement in media operations, number about 80.[13]

The easiest way in the early 1980s to go into business was to take over management of an ailing State asset or else receive government funding for a new venture. Publishing was no exception. The period 1980–84 saw huge growth in the publications sponsored by government ministries, a class of publications that enjoyed relatively little ideological and Party oversight and that were supposedly limited to "internal" circulation within the ministry— although in fact they circulated the same way as any conventional magazine or newspaper. Ultimately, the central government grew displeased with this obvious drain on resources and commissioned a survey of publications by People's University in 1986. Leaders concluded that the great majority of new publications did not, in fact, support any political agenda, and there were new efforts to cut off subsidies to the media.

The withdrawal of funding unleashed an era of intense media competition. The public, before the 1980s, had lacked for reading material. Official newspapers, reserved by mandatory subscription by all government companies and organizations, were generally four pages long and contained didactic editorials almost entirely concerned with internal Party debates. The first 500 words of a report on a national celebration, for example, would list all the officials who attended in order of rank, attaching all their titles, and would contain hints about the current political standing of the leaders so subtle that combing the grammar and usage for such hidden comment became a national pastime. Newspapers formed the syllabus for Saturday "study groups" at all domestic organizations but were certainly not considered recreational reading.

In the late 1980s, that changed. Media managers faced an oversupply of boring publications competing for a limited consumer appetite or ability to pay. As a result, publications grew in size and variety and began to seek more muscular distribution strategies. Every publication sought some connection with a government organization engaging in local distribution in order to move more newspapers and magazines to the public more quickly. Quasilegal distribution organizations grew up on the city and provincial level to compete with the Xinhua chain and the postal system. This was the period in which star journalists, like Liu Binyan, emerged on the staffs of prominent dailies.

The advent of commercial advertising also drove a shift toward bread-and-circuses populism. Shanghai TV had aired the first commercial in post-Liberation China in January 1979. By the late 1980s, a commercial advertising market was emerging, though mostly in the form of paid editorials. Publishers borrowed the name of a popular play to describe their plight—"One Servant, Two Masters"—meaning that they had to serve both the interests of their political overseers and those of advertisers. As circulation began to be the most important driver of revenue, a third master was added—the general public. Publishers with the strongest political connections engaged popular taste with their editorial content as much as they dared to, seizing on campaigns around revising the Marriage Law or promulgating an Unfair Competition Law to open up new topics of discussion. Competing for circulation, newspapers and magazines began to write about divorce, shoddy products, and the plight of the average Chinese faced with job competition and government layoffs. The publications most willing to challenge the status quo, then as now, were those reporting to powerful local governments, especially Guangzhou, Shenzhen, and, to a lesser extent, Shanghai and Beijing.

The media growth of the late 1980s set the stage for the cracking of the distribution monopolies, which, in turn, prepared the ground for private involvement in the print media. The formation of new, alternative distribution networks lowered the barrier to entry for new publications, as well as made it easier for publications to evade official notice, at least for a time.

In publishing, Xinhua, the government news agency reporting directly to the State Council but with its closest bureaucratic ties to the security agencies, operated the longstanding State monopoly on book distribution through a nationwide chain of printing plants, stores, trucks, and warehouses. The postal system, formerly part of the national telecommunications ministry, monopolized the distribution of print publications. That monopoly had been established by Premier Zhou Enlai at the founding of the People's Republic. Since, in

1949, the postal system was the only organization with reach into every town and village in China, the post office was the only organization formally permitted to accept subscription fees or distribute newspapers and magazines to subscribers. Before the formal breakdown of the monopoly—regulations describing how companies could qualify as publication distributors were issued only in 1999[14]—many competing distributors had grown up under protection of local governments. Nevertheless, nonpostal authority companies are still not permitted to distribute directly to the customer's door or shop.[15]

The post office has defended its monopoly only weakly. The main reason seems to have been the post office's relative weakness in local politics. The postal system derives its important revenues on the local level with profit deriving from the major cities. But postal policy is made on the national level. To protect their interests, local postal administrations have traditionally failed to account clearly for their costs, even internally. Once a real opportunity to engage in a commercial business arose, the postal authorities were ill-equipped to compete.

For example, the post office collects between 35 percent and 40 percent of the cover price of a magazine or newspaper from the publisher as its distribution fee. But, as publications have grown in page count, the cover-price proposition has become less attractive.[16] Rural distribution has always operated at a loss. In the early 1990s, some publications with subscribers nationwide attempted taking over their own distribution; *People's Daily* was one, but it wanted to leave rural distribution in the hands of the postal system. The post office reportedly complained to Premier Li Peng, who ruled that *People's Daily* could not take over only the most lucrative portion of its distribution business.[17] Gradually, though, urban-based publications began establishing their own networks, by poaching postal employees while simultaneously shoring up support from competing bureaucracies. In 1996, *Beijing Youth Daily* established its own distribution company, Little Red Cap (sometimes translated as "Little Red Riding Hood"), by hiring members of the Post Office Publication Distribution division at high salaries and having them set up a network of delivery stations, warehouses, and part-time employees to do house-to-house delivery. Little Red Cap reached agreement with the Bank of Industry and Commerce to have subscription fees accepted at any bank branch, which solved the problem of consumer trust and took the financing stream out of the hands of the post office. Little Red Cap worked hard to build a reputation as a supporter of the local government by publicizing its policy of hiring workers who had been laid off from State-owned enterprises. Although much attacked by the postal administration, Little Red Cap had the support of the Beijing local government, and, ultimately, the nationally based postal administration could not penetrate Beijing's protectionism.[18]

Shortly after Little Red Cap's advent came Little Yellow Cap (*Beijing Morning News*) and Little Blue Cap (*Beijing Economic Daily*) as well as a dozen other imitators. Soon, any daily with enough circulation to support its own distribution company established one, and, as of a year ago, there were about 800 newspaper-distribution companies under dailies nationwide.[19]

Magazines with multicity distribution tried to follow the Little Red Cap example; *New Weekly*, under the 999 Group, a pharmaceuticals company formerly owned by the military, was among the most notable examples, claiming to have invested millions in 1999 to establish distribution through about thirty offices nationwide.[20] *New Weekly*'s effort, however, like those of other multicity distribution organizations, failed because of the tremendous obstacles to running a logistics business efficiently across provincial or even city lines.

While, formerly, newspapers sold 70 percent of their copies by subscription, now the balance has shifted toward newsstand sales, thanks to the demise of compulsory subscription and to independent distribution schemes, both of which have had profound effects on the popularization of editorial content. The ability to put together a distribution team to sell on the street, or to piggyback on an existing distribution network, has lowered the barrier to entry, making it possible to take circulation away from an established publication quickly. Because newspaper publishing in China's cities is essentially a circulation business (circulation on average accounts for about six times the amount of advertising revenue in newspapers,[21] an investor in a new publication need only deploy more people in more locations, selling a publication that appeals to the average person, in order to cut into the market of the established daily. Perhaps more significantly, the ability to maintain an on-the-ground distribution team enables publications to target particular demographic groups within a market that so restricts the flow of information that the relative wealth or poverty of city neighborhoods is considered a State secret. Using an existing distribution team—cable TV installers, Street Committees, parcel-delivery services, or any other type of company that goes door to door—permits a new publication to choose a roughly predefined demographic target. Employing people to hawk papers or to sell door to door, on the other hand, permits some informal targeting—for example, at sports stadiums, on college campuses, at auto repair shops, or other places that might attract the desired reader.

The Entry of Private Capital

Opening up distribution networks made the establishment of privately sponsored publications a practical possibility. Initially, the ground was prepared by the government requirement that media organizations become independent *danwei* or accounting units under government organizations. This meant that they had to have their own budgets and profit and loss accounts. From there, it was not hard to split off some parts of media organizations as companies. This "corporatization" tended to unbind portions of media organizations, so that advertising, distribution, and editorial were often established under separate companies. Once this began to occur, it became easy for private and foreign capital to enter into the less sensitive parts of the publishing enterprise.

First, the most commercially successful Chinese publishers split their departments into separate companies then applied for the status of "group corporation," of which there are currently sixteen in the print media.[22] The "group corporation" represents an attempt to permit successful government-owned businesses to operate as integrated corporations, binding operating units into a structure that permits more discretion in financing and more independence from supervising ministries. The group corporations bring together editorial departments of several publications with advertising companies, distribution companies, and unrelated units. The financing that becomes available to the groups through intercompany transfers has made it easier for these publishers to start new magazines and newspapers. The Southern Group's establishment of *Southern Metropolitan News* in Shenzhen is one good example.

Next, private players began to set up or invest in advertising and service companies attached to publishing operations. To obtain direct control over editorial, the private companies publish within regulatory loopholes, distributing a magazine as free advertising material, buying International Standard Book Numbers (ISBN) used for book publishing and putting out magazines as a "series of books," or taking over a bankrupt publication for the price of a fee to the bureaucrats in charge of license renewal and running political interference. Nearly all mainland-based foreign involvement in publishing employs service contracts to operate: the foreign investor establishes a consulting or advertising company that writes an exclusive service contract with a government-owned organization that holds a publishing license. Such contracts, in various forms, are used by IDG Corp., Hachette-Filipacchi, McGraw-Hill, Figaro, Ringier, and many others.

Private Chinese interests follow the same pattern, but often with more flexibility. Cheng Cheng and Science and Culture are examples of wholly private companies that, through contractual arrangements, have established themselves as publishers of significant size. Another example is *Chengdu Business News*, a popular newspaper in Sichuan Province dealing with crime and scandal, which was formed in 1999 and became the principal shareholder of Borui Investment Co.[23] Borui then bought a 29.5 percent stake in Sichuan Electrical, a listed company. Sichuan Electrical in turn purchased nearly all of *Chengdu Business News*'s independent distribution company. Gradually, the staged purchases made this private investment and advertising company owner of a media business.

In newspaper publishing, *Shu Bao* (Sichuan News) until recently was published in Chengdu under the Sichuan Top Group, a software company listed as the Sichuan Tuopu Software Co. Ltd. (Shanghai: 0583). Sichuan Top had purchased the noneditorial assets in two failing local newspapers, *Shu Bao* and *Morning Business News*, investing 20 million RMB and later losing 43 million RMB more, according to a report on the China Securities News Web. In order to fit within the most narrow interpretation of Chinese policy and regulation, private media organizations like Borui and Top have often purchased distressed, publicly traded companies in order to acquire a financing vehicle. The entity then is reorganized, with a spin-off of the most sensitive portions of the business, dealing with editorial. The spun-off units normally sign exclusive contracts with their original parent companies. This tactic has also been used to advantage by foreign-invested Internet portals, which were not allowed to list on public exchanges as long as the editorial portions of the company had foreign investment. Both Sohu and Sina divested their content departments into the hands of Chinese partners before they listed.

Some media organizations, operating through advertising companies under contractual arrangements, have managed to list on domestic markets without restructuring. China Television Media, Ltd., Oriental Pearl, Shandong Sanlian, and Dianguang Broadcasting all feature media components within their operations, particularly in film and television production.[24]

Since they lack a personal stake in the Party organization, private operators have tended to stretch the boundaries of publication content and style. Well-known examples are the Trends Group, which started its flagship title with the cooperation of the Tourism Bureau and now publishes *Cosmopolitan*, *Esquire*, and its own fashion and lifestyles titles; *Jing pin gou wu zhinan* (Shopping Guide) in Beijing, formed by individuals using a publishing permit owned by the Chinese Academy of Social Sciences; and *Cai Jing* (Money), formed by private entrepreneurs with the sponsorship of the Stock Exchange Executive Council and using a publishing permit from the preexisting *Securities Market Weekly*. Each of these organizations broke new ground for the Chinese publishing world: *Trends* because of its high-quality design and printing and its reliance on advertising instead of circulation revenue, *Shopping Guide* because it was the first well-known publication to rely on free distribution and content that appealed to consumers, and *Cai Jing* because of its on-the-edge investigative reporting on economic scandals.

Papers in outlying provinces have contended to attract readers with exciting stories and promotional events. In October 2001, several newspapers eagerly reported on and photographed promotions at department stores that had customers walk through clad in only underwear in order to win prizes. The rousing *Sichuan News* on the eve of the new year in 2000 organized a mass wedding ceremony.[25] But *Sichuan News*, and its companion *Morning Business News*, were closed in fall 2001 by the propaganda authorities. The splashy style bothered staid officials, and *Sichuan News* was rumored to have gotten into trouble for writing disrespectfully about President Jiang Zemin's (widely ridiculed) eyeglasses.[26] Since the organization was not making money, it was weakly positioned to call on local authorities for help in mounting a defense.

Unintended Pluralism

Over twenty years of growth in the media, the number of officials charged with supervising media content stayed constant and then dropped, at least at the national level, with the already diminished staff at the State Press and Publications Administration (PPA) finally cut in half, to about 150, during the 1998 government-reduction campaign that followed the Fifteenth Party Congress. The inability of the ideological censors to keep up with the pace of change in the media market was an important stimulus to the relaxation of content controls.

The government employs two basic means of control: direct supervision of content and regulation of media structures. To make the best use of a small number of staff, direct supervision is focused on the media organizations considered most likely to be apostate. The central-level PPA, for example, has members of the staff exclusively devoted to reading *Beijing Youth Daily* and *Southern Weekend*, newspapers that have a following among well-educated urban Chinese and that frequently pursue stories on official corruption.[27] The editors of *Southern Weekend* have been removed twice in two years, and the newspaper's print run is controlled, as is its circulation outside of its home Guangdong Province. The Propaganda Bureau also sponsors groups of retired editors in each city to read newspapers and magazines for content that does not conform to current Propaganda instructions. These editorial review groups often receive letters from competing publications making a political case against a particular editorial direction. Should the editors flag something as nonconforming, an internal Party report goes to the PPA, which makes a phone call or issues a notice to the publication's editor. Such notices are received with great seriousness, because the PPA has the preemptive right to stop publication without notice, while Propaganda may remove editors from their jobs. In a serious case, the Party's report will also lead to administrative detention ("reform through labor") for an editor or lead to civil charges that put him or her in jail.

For day-to-day administrative purposes, the CCP through its Propaganda

Bureau issues directives on how the press should regard particular issues of concern to the leadership. Particularly long-lived campaigns in recent memory include the antispiritual pollution campaign of 1983 and the antibourgeois liberalism campaigns in 1987 and 1989. More often, the propaganda bureaucracies use monthly meetings with editors-in-chief and internal policy notices to press particular points of view on international or domestic issues: The press was not permitted to print anything that did not condemn the United States for the NATO bombing of China's embassy in Yugoslavia, for example, and media outlets that released information about the September 11 terrorist attacks on the United States prior to the issuance of instructions from the Propaganda Bureau in Beijing were criticized.

The second means of control consists of administrative rights over business establishments. The right to publish, awarded only to government institutions after a three-year qualification process, may be withdrawn by the "department in charge," which, for openly circulating publications, is the PPA at the appropriate level. In the ideological bureaucracy, the Propaganda Bureau of the CCP has actual authority, but regulations are issued and direct control over business establishments is exercised through the State Council Office of Information and the PPA, civil institutions reporting to the State Council. The PPA was formed only in 1986, as the State Media and Publications Office, in order to reflect the new corporatizing of media organizations, which removed them from direct Party control. The first director of the PPA, Du Daozheng, was transferred by the Party from his former job as editor-in-chief of *Guangming Daily*,[28] one of the Party's chief mouthpieces, still directly funded and controlled by the CCP at the central level. As media organizations began to incorporate as companies, the Party was obliged to rely on civil organizations for regulatory control, and its ability to reach through the civil bureaucracy to the offending media outlets was necessarily diluted.

Neither the central government nor the Party apparatus has funded a growth concomitant with the proliferation of media in the bureaucracies that supervise ideological content. Instead, the Propaganda Bureau has retreated to a defense of what it considers core political principles. International news (as long as it does not touch upon China's foreign policy concerns, describe China's leaders in unflattering ways, or disclose economic, commercial, or social issues considered inimical to China's image development at home and abroad), leisure and entertainment, marriage and family, and examinations of official corruption (as long as the corruption is not too high up in the political hierarchy) have all become permissible areas for discussion. The most powerful new entrants into the print media fray seek safe harbor by concentrating in a less-sensitive information niche—shopping, sports, technology areas, for example. IDG, which may be the most successful foreign publisher operating in China and which has operated a publishing joint venture since 1980, for its first fifteen years in business eschewed almost anything but high-tech and computing. Media organizations rely on the delicate interplay between local and national power centers, as well as between domestic and international news organizations, to break open previously untouched areas. Often, a news organization will break a story about a scandal in another province, or a local paper will pick up a story that has already been broken in the international media. Even the crusading *Southern Weekend* seldom writes about scandals in its own Guangdong Province.

Instead of approving the less-sensitive content areas before publication, authorities now rely on the chill effect of dismissal or even arrest for editors and reporters who went too far, particularly when a press report, whether on a soccer competition or on ethnic issues, is perceived as having led to civil unrest. Publications remain subject to the prepublication review process (*zhongshen*), which is the responsibility of the editor-in-chief, who is generally directly appointed by the Party but who lately may have diminished influence within press organizations. The postpublication review by local propaganda authorities and monthly meetings and directives on ideology content, called "blowing the wind" (*chui feng hui*) meetings at which publications are told how to treat hot topics and what to avoid, provide another check valve. The *chui feng hui* are also used to criticize apostate publications, announce temporary stops to publication, and praise reports that support government policy particularly effectively.

The shift from direct, prepublication content control to after-the-fact penalties has had profound effects on China's ideological environment, as the diffusion of authority has tended to accentuate the usual conflict of interest between editors seeking readers and censors seeking political safety. Although the disproportionate penalties that often apply to incautious editorial content create a chill on the media, nevertheless, being threatened with penalty after publication tends to give media organizations time to lobby with bureaucratic allies and build a defense against closure of the publication.

The publications that have been best equipped to take advantage of this new political permissiveness are not those run behind the scenes by private organizations—which are influential but remain small—but instead those sponsored by quasi-independent government organizations or localities: the Beijing-level Communist Youth League (sponsor of the *Beijing Youth Daily*), the Sanlian Group (*Sanlian News Weekly*), the Southern Group (under the Guangzhou government), and the Xinmin Group (under the Shanghai city government). Protected by localities, these organizations have grown large and mostly very profitable.

In the meantime, no national leader has been willing to take on the task of systematic reformulation of media policy. The bureaucratic agenda of deliberate reform has from time to time been accepted by certain high-ranking officials, notably Vice Premier Li Lanqing. But unlike industries that produced revenue, however inefficiently, before the reform period, such as machinery and telecommunications, the media operated directly by the Propaganda Bureau have always lost money, while those media outlets sponsored by organizations with indirect reporting relationships to the central ministries have more often managed to become profitable. In the Chinese system (as in most companies), those responsible for bringing in revenue have the most clout. Therefore, any State Council official who takes media into his or her portfolio can count on attracting Politburo discontent for allowing too much free speech but cannot anticipate any counter-balancing rewards for strong financial performance. In the policy gap, officials limit their risk by engaging in periodic efforts to reduce the growth and independence of any particular media outlet.

Reasserting Control

Over the past two years, the central government has been engaged in an attempt to understand the changed media market in China and begin to formulate policies that will secure the form of control that matters most to the political leadership: the ability to start or stop political campaigns by using the media. Since 1999, the issuance of new publishing permits for periodicals has been frozen, although many organizations have been successful in recycling old permits for the launch of new titles. Several crackdowns, starting in the summer of 1998, have been leveled against the use of book publishing permits to publish magazines and the use of advertising permits to publish magazines with editorial content. In November, Xinhua reported, the PPA issued "stop business for rectification" orders against five publishing houses—the China Geological University Publishing House, Taihai Publishing House, Arsenal Industry Publishing House, the Chinese Ancient Medical Books Publishing House, and the China Industry and Commerce Publishing House—because they had been selling their ISBNs.[29]

Through the issuance of policy clarifications and sweeps by an inspection team, the PPA managed to remove from the market many privately run magazines that were purchasing book numbers from official publishing houses. The PPA has tightened up on ministry-sponsored magazines, issuing a notice in 1999 to local governments requiring all ministry-sponsored publications to reapply for their publishing numbers, which are controlled by the central-level PPA. Most of the publications deemed legitimate were shifted under direct Party control, while ministries—which are hard or impossible for the PPA to control—lost most of their publishing numbers. The PPA's newspaper reported that, in 1998, the campaign to reduce the number of publications stopped publication of 300 "openly circulating" national newspapers and 3,773 "internally circulating" publications published by government organizations. In television, stations have been required to split programming from broadcasting, which has led to vigorous growth in independent programmers.

A few attempts to establish a more modern and transparent policy on the media have been blocked, most recently because of concern over maintaining a "good environment" for the Sixteenth Party Congress in fall 2002. A May 2001 "clarification" on media policy reportedly originally contained reference to a policy intention to allow foreign investment in the media.[30] But, anticipating the Beidaihe government meetings in August to discuss the Sixteenth Party Congress, the State Council reportedly removed reference to foreign investment. As finally issued, internally, to Party secretaries of media organizations, the joint State Council and State Council Office of Information document reportedly contained the following reforms planned for the media:

1. Media outlets will be permitted to distribute outside the provinces in which they originate.
2. Officially approved organizations will be allowed to cross media lines. That is, a television station may receive approval to publish a magazine and a newspaper may apply for a broadcasting license.
3. Media organization will be permitted to accept investment from nongovernment organizations, as long as the government retains editorial control.

Still stalled within the pre–Party Congress gridlock are a Press Law to define the rights of journalists, the issuance of permits to foreign-invested companies that would legalize their publication of information on the Internet, and the promulgation of an official policy establishing an "experimental area" for foreign participation in broadcasting in Guangdong Province. Efforts to catalogue foreign and private involvement in the media and to gain more direct levers of control over foreign-owned media outlets being viewed within China suggest that that policy options are being prepared for the post–Party Congress period.

Clearly, though, more formal reform measures are in store. The establishment of official landing rights for Phoenix TV and AOL Time Warner in Guangdong Province is widely seen as the opening of an "experimental zone" for foreign-invested media. A policy permitting media organizations formally to seek market listings is also in preparation: In April 2001 the China Securities Regulatory Commission (CSRC) issued a reclassification of enterprises eligible for market listing in which the media, broadly defined as "broadcasting" and "art" industries, was named as one of thirteen "fundamental" industry sectors eligible for market listings.[31]

Keeping Them Small

Change came about through a mix of policy and absent-mindedness. Jiang Zemin, through repeated statements exhorting the Chinese press to become internationally competitive and the foreign press to have limited involvement within China, has established a broad policy framework in which some form of "opening" is anticipated. In a March 2001 meeting with the chairman of Viacom, Inc., producer of MTV, for example, Jiang said that "international media could play an active role in helping deepen understanding between China and the rest of the world," according to *People's Daily*.[32]

Why? Foreign observers conventionally agree that the realm of public information is the most dearly held bastion of Party power, and that letting the media become independent would spell the end of the Party. In fact, China's leadership takes a more nuanced approach, whether or not it is a realistic one. As economic development has stimulated the growth of formidable centers of power in the provinces, Beijing has repeatedly demonstrated that it will sacrifice control over the general populace in favor of control over its own departments and regions. One of the best examples has been the central government's "Golden Projects" to bring communication and information technologies into government agencies, causing a not-unanticipated side effect in the delivery of Internet services to the general public. In 2001, although China still blocks Internet sites it considers dissident, jails people for posting politically offensive content, and requires active censorship of Internet content and chat rooms, still, the government predicts and even welcomes the egress to Internet browsing of 200 million people in China by 2005,[33] according to State Council Office of Information Director Zhao Qizheng. The government has been willing to permit such slippage in control over access to information because the "Golden Projects," in government estimation, have had such an overwhelmingly positive effect on the central authorities' ability to monitor local tax, Customs, police, trade, and other agencies—and because the potential negative impact of more severe Internet controls on China's public dream to become an information intensive, high-technology economy would be devastating.

Equally important, with the devolution of both political control and revenue from central to local governments over the period of economic reform, China's political leadership has found itself increasingly reliant on media exposure to regulate both official behavior and the marketplace. This reliance has taken two forms: first, State Council leaders, with much reduced staff resources at their disposal in the government think tanks, have increasingly used journalists in localities to provide confidential reports on situations that the local governments might prefer to leave unexposed to their political masters. *People's Daily* articulated the situation in an August 27 editorial on the flooding of a tin mine in Nandan, Guangxi, which reportedly killed eighty-one people: "Since last July, we've seen serious accidents taking place one after another in Guangxi, Shaanxi, Shanghai, and Jiangsu. News about the accidents spread fast by way of television, newspaper and the website. Especially in the case of the Nandan mine flooding, it was only due to the great efforts by journalists that the 'Iron Curtain' [of official silence] of the fact was torn apart. Afterwards, the accident aroused high attention of the Party and the State Council and the investigation on the accident was thus brought onto a right track."[34]

The leadership, along with the rest of society, has discovered how potent exposure in the press can be for pressuring corrupt officials, vendors of substandard products, autocratic employers, and other oppressors small and large. The leadership has repeatedly praised media outlets for "supervising" the work of government itself. During a much-discussed visit to CCTV on October 7, 1998, for example, Premier Zhu Rongji met reporters from the popular news magazine show *Focus*. "Through media supervising, the press can help us correct our mistakes and listen to the public opinions," he said, calling on Chinese journalists to be the "throat and tongue of the masses, mirror of the government, and pioneer of the reform."[35] Examples abound. At Mid-Autumn Festival in 2001, local governments throughout the country launched investigations of bakeries making "mooncakes" following a CCTV exposé on unsanitary conditions in mooncake factories. Press exposés have become such a potent social tool that companies and individuals throughout China have begun to use the media to seek satisfaction in disputes ranging from commercial, labor and environmental issues to wrongful arrest. The consumer crusader Wang Hai now has his own Web site, www.wanghai.com, which posts consumer bulletins and product warnings. Wang Hai himself has been targeted by the media for allegations that he has been in the employ of companies wanting to prove that competitors' products are shoddy.[36]

Having lost so much control over the economy in particular and society in general, the CCP has deliberately used the media as a watchdog on powerful local and corporate interests. This policy was carefully developed in accordance with the Party principle of "supervision by public opinion," an essentially Confucian system of checking power by exposing officials to normative criticism. Nearly all national leaders in China invoke this principle as a motive for economic and social reform. In his work report to the National People's Congress in 1994, for example, then-Premier Li Peng, not best known as a proponent of balance of power, said, "We must consciously accept supervision . . . by the broad masses of people. We must . . . give play to the supervisory role of public opinion. We must attach importance to letters and visits by the masses, and grasp people's feelings by opening and unclogging a multitude of channels."[37]

Additionally, the Internet investment boom, now being followed by a more modest explosion in speculative media investment, has created a new class of media compradors, some of whom have the trust of the political leadership, to present cautious arguments in favor of media reform. They include AT&T/ TCI's John Tse, an indefatigable organizer of delegations and conferences on commercial television broadcast and production; Pacific Century Holdings' Richard Li, whose "Network of the World" receives skepticism from the rest of the world but financing from the Bank of China; his father, Li Ka-shing, whose Tom.com venture is buying up stakes in China's media; and Wang Zhidong, founder of Richsight Technologies, which was one of the companies that merged to form Sina.com.

Divide and Conquer

Jiang Zemin is said to have watched Russia's Most Media case with appalled interest and to have drawn the lesson that media monopolies may not be permitted to rise.[38] It is no mistake that, in China, a newspaper is the hardest of all mass media to get licensed, as well as the most tightly monitored, because the frequency of publication makes newspapers hard to shut down without some public outcry. Books, on the other hand, enjoy the most permissive of the control regimes around the media; once printed and distributed, their sale can nevertheless be stopped with an order, and almost no one knows the difference. Throughout all the liberalization of media investment structures and managerial regimes, discretionary control over ideological content has never been loosened; in fact, the administrative measures available to officials from the Propaganda Bureau of the CCP and its civil arm, the State Council Office of Information, have only become stronger. For example, upon his assumption of the directorship of the Propaganda Bureau, Ding Guangen was given direct, personal authority to remove editors-in-chief of media outlets at will, which was an authority generally acknowledged to belong to the Propaganda Bureaus at the provincial level.

What may appear externally to be a cyclical policy of laxness followed by paranoiac crackdown follows a time-honored Chinese regulatory tradition of relaxation of control in order to encourage growth, co-optation of a portion of that growth for the benefit of the central government, and further regulation to keep any particular nongovernment organization from growing large enough to wield threatening political and economic power. China's leadership has permitted, both actively and passively, the advent of new and contentious voices in the media, but the leadership has also made it clear that the Chinese Communist Party will maintain ultimate authority to close down media outlets, require media to carry government messages, and generally use the media to form public opinion. What will be interesting to watch in years to come will be the ability of central government authorities to ride the tiger they have unleashed. Internal Party debate already revolves around the wisdom of exposing too many cases of official corruption in the press,[39] and the fiercely nationalistic press campaigns directed by the Propaganda Bureau after the NATO bombing of China's embassy in Yugoslavia in 1999 and the plane collision off Hainan in 2001 may have had unintended repercussions: After the September 11 attack on the United States, for example, the chatrooms of the Chinese portals were filled with people talking about how China "needs its own bin Laden" and how, in a sarcastic reference to the reportedly unintentional NATO bombing of the Chinese embassy, the pilots of the two planes that hit the World Trade Center must have been "using maps from 1972, when the World Trade Center was built in 1973."[40] By the third day after the incident, once the Propaganda Bureau had come out with its "guidance" for the media, the "chatroom ayis" or political monitors stopped permitting the expression of strong nationalist views.

The extent to which the clear rise in Chinese nationalism results from a freer and more commercial press that gives voice to the "little man" is highly debatable. Whether or not the Chinese government can be successful with its tactic of controlling the press by keeping its outlets small and subject to preemptive control will be seen only in years to come.

Appendix: Selected Regulations on Publishing

On Means of Publishing:

Press and Publications Administration 1991: "Notice on the Approval Process for Establishing Foreign-Invested Enterprises in News and Publishing"

Reiterates the principle that foreign investment is not permitted in publishing and foreign cooperation is not normally allowed. If such cooperation is "truly necessary," it can be approved through the central-level PPA. The notice calls for an inventory of existing projects that have not been centrally approved and reapproval or elimination by the end of February 1992.

Press and Publications Administration November 6, 1993, No. 1486: "Notice on Reiterating That No Department or Organization May Independently

Approve the Establishment of a Foreign-Invested Enterprise in News or Publishing"

Press and Publications Administration, November 24, 1988, No. 1359: "Provisional Regulations on Publication Management"

PPA Notice 966: "Notice Regarding Further Strengthening of Management in Publication Distribution," effective January 1, 2000

Press and Publications Administration, February, 28, 1989, No. 140: "Forbidding the Use of Book Numbers to Issue Periodicals"

Press and Publications Administration, November 26, 1993, No. 1556: "Means for Carrying Out and Implementing the Central Propaganda Bureau's and Press and Publications Administration's Notice Regarding a Ban on the Sale of Book Numbers"

1995 Propaganda Bureau and PPA "Notice Forbidding the Purchase and Sale of Publication Numbers"

Central Propaganda Bureau and Press and Publications Administration: October 26, 1993, No. 13: "Notice Regarding a Ban on the Sale of Book Numbers"

Central Propaganda Bureau and Central Foreign Propaganda Working Group 1985: "Decision on Establishing a Publication for Overseas Propaganda and on the Creation of Foreign Editions by Publications"

An effort to tighten up on the approval of overseas editions of publications. Specifies that such editions should be approved only rarely and should have clear propaganda value.

On Editorial Content:

State Council "Notice on Resolutely Banning Illegal Publishing Activity," January 25, 1996

Considered illegal is any content that is "counter to China's laws and regulations, reveals State secrets, threatens State security, harms the national advantage, violates the Party's policies or national minorities' religious principles, destroys national unity, advocates obscenity, promotes violence or illegal activity . . . [or] . . . other activities."

On Imported Publications:

Central Propaganda Bureau Document 20, December 12, 1989, co-signed by the Press and Publications Administration: "Opinion on Strengthening Management of the Import and Sale of Foreign, Macao, Hong Kong, and Taiwanese Publications"

Partial text:

From now on, the import and subscription sales of publications from abroad and from Hong Kong, Macao, and Taiwan will mostly be managed by the China National Periodicals Import and Export Corp., while import and sales of publications for the educational system may be handled by the Educational Publications Import and Export Corp. No government department or organization may import or sell any publication that has not received approval from the Central Propaganda Bureau and the Press and Publications Administration.

Principles of Control and Important Points:

Imported publications should more seriously adhere to the principles of choice, control, distinguishing different types of content, and strict grasp. Currently, the principal areas for control are Chinese-language publications from Hong Kong, Macao, and Taiwan, particularly publications about current affairs and politics. The domestic sale of a few foreign publications that carry unusually sensitive content is prohibited other than to foreigners in China.

Readjusting the Standards for Categorizing Publications, Subscribing, and the Approval Process

First Category: Publications on economics, science and technology, and politics and those taking a neutral political stance; in technical publications, those foreign publications analyzing value. These publications may be broadly imported, but care should be taken to avoid repetition and waste. When issues suddenly arise with respect to publications formerly classed I, the first category, adjustments can be made. Publications imported on the central level may be imported following approval by all the relevant central-level government departments; local-level publications must receive approval from the provincial-level Press and Publications Administration, which solicits approval from the Party Propaganda Commission.

Second Category: Publications that have some negative and even reactionary content but have reference value. The variety and number of these publications is restricted for import, and subscriptions are strictly limited to organizations with a special, work-related interest in the content, central and local Party, military, and leading governmental organizations, and a few general universities. Some of these publications that are imported in large number and have sensitive content should be severely limited in the number of subscribers. All publications of the second category should be approved by the China National Periodicals Import/Export Corp. or the China National Educational Books and Periodicals I/E Corp., following examination by the central and provincial-level Press and Publications authorities and comment by the Central Propaganda Bureau.

Third Category: Publications that are reactionary or politically harmful. These publications can be subscribed to for use as intelligence material by central and provincial Propaganda Bureaus, Unified Army Command, State Security, PPA, and other government and military organizations.

Procedures for military organizations seeking to subscribe to foreign and Hong Kong, Macao, and Taiwanese publications are determined with the Central Political Commission in accordance with these rules."

State Council Office of Information, Press and Publications Administration, March 11, 1994, No. 1: "Notice Specifying That Foreign Publications Should Not Handle Their Own Distribution in China"
Includes books, newspapers, magazines, and sound and video recordings.

Central Propaganda Bureau and Press and Publications Administration July 31, 1993, No. 10: "Notice Regarding the Strengthening of the Press Corps' Professional Ethics and Building a Ban on 'Compensation for News' "

Central Propaganda Bureau Document 20, December 12, 1989

1. The CNPIEC and the Educational Periodicals I/E Corp. with the PPA have the right to stop delivery of periodicals of the second and third category that have unusually sensitive content, and they are not required to refund subscription fees. These organizations may also remove the offending pages. Customs also has the power to stop import of publications that have received full approval.
2. The CNPIEC is charged with handling import of publications to hotels, Friendship Stores, and foreign-invested companies, which may not import themselves and may not resell.
3. The PPA is charged with examining and approving imported publications within the framework of policy guidance from the Propaganda Bureau.

Notice That Overseas Publications May Not Themselves Engage in Subscription Work or Distribution on the Mainland
The State Council Office of Information and the Press and Publications Administration Document 1, March 11, 1994

The mainland offices of overseas publications may not involve themselves in the domestic distribution of their publications. Overseas publications should not use other domestic channels, including the foreign offices of domestic organizations, to organize mainland distribution of their publications.

Customs Administration of the People's Republic of China: "Management Regulations on the Import and Export of Printed Materials and Audio-Visual Products Via Carrying In or Mail," Temporary 2 No. 700, June 11, 1991.

Such materials must be declared to Customs, and content that opposes the government, supports superstition or feudalism, promotes violence, harms moral character or Chinese culture may be impounded.

State Administration of Industry and Commerce, January 9, 1988: "Detailed Rules on the Advertising Management Regulations."

Article 17: Any foreign company, organization, or individual wanting to advertise in China must go through an advertising agency that is approved to handle foreign advertising.

According to Article 16, the fee for this service should be 15 percent.

1997 Regulations on Publication Management
1997 Regulations on the Management of the Printing Industry
1998 Regulations on Electronic Publishing
January 25, 1996 State Council Notice on Resolutely Banning Illegal Publishing Activity
State Planning Commission and the Ministry of Foreign Trade and Economic Cooperation, December 31, 1997: "Catalogue for the Guidance of Foreign Investment in Industries" (first revision)

The catalogue lists industries in which foreign investment is restricted or prohibited. Publishing is among the prohibited sectors.

On the Internet:

Orders Nos. 291 and 292 of the State Council of the People's Republic of China: "Telecommunications Regulations of the People's Republic of China" and "Measures for the Administration of Internet Information"
Beijing Municipal Telecommunications Administration, November 3, 2000: "Notice on Issues Relevant to Carrying Out the Procedures for Operating Permits and Registration for Internet Information Services"
Ministry of Information Industries, November 7, 2000: "Regulations on Management of Internet Electronic Bulletin Board Service"
Ministry of Posts and Telecommunications: "Management of Multimedia Telecommunications for a Mass Audience"

Public Security Bureau, December 30, 1997: "Means for Protecting the Security of Computer Information on the International Web"

State Council Order 147, February 18, 1994: "Regulations of the People's Republic of China on Protecting the Security of Computer Systems"

"The Provisional Management Means for Registration of Chinese Domains"

State Council Order 195, February 1, 1995: "Provisional Regulations of the People's Republic of China on Managing Computer Information on the Internet"

PRC Measures on the Regulation of Public Computer Networks and the Internet, Issued by the Ministry of Post and Telecommunications (MPT, predecessor of the Ministry of Information Industry) on April 9, 1996

PRC Interim Provisions on the Regulation of Computer Networks and the Internet, Issued by the Secretary Bureau of the State Council General Office on February 1, 1996

PRC Interim Provisions on the Approval and Regulations of Businesses Engaging in Opened Telecommunications Services, Issued by the Ministry of Post and Telecommunications (MPT, precedessor of the Ministry of Information Industry) on September 11, 1993

PRC Measures on the Regulation of Public Computer Networks and the Internet, Issued by the Ministry of Post and Telecommunications (MPT, precedessor of the Ministry of Information Industry) on April 9, 1996

PRC Interim Provisions on the Regulation of Computer Networks and the Internet, Issued by the Secretary Bureau of the State Council General Office on February 1, 1996

PRC Interim Provisions on the Approval and Regulations of Businesses Engaging in Opened Telecommunications Services, Issued by the Ministry of Post and Telecommunications (MPT, predecessor of the Ministry of Information Industry) on September 11, 1993

Interim Provisions on Guidance for Foreign Investment, Jointly Promulgated by Decree No. 5 of the State Planning Commission, the State Economic and Trade Commission and the Ministry of Foreign Trade and Economic Cooperation on June 20, 1995

Catalogue for the Guidance of Foreign Investment Industries, Promulgated by Decree No. 5 of the State Planning Commission, the State Economic and Trade Commission and the Ministry of Foreign Trade and Economic Cooperation on June 20, 1995

State Council Directive on Strengthening Regulations in the Management of the Telecommunications Sector, The State Council (SC) formally issued a Notice on Reinforcing Regulations of the Telecommunications Sector on August 3, 1993

Notes

1. "Notice Regarding the Strict Management of Publication Numbers," State Press and Publications Administration, September 8, 1999.

2. On the closing of *Shu Bao* in Sichuan, see, for example, "'Economic News' Receives a Stop-Publication and Rectification Order," *China Press and Publishing Journal*, November 14, 2001.

3. "Notice on Issues Relevant to Carrying out the Procedures for Operating Permits and Registration of Internet Information Services," Beijing Telecommunications Administration, November 3, 2000. A new wave of closings nationwide occurred in July 2002, following the death of 25 customers at an unlicensed Internet cafe in Beijing that was allegedly set afire by two teenage arsonists on June 16. See, for example, *Beijing Youth Daily*, July 18, 2002. Concern about fire safety was quickly extended by Beijing Mayor Liu Qi, then central government officials, in the crackdown campaign, to encompass a number of social ills that Internet cafes supposedly promote.

4. "Notice on Clarifying and Rectifying News Reporting on Military Affairs," summarized in *China Press and Publishing Journal*, February 6, 2001.

5. Interview with government researcher on media trends, October 2001.

6. "Ideological Propaganda Work Must Create a Good Atmosphere for the 16th Party Congress," *China Press and Publishing Journal*, November 6, 2001.

7. Interview with Yu Guoming, Director of Public Opinion Research, People's University, Beijing, October 2001.

8. The Third Plenary Session of the Eleventh Party Central Committee, December 1978.

9. Yu Guoming, Director of Public Opinion Research, People's University, Beijing, October 2001, based on a 1986 survey by People's University.

10. Report by Universal McCann Advertising, Shanghai, fall 2000.

11. According to a People's University report, 1,800.

12. From data collected by Universal McCann Advertising Agency in Shanghai, July 2000. Official and non-official sources provide dramatically varying figures for the number of media outlets in China, depending on whether the count includes small, private outlets (cable TV for a housing compound or a factory, for example) and non-commercial outlets (for example, fixed-line radio, which may be used simply as a public address system in schools, factories, etc.). The number of commercial media outlets is much lower than the figure presented here.

13. Interviews with researcher from government research institution and member of the State Press and Publication Administration.

14. PPA Notice 966: "Notice Regarding Further Strengthening of Management in Publication Distribution," effective January 1, 2000.

15. Interview with Jesse Ning, international publisher, Figaro Publications.

16. Interview with Beijing Postal Administration official.

17. Interview with Postal Administration official.

18. Discussions with a Little Red Cap director, 1996, and with a Beijing Postal Administration official, 2001.

19. Interview with Yu Guoming, director of Public Opinion Research, People's University, Beijing, October 2001.

20. Interview with *New Weekly* editors, Guangzhou, 1999.

21. Tim Murray, general manager, Beijing Ringier Advertising Co., Ltd.

22. See, for example, "China's Media Rush" by Lu Yi in *Beijing Review*, April 2001.

23. *China Media Update*, October 1999, and *China Print Media*, June 2001, and *China Print Media*, June 2001, published by Capital Strategies/66cities.com Co., Ltd. in Beijing.

24. See, for example, *China Money*, February 2002 and the first quarter 2002 report of China Television Media, Ltd. (Shanghai: 600088), available on the Homeway network at www.hexun.com.cn.

25. See *Shenghuo Ribao*, "Life Daily;" October 22, 2001; *Dazhong Ribao*, "Masses Daily," October 25, 2001; and *Shubao* "Once in a Thousand Years, Weddings for the Century," December 31, 1999.

26. Discussion with Chinese news reporter, November 2001,

27. From discussions with PPA officials in the Newspaper and Periodicals Department, 1999–2000.

28. *China Directory*, Japan Radio Press, 1987, 1988, and 1989.

29. Book publishing in China is regulated through the issuance of a number and a bar code for each book. State publishing houses, which number about 550, receive an annual quota of numbers. Over the years of reform, numerous private publishing concerns have been established that are better equipped than the State sector to create or procure commercial book content. Because they cannot be approved as official publishers, most State publishing houses have become, in effect, sellers of permits, overseeing the political content of the books and sometimes providing distribution service in return for the publishing right. The sale of book numbers, however, remains illegal.

30. Interview with government researcher on the media, November 2001.

31. *China Print Media*, June 2001.

32. *People's Daily*, March 30, 2001.

33. State Council Office of Information Director Zhao Qizheng speaking at the 2001 Beijing Internet Development Forum, quoted in *People's Daily*, September 7, 2001.

34. Du Minghua, *People's Daily*, August 27, 2001, English translation by *People's Daily Online*.

35. Cited by Li Xiguang, "Great Sound Makes No Noise."

36. *City Weekend* magazine, 2000.

37. The full excerpt, translated by Xinhua News Agency, reads as follows: "We must consciously accept supervision of the people's congress and its standing committee at the corresponding level and supervision by the broad masses of people. We must further bring into play the roles of the CPPCC, democratic parties, and nonparty people in political consultation and democratic supervision. We must attach importance to the roles of trade unions, the Communist Youth League, women's federations, and other mass organizations as bridges and links; and give play to the supervisory role of public opinion. We must attach importance to letters and visits by the masses, and grasp people's feelings by opening and unclogging a multitude of channels. We must continue to strengthen the building of political power at the grass-roots level, perfect the democratic management system in enterprises and the urban neighborhood and village self-management system, perfect the democratic supervision system, and ensure that citizens' legitimate rights and interests are not encroached upon. We must attach great importance to building the socialist legal system. The establishment and perfection of a socialist market economic structure relies on a comprehensive legal system to provide a safeguard. Since the start of reform and opening up, the NPC and its Standing Committee have speeded up the pace of legislation."

38. Interview with government researcher on Russia, November 2001.

39. A *Southern Weekend* reporter commented in a private conversation that the paper cannot write about corruption anymore unless the amounts are in the millions of dollars and central-government officials are involved, because their readers are immune to shock.

40. Comments in Sohu chatroom, September 11, 2001.

— V —

The Generation After Next and Future Prospects for the CCP

——— 12 ———

The Generation After Next in Chinese Politics

Willy Wo-Lap Lam

Introduction: Enter the Fifth Generation

The Fifth Generation (*diwudai*) leadership is tipped to begin running China from the early 2010s. It will succeed the Fourth Generation headed by cadres such as Vice President Hu Jintao and Vice Premier Wen Jiabao. The tenure of the *disidai* (Fourth Generation) is expected to stretch from the Sixteenth Chinese Communist Party (CCP) Congress scheduled for late 2002 to the Eighteenth Party Congress, to be held in 2012.

While no definition of the *diwudai* leadership has been given by official sources, the Fifth Generation can generally be characterized as cadres now in their late 30s to early 50s.[1] Almost all of them were trained in Chinese universities. Most *diwudai* cadres attended college in the mid-1970s and 1980s, and joined the CCP from the late 1970s onward. The single most important influence in their lives and careers is probably Deng Xiaoping's era of reform rather than earlier events such as the Cultural Revolution of 1966 to 1976.

In terms of education and professional experience, *diwudai* cadres are better qualified than their forebears. Many have master's degrees or doctorates. While only a minority of Fifth Generation cadres has degrees from American or Western universities, most of them have had ample exposure to the West through short-term courses, visits, or interactions with Western officials and business executives. Most of them can read English and handle computers with ease.[2]

In the wake of China's accession to the World Trade Organization (WTO) in late 2001—and the need for the Party, the government, and enterprises to recruit thousand upon thousand of English-speaking, globally minded professionals—the proportion of senior posts being given to officials in their early 40s or even late 30s is expected to increase dramatically. Indeed, by 2001, there were at least two cadres in their early 40s—the secretary of the Communist Youth League (CYL), Zhou Qiang, 41, and the vice governor of Jiangsu Province, Zhang Taolin, 40—who had already been appointed to senior posts. The youngest governor, Zhao Leji of Qinghai Province, was only 44.[3]

Given that most *diwudai* cadres have developed their careers in the epoch of market reforms, it seems safe to assume that it is in their vested interests to continue with economic liberalization. This is particularly true for cadres in departments such as foreign trade or financial regulatory agencies, which either did not exist or were not considered important in the prereform era. As ensuing sections will make clear, however, *diwudai* officials may not necessarily embrace radical or pro-West postures in political reform or foreign policy. More of their policy orientation will be made clear as we examine the background and factional affiliation of likely Fifth Generation leaders.

Major Groups and Factions Within the Fifth Generation Leadership

Major Diwudai Factions

Fifth Generation leaders will be picked through both conventional and unconventional means. As with past practice, major factions among the Third- and Fourth Generation cadres had already started grooming their *diwudai* successors in the 1990s. Thus, a number of up-and-coming officials associated with such well-known groups as the Shanghai Faction and the CYL Faction can be identified.

The Communist Youth League Faction

Among the various cliques, perhaps the CYL Faction has been most successful in propagating *diwudai* successors. After all, the very function of the league is to identify potential leaders from the younger generation. CYL affiliates can also look for leadership to Vice President Hu, a former league chief and the likely "core" of the Fourth Generation cadres.[4]

A number of Beijing-based cadres who are in their late 30s to early 50s are CYL alumnae and considered Hu protégés. Foremost among them are the vice director of the CCP General Office, Ling Zhihua, 46; vice minister at the State Development Planning Commission, Wang Yang, 46; and the vice head of the CCP Propaganda Department, Liu Peng, 50.

Hu has been particularly successful in grooming CYL alumnae for positions in the regions. By late 2001, there were more than twenty league affiliates holding positions such as vice Party secretary or vice mayors of provinces and major cities. These regional young turks included governor of Henan Province, Li Kejiang, 46; vice Party secretary of Beijing, Qiang Hui, 48; vice Party secretary of Shandong, Jiang Daming, 48; vice Party secretary of Guangxi, Liu Qibao, 48; vice Party secretary of Anhui Province, Shen Yaoyao; mayor of Lhasa, Luosang Jiangcun, 44; and Party Secretary of Zhengzhou, Henan Province, Li Ke, 45.[5]

Among the CYL rising stars, Ling and Li Keqiang have attracted the most attention. Ling, who once headed Hu's personal office, is tipped to be made director of the General Office at the Sixteenth Congress. Former directors have included luminaries such as Wen Jiabao and Zeng Qinghong. So far, Ling has kept a low profile. His main job has been to prepare documents and speeches for Hu.

Li Keqiang, is a distinguished Peking University graduate who built his career in the CYL, rising to Party secretary of the league in the mid-1990s. He was appointed governor to a major agricultural province, Henan, in 1998 mostly to test his mettle. While his reputation was dented somewhat by incidents such as a fire that killed more than 200 when it gutted a Zhengzhou discotheque in 2000, Li is still tipped for a promotion post–Sixteenth Congress.[6]

The Shanghai Faction

The dominant position of the Shanghaibang or Shanghai Faction in Chinese politics is expected to come to an end at the Sixteenth Party Congress. However, Fourth Generation Shanghaibang stalwarts such as Zeng Qinghong and Wu Bangguo are expected to go on grooming *diwudai* cadres with a Shanghai affiliation.

A number of Fifth Generation cadres have already been promoted to senior positions in Shanghai itself. They include Vice Mayor Han Zheng, 47; head of the municipal Propaganda Department, Yin Yicui, 46; and head of the municipal United Front Department, Huang Yuejin, 48. It is likely that in the five years covered by the Sixteenth Congress, these and other Shanghai-based cadres may be elevated to senior positions either in Beijing or other provinces. This is in the footstep, for example, of Fourth Generation cadre Meng Jianzhu, a vice Party secretary of Shanghai who was promoted to Party secretary of Jiangxi Province in early 2001. In mid-2001, another well-known Shanghai cadre, former municipal Secretary General Huang Qifan, 52, was made vice mayor of Chongqing.[7]

Perhaps the majority of Shanghaibang affiliates are cast in the mold of faction chief President Jiang Zemin, who is known for his middle-of-the-road tendencies. A good example is Jiang's son, Jiang Mianheng, 44, a vice president of the Chinese Academy of Sciences. A computer and telecommunications expert, the younger Jiang has advised his father on how to keep the balance between introducing foreign capital and maintaining a tight grip on ideology.[8]

However, quite a few faction members have come up with radical ideas for reform, including political liberalization. A notable example is Wang Huning, 46, who, at least in terms of experience, straddles the Fourth and Fifth Generations. As vice head of the Policy Research Center of the CCP General Office, Wang wrote policy papers on topics including the prospects for the expansion of village-level elections and the "civilianization" of the People's Liberation Army (PLA).[9]

The Zhu Rongji Faction

Among Third Generation cadres, Premier Zhu Rongji is perhaps the least given to factionalism. However, it is a political reality within the Party that a senior cadre can be effective only if he has a large following, at least in departments that lie within his portfolio.

Because Zhu has run the financial portfolio since the early 1990s, it is not surprising that he has been able to install quite a number of protégés in units such as the Ministry of Finance, the banks, the Ministry of Foreign Trade and Economic Cooperation (MOFTEC) and the China Securities Regulatory Commission (CSRC). A number of key Zhu affiliates among the Fourth Generation such as the People's Bank of China (PBoC) Governor Dai Xianlong, State Councillor and former MOFTEC chief Wu Yi, and MOFTEC Vice Minister Long Yongtu, are tipped for senior Party and government positions to be announced at the Sixteenth Party Congress and the Tenth National People's Congress (NPC) of early 2003.[10]

A number of Zhu affiliates who straddle the Fourth and Fifth Generations have already risen to senior positions. Prominent among them are executive vice minister of finance, Lou Jiwei, 51; vice governor of the PBoC, Guo Shuqing, 46; and CSRC vice-chairman, Gao Xiqing, 48. Up-and-coming Zhu Faction affiliates include PBoC vice governor, Wu Xiaoling, and MOFTEC head of department, Yi Xiaozhun.[11]

The "Gang of Princelings"

In the two to three years before the Fifteenth Party Congress, Deng Xiaoping laid down an internal dictum that the Party leadership must be careful not to elevate too many sons and daughters of Party elders (the "gang of prince-lings") to the Central Committee or other top-level councils. By around 2000, however, Jiang decided it was proper to absorb more princelings to senior positions.[12]

The elevation of a relatively large number of princelings to the top echelon has led to speculation that among Fourth Generation, and perhaps also Fifth Generation cadres, members of the CYL Faction will "split the sky" with princelings.

Prominent examples of princelings in their 40s who have already occupied vice-ministerial positions or above are Fujian Governor Xi Jinping, 48; Chinese Academy of Science Vice President Jiang Mianheng, 44; vice head of the Office for Restructuring the Economy, Pan Yue, 42; and a vice commissar of the People's Armed Police, Liu Yuan, 49. They are, respectively, the son of party elder Xi Zhongxun; son of Jiang Zemin; son-in-law of General Liu Huaq-ing; and son of the late president Liu Shaoqi.[13] There are also a considerable number of *diwudai* princelings among People's Liberation Army officers.

The Leftists and Nationalists

One of the most significant developments in Chinese politics since the late 1990s has been the marriage of Leftists—loosely defined as quasi-Maoists opposed to market reforms—and nationalists. These two camarillas are drawn together by common causes such as the opposition to the United States and globalization under U.S. terms as well as the "infiltration" of U.S. capital into China post-WTO.

As of late 2001, Leftist patriarch Deng Liqun, in his early 80s, remained the godfather and Third Generation leader of the remnant Maoists. Deng and his followers, however, were dealt a big blow in mid-2001 after they dared openly to oppose Jiang's Theory of the Three Represents and the latter's de-cision to allow private businessmen to join the CCP (see following section). Moreover, given the fact that economically, the entire country is going down the capitalist road, Leftists have had difficulties recruiting Fourth or Fifth Generation successors.[14]

Most of the Fifth Generation conservatives are first and foremost nation-alists, particularly in the sense of their anti-American and anti-West stances. Quite a few of them are much-published professors and journalists in their late 30s and 40s who have a wide following among the public. Almost invariably, they have endeared themselves to their readers through putting stress on Chi-nese pride. The Leftist-nationalists have also represented themselves as the champions of workers and farmers, who, they claim, are in danger of being exploited by the "collusion" between cadre-capitalists and multinationals.

The best known among the nationalists include academics and authors

Wang Xiaodong, Lu Zhoulai, Fang Ning, Yang Fan, and Han Deqiang. They have warned the Party and nation against leaning too close to the United States. The radicals are also opposed to privatization of State-owned enterprises using methods that include the incorporation of American capital.[15]

Unconventional Methods for Selecting Cadres

Open Recruitment of Fifth Generation Officials

A major thrust of political reform under the Fourth Generation could be the open recruitment of officials, seen as one way to broaden the base of the Party's elite without having to dilute one-party dictatorship. It is thus to be expected that, as compared to the Third or Fourth Generation, more *diwudai* leaders may be picked from diverse backgrounds.

The official Xinhua News Agency reported in mid-2001 that, since 1995, more than 1,000 officials with ranks of vice head of department or above and more than 10,000 officials with ranks of vice head of office had been recruited through open exams. This is a radical departure from the long-standing practice of the party's Organization Department picking all mid- to top-ranked cadres. According to one proposal for speeding up the "democratization" of cadre selection, a third of all positions at the level of heads of bureaus and departments in provinces and cities may be openly recruited by the mid-2000s.[16]

Experiments so far conducted in several Guangdong cities have yielded interesting results. In applying for the jobs, which are advertised in newspapers, CCP members are, at least in theory, given no preference over nonparty members. In addition to a written exam on professional knowledge, candidates must sit for an oral test on political skills. Guangdong authorities have asked a number of "people's representatives," mostly deputies to local-level people's congresses and people's political consultative conferences to be oral examiners.[17]

It is envisaged that if ongoing experiments are successful, a proportion of cadres at the level of vice ministers and vice governors could, toward the end of this decade, be openly recruited. Deng's old ideal of the "five lakes and four seas" may to some extent be achieved in the selection of Fifth Generation officials.

Prominent Role for Holders of Foreign Degrees

Immediately after China's accession to the WTO in November 2001, Premier Zhu said his main task would be to search for talent. In foreign trade alone, China is said to be in need of 180,000 professionals.[18] Obviously, holders of foreign degrees, many of them in their 30s, are a major talent pool for WTO-conscious leaders.

An estimated 380,000 Chinese have gone abroad for studies since the early 1980s, and 130,000 have since returned. In mid-2001, some departments, including the Ministry of Personnel, the Education Ministry, the Ministry of Science and Technology, and the Ministry of Public Security, published an internal document on ways to encourage holders of foreign degrees to return to work in China. The gist of the incentives included pay according to international norms, and special help with housing and other perks. Those wanting to set up businesses would be given preferential tax and other favorable treatments including funds for developing high technology and guarantees of intellectual property rights. Returnees who wanted to retain their overseas citizenship would be able to get multiple-entry and work visas.[19]

Naturally, the majority of holders of advanced American or Western degrees have found gainful employment in Chinese universities. Prominent *disidai* and *diwudai* cadres who have Western qualifications such as doctorates, MBAs, or law degrees include the SCRC vice chairman, Gao Siqing, 48, and the vice chief of the Taiwan Affairs Office, Zhou Mingwei, 46. Most of these Western-trained cadres are employed in departments having to do with finance, law, the stock market, or foreign trade.

Liu Hong and Fang Xinghai, both 37, are billed as the first thirty-something returnees who are employed in a senior capacity by government units. Liu, who has degrees from Oxford and Harvard, headed the CSRC's Department of Legal Affairs before he went into private business in 2000. Fang, with a Ph.D. from Stanford, went in the opposite direction. He first worked for a private securities firm before joining the Shanghai Stock Exchange as assistant to the general manager in 2000.[20] Indeed, heads of ministries and commissions have allowed a growing number of bright and reliable returnees from the United States to take the proverbial "helicopter ride" to the top.

And in the wake of the much-noted appointment of a U.S.-educated Hong Kong lawyer, Laura Cha, as CSRC vice chairman in early 2001, a good number of Hong Kong and overseas-Chinese professionals are expected to be selected for vice ministerial–level positions, particularly in banks and other financial departments on the mainland. However, Chinese citizenship is a prerequisite for such appointments, and Cha had to give up her U.S. citizenship prior to taking up the high-profile post.[21]

The Rise of the Entrepreneurial Class

A major reason behind Jiang's decision, as announced on July 1, 2001, to admit members of the "new classes" to the Party is that the CCP can no longer afford not to absorb the cream of the entrepreneurial and professional sectors into the Party. At the Beidaihe leadership meetings in the summer of that year, the point was raised that the eight *minzhudangpai* ("democratic parties") had aggressively recruited a large number of young and successful private businessmen, and that the CCP would be at a disadvantage if this trend were to continue.[22]

By mid-2001, there were 1.5 million private businesses in China, and another 31 million *getihu*, or self-employed business households. This "private sector" contributed an estimated half of China's GDP. Moreover, there is also a fast-rising middle class. The official State Information Center indicated in 2001 that the size of the middle class should reach 200 million in five years' time. In China, a middle-class family is defined as one that has steady income, that can afford its house and car, and that has the means to travel abroad or to send its kids to private or overseas schools.[23]

As of late 2001, the CCP had no mechanism for plucking politically active and trustworthy "red bosses" to become cadres. In a tradition going back to the 1950s, entrepreneurs have been inducted into the Chinese People's Political Consultative Conference (CPPCC) and other advisory bodies. And those who have distinguished themselves in the *minzhudangpai*, particularly the Federation of Industry and Commerce, may be given senior positions in the National People's Congress or the CPPCC.[24]

According to the *Forbes Magazine* tally of the twenty richest private businessmen in China in 2001, thirteen were in the age group of 30 to 49. Three within the top ten—Yang Bin, Sun Guangxin, and Zhang Simen—were in their 30s. The richest of them all, the Liu brothers headed by Liu Yonghao, had assets worth 8.3 billion yuan. Liu is active as a Standing Committee member of the CPPCC.[25] However, it is likely that the younger generation of the well-heeled would not be satisfied with "flower vase" or decorative positions such as senior government advisers.

In fact, beginning in the mid-1990s, hundreds of red capitalists had purchased positions starting from grassroots levels. These so-called *maiguan* (buying posts) scandals, which have hit areas ranging from rich Guangdong Province to relatively backward Shanxi Province, have been described in detail in the official media. Positions bought ranged from seats in local-level people's congresses to the vice mayor or even mayor of a medium-sized city.[26]

Journalists from the business newspaper *Fazhan daobao* conducted investigations into the *maiguan* phenomenon in the city of Yuncheng, Shanxi. The paper concluded that rich people were snapping up positions for three reasons: to enhance their political standing, to facilitate business, and to seek a "protection umbrella" for dubious deals.[27]

Policy Orientations of the Fifth Generation

The Fourth Generation leadership will likely be in power until the Eighteenth Party Congress of late 2012 and the First Session of the Twelfth NPC in early 2013. The "first term" of the *disidai* leadership—up to 2007/2008—would likely be spent rounding out the unfinished agenda of the Third Generation such as fulfilling the country's WTO obligations. The theory has thus been advanced that perhaps the *disidai* will prove to be a transitory generation, meaning that a number of its policy initiatives cannot be carried out within a short "second term."

If this is true, observers of China who are after dramatic reforms in either the economic or political arena can perhaps look only to the Fifth Generation. For example, it is possible that CYL alumnae among the *diwudai* leaders may be in a position to develop the league's well-known reputation as a reformist organ. After all, a number of *diwudai* cadres had benefited from the teachings of Third Generation reformers and former CYL chiefs such as Hu Yaobang and Hu Qili.[28] Several reform initiatives that may be undertaken by the *diwudai* leadership are outlined below.

Prospects for Political Reform

High Possibility for a Cautious Pace of Reform

It will be unrealistic to expect that the *diwudai* leadership's exposure to Western values will necessarily translate into an inclination toward faster political reform. Fifth Generation cadres will likely carry on the cautious philosophy of such Fourth Generation stalwarts as Hu Jintao and Wen Jiabao, that is, to liberalize the political structure in such a way as to avoid hurting social stability or the CCP's hold on power.[29]

It is instructive to study the reform orientation of the vice head of the Office for Restructuring the Economy, Pan Yue, who is perhaps the best-known theorist among *diwudai* cadres. In a paper on reform that was circulated in Beijing in early 2001, Pan advocated that more businessmen and members of social groups be co-opted into the system. There were also reports that Pan, like such *disidai* leaders as Hu, was interested in the ideas of a European-style Social Democratic Party (see following section). However, Pan, the former son-in-law of General Liu Huaqing was opposed to democratic principles such as popular elections. He also believed in a form of "neo-authoritarianism," meaning that reform can be carried out only incrementally under a strong party leadership.[30]

Nor are the "new classes" of newly enfranchised private businessmen eager for fast-paced political liberalization. Like bureaucrats and apparatchiks, CCP-affiliated businessmen are also holders of vested interests. Their major political goal is likely to be to guard their privileges and to ensure a say in economic policymaking, rather than to go after a wholesale changing of the system (see the following section). This mindset is radically different from that of the early generation of private entrepreneurs, who had yet to gain either economic or political stature.

In the run-up to the massacre of June 4, 1989, a number of private businessmen were prominent supporters of the student protestors. This was behind Jiang's now-famous saying in late 1989 that he would "bankrupt" the red bosses.[31] In the new century, however, most red capitalists have been co-opted by the system. Quite a few among them have formed joint ventures—or at least cemented lucrative relationships—with the cadre-bureaucrats. It is therefore not in their interests to rock the boat.

One harbinger of future trends is that the CCP seemed to have frozen a major reform initiative—the expansion of village-level elections—on the eve of the Sixteenth Party Congress. In the late 1990s, a number of Fifth Generation think-tank members, including Wang Huning, had proposed the gradual upgrading of the polls. For example, village elections should be extended to the county level by 2003, and to the municipal, provincial, and, to some extent, the national levels by 2008, 2013, and 2018, respectively.[32]

Indeed, indicators in 2001 and 2002 are that the *disidai* as well as the *diwudai* would opt for the strategy of broadening the basis of the CCP elite in the absence of Western-style institutions such as the ballot box or multiparty politics. Apart from inducting more members of the "new classes" into advisory or even policymaking councils, throughout the coming decade or so, the CCP will consolidate the practice of the open recruitment of officials up to the level of vice ministers. As of the early 2000s, hundreds of cadres up to the rank of heads of bureaus and departments have been selected via public examinations where candidates with no CCP affiliation are not discriminated against (see earlier section). The CCP leadership seems confident that if the ruling elite is broad-based enough, its mandate of heaven can be considerably extended.

A Chinese Social Democratic Party and Multiparty Politics?

A good test of how far down the reform path the Fifth Generation is able to go in the 2010s and beyond is demonstrated in the extent to which it can bring about the actual or virtual transformation of the CCP into some kind of a Chinese Socialist Democratic Party (CSDP).

The basis for this dramatic transformation was laid by the Third Generation leadership in 2001. Implicit in Jiang's theory of the "Three Represents," and in the admission of private businessmen to the CCP, was the idea that the Party needed to break with tradition so as to preserve its ruling status. Chinese sources in Beijing said leaders such as Jiang, Zhu, and Hu realized there was no choice but to change the CCP from a party of workers, farmers, and other proletarians to a *quanmin dang*, or party for all the people.[33]

After all, the theory of the "Three Represents" had already laid bare the fact that in the information age, peasants and workers could no longer claim to be "representative" of the foremost production or cultural trends. That was why Jiang pronounced, on July 1, 2001, that the CCP had to throw open its doors to the "new classes" of private businessmen and professionals. Moreover, Jiang and company also understood that the Party had to drop the long-standing goal of "class struggle" and focus on economic development. This economics-first persuasion was behind the "third represent": that the CCP must represent the comprehensive interests of the broad masses, a reference to their living standards and other economic criteria.[34]

Jiang's so-called new thinking has indeed contravened many orthodox Marxist edicts. For example, Marx and Lenin had insisted on the primacy of class distinctions and class struggle, meaning the proletariat fighting capitalist exploiters. Moreover, if the CCP has become a *quanmin dang*—and one that pursues market economics—how different will it be from bourgeois socialist-democratic parties in Europe?

Jiang's answer was that the Party must undergo a new thought liberation akin to that staged by Deng Xiaoping soon after the fall of the Gang of Four. In 1979, Deng launched the campaign of "seeking truth from facts"—whose slogan was "practice is the sole criteria of truth"—as a retort to the Maoists' attack on his economic reforms as having contradicted Marxism and Mao Thought.[35]

The big question: when will the CCP leadership push the idea of a *quanmin dang* to its logical conclusion? When will the CCP change its nature—if not also its name—to that of a European-style socialist democratic party? Analysts in Beijing say it is unlikely that this radical transformation can be consummated under the watch of the Fourth Generation.

If the *diwudai* is inclined toward change—and the requisite socioeconomic criteria are available—they might push through a sizable number of reform initiatives that are consistent with a CSDP. First, there may be some form of Party politics with Chinese characteristics. While the *diwudai* may find it premature to lift the ban on the formation of new parties, a limited degree of Party politics might be achieved through the empowerment of the eight *minzhudangpai* or "democratic parties." Founded in the 1940s and 1950s, these entities consist of non-CPP politicians, professionals, and intellectuals who have pledged, at least in theory, to "discuss policies and take part in politics under CCP leadership." For the eight *minzhudangpai* to act as viable parties, this "subservience clause" must be removed. Moreover, they need to have the wherewithal to achieve financial independence instead of remaining beholden to the CCP.[36]

Moreover, the *diwudai* will come under pressure to expand and upgrade the village elections. Alternately, they will, at the least, have to come up with measures to induct more members of rising sectors such as the entrepreneurial and professional classes to leading councils. More well-educated returnees from abroad as well as professionals living in Hong Kong and overseas may also be tapped for senior-level positions.

Then there may be significant changes regarding the status of the PLA as a virtual Party army. If, under the *quanmin dang* concept, the CCP has abandoned class warfare, the PLA should cease to remain either a "Party's army" or a tool for exercising proletarian dictatorship over the exploiting classes. There will be clarion calls for turning the PLA into a "State army," that is, a military force led by a civilian minister of defense and one that is answerable to the NPC or other representative bodies.[37]

Economic Reform: The Unfinished Revolution

Weaning Business from Government and Party

Even though sizable steps in economic reform have already been accomplished by Third Generation and Fourth Generation leaders, the challenge to *diwudai* leaders in this area could still be daunting. At least in theory, the Fifth Generation has ample bushwhacking opportunities in the brave new world of a globalized, knowledge-based economy. By contrast, most *disidai* stalwarts still have to labor under the shibboleth of something called the "socialist market economy." *Diwudai* affiliates may perhaps find it easier to jettison traditional socialist concerns and concentrate on the marketplace.

Much of the energy of *disidai* leaders such as Hu and Wen will be focused on ensuring that the benefits of WTO accession will be maximized and the downside minimized. A key task of Hu and company would be to change the role of government so that the economy can function according to market— and WTO—norms. Thus, just prior to China's induction into the WTO in November 2001, the State Council abolished in one stroke 221 laws and regulations deemed to be WTO-incompatible. The central government also pledged to drastically reduce the estimated 2,000-odd executive fiats, or government edicts on how the economy should be run.[38]

The leaders of coastal cities also came out with unequivocal statements about the new goal of "small government, big society," or "small government, big service." As Shanghai Major Xu Kuangdi put it in late 2001, "What we must do immediately is to change the functions of the government." Likewise, Shenzhen Executive Vice Mayor Li Decheng said governmental structures and behavior would be transformed in three to five years. "A government based on law and regulations will replace one based on power," Li said. "A service-oriented government will replace a command-type government."[39]

However, it is important to note that the CCP still maintains a large say in economic policies as well as mechanisms galore for interference in the marketplace. For example, top Party organs such as the secretive Leading Group on Finance and Economics still call the shots in policy formulation. And the Party's Organization Department still appoints top managers to dozens of large State-owned enterprises (SOEs). Given the *disidai's* respect for Jiang's dictum about Party supremacy, it is likely that the Fourth Generation cadres may only be able to separate government and business. The task of genuine separation of Party and business could rest on the shoulders of the *diwudai*.[40]

The Road Toward Privatization

The *diwudai* may also be called upon to finish a long-standing goal of economic reform: the restructuring, and to a large extent, privatization of State-owned enterprises and financial institutions. A notable achievement of President Jiang and Premier Zhu was in effect to privatize most of the small- and medium-sized enterprises among State units.[41] And from the late 1990s onward, most municipal governments had passed regulations forbidding the formation of new SOEs.

It is expected that during the *disidai's* tenure, a good proportion of the 800-odd large-scale SOEs will also be restructured mainly through floatation in the stock market. However, the restructuring of institutions, particularly the four major banks, may be attained only under the Fifth Generation leadership.[42] Western economists have pointed out that the marketization of the Chinese economy will be incomplete unless the banks are run in full accordance with the forces of supply and demand.

The status of private enterprises and private property should also be considerably enhanced. A key goal of business groups including the Federation of Industry and Commerce is to ensure a level playing field for private businesses. Since the mid-1990s, they have been lobbying for revisions of the State and Party constitutions to guarantee the status of private enterprise and the inviolability of Party property. Other businessmen want explicit clauses stipulating that businessmen are not exploiters.[43] Moreover, newly assertive private-sector bodies such as chambers of commerce hope they will be given a much bigger role in coordinating economic policy.

It is expected that in both the political and economic fields, private businessmen will be packing a bigger punch under the *diwudai*'s tutelage. In late 2001, Yunnan Party Secretary Linghu An raised eyebrows when he said government units must be more "business-friendly." "We must become friends with entrepreneurs both in and out of the province," Linghu said. "We must take an active stance in solving the problems of enterprises and consolidate our relationship with them." And according to mergers and bankruptcy expert Cao Siyuan, private entrepreneurs—who should be given more prominent positions in the NPC and other organs—as well as their trade associations will be playing a much bigger role in economic policymaking in the next decade.[44]

Foreign Policy: The Nationalistic Temptation

By the time the Fifth Generation takes over, the Chinese economy may be within striking distance of overtaking Japan, and China may already have attained the status of "regional superpower." A big challenge for the *diwudai* is to gain a diplomatic status for China that is commensurate with the country's economic and military clout as well as with the aspirations of the people.

Another area that might predispose Fifth-Generation politicians to be more assertive in foreign policy is the energy sector, in particular petroleum. China is expected to import as much as 40 percent of its energy needs to fuel its aggressive industrialization and infrastructure programs. In late 2001, much of Beijing's concern about America's war in Afghanistan was that the United States might take advantage of the antiterrorist campaign to establish a foothold in Central Asia, and to exploit its oil potential to the detriment of other countries including China.[45]

A key test of the diplomatic skills of the *diwudai* will be relations with America. Can Beijing avoid a clash with the United States, which will likely continue to maintain a massive presence in Asia, including in areas that China considers to be its backyard? After all, Fourth-Generation leaders will likely follow the so-called "pro-U.S." policy of Deng Xiaoping and Jiang Zemin. This policy is epitomized by Deng's well-known instructions of the early 1990s: "Keep a low profile; never take the lead"; "Seek cooperation [with the United States] and avoid confrontation."[46]

Diwudai cadres, however, will likely make significant modifications to the pro-U.S. policy of Deng, Jiang—and very possibly—Hu. The late 1990s witnessed a rise of nationalism among sectors ranging from the Army to students. The most obvious manifestation of patriotism and nationalism has been anti-Americanism, which first became evident in the two days of rioting that followed the NATO bombing of the Chinese embassy in Belgrade in May 1999. Chinese reactions to the April 2001 spy plane incident and the September 11 terrorist strikes in New York demonstrated that anti–United States feelings had spread to wider sectors of society.[47]

Nationalists have accused the central leadership of being "soft and weak" with regard to U.S. "hegemonism." They have claimed that part of the reason for this weakness is that Party bureaucrats and their allies, the crony capitalists, have formed lucrative deals with American multinationals to exploit the riches of the land.[48]

Diwudai leaders may have to seek some form of accommodation with the nationalists. After all, it is evident that in times of crisis such as the spy plane incident, anti–United States feelings have struck a chord of resonance with a large segment of the populace. And Sino-U.S. conflict, whether over Taiwan or other issues, is tipped to be more serious and frequent as China is more conscious of the need to project its power in the Asia-Pacific region.[49]

After all, the Afghan war and antiterrorist campaign of 2001 have already fully demonstrated the potential global rivalry between China and the United States, which cannot be papered over by platitudinous phrases such as "cooperative relationships" or "constructive partnerships." American actions in Afghanistan as well as in Central Asian countries such as Tajikstan and Uzbekistan—in addition to even more intimate relationships between the United States and its Asian allies such as Japan—have revived Beijing's fears about an anti-China containment policy.[50]

Conclusion: Can a Soft Landing Be Achieved?

The year 2001 was a momentous one for China. The giant country gained accession to the WTO, and acquired the trappings of a great power, for example, by hosting the APEC summit in Shanghai and gaining the right to stage the Olympics in Beijing in 2008. However, the question on the minds of many China observers is whether a soft landing can be achieved on both the economic and political fronts.

On the economic front, Premier Zhu achieved some form of soft landing through the 1990s not only by reducing inflation but by achieving a transformation of the economy from quantity-based to quality-based growth. In the wake of WTO accession, a bigger challenge looms with regard to weaning the State from business, privatizing more thoroughly, and doing business according to global norms of corporate governance. It seems likely that much of this agenda could be achieved by a relatively reform-minded *disidai* leadership in the coming decade or so.

Soft landing on the political front, however, will be a taller order. This refers to ways and means by which the relatively monolithic, one-party state machinery could be liberalized. While it may be far-fetched to expect Western-style democracy to develop within the tenure of the Fifth Generation, there are expectations that, as the economy and education levels develop, China might gradually go down the road of South Korea and Taiwan in political pluralism. To use the Taiwan example, it was a sizable leap forward from the dictatorial one-party rule of Generalissimo Chiang Kai-shek to the last years of President Chiang Ching-kuo, when the seeds of liberalization and multiparty democracy were sown within the confines of a fast-reforming one-party milieu.[51]

As discussed earlier, efforts by the *disidai* and *diwudai* in areas such as incorporating elements of the socialist democratic party model, empowering the business sector and the *minzhudangpai*, and expanding village-level elections will yield important pointers on the pace of change. However, just as in economic development, what is required in political liberalization is a leap from quantitative to qualitative change. A paradigm shift—what Deng liked to call *huan naojin*, or "changing the mindset"—is required. Cadres including many *disidai* officials are obsessed with the zero-sum game mentality of not yielding one bit of the CCP's prerogatives.

In the twenty-first century and post-WTO world, however, *disidai*, and certainly *diwudai* cadres need to acquire the mentality of win-win: that by sharing power, the CCP is actually making the transition from an unstable, angst-ridden, and ultimately doomed one-party dictatorship to a pluralistic system where a liberalized CCP may have the chance of running China under stable conditions that are based on openness and equal competition. Of course, tendencies to learn more from the West as well as from former Soviet-bloc countries may do battle with the temptation to wrap China in a cocoon of self-satisfied nationalism. Whether such a leap forward in worldview can be accomplished could be the biggest challenge facing the Fifth Generation.

Notes

1. There are different definitions, particularly in terms of the "age range," of the Fourth Generation or the Fifth Generation. Some commentators, including Hong Kong's respected CCP researcher Ting Wang, have classified *diwudai* cadres as those in their early 30s to early 40s.

2. The tradition of sending officials for post-graduate courses in Western universities began with Fourth Generation officials. Examples of *disidai* cadres with foreign degrees include China Securities Regulatory Commission Chairman Zhou Xiaochuan; Ministry of Foreign Trade and Economic Cooperation Vice Minister Long Yongtu; and Shanghai Vice Mayor Zhou Yupeng.

3. For a discussion of the accelerated promotion of young cadres, see "More Senior Officials in Their 30s Handling the Task of WTO Accession," *Ming pao* (a Hong Kong newspaper), November 17, 2001.

4. For a discussion of Hu Jintao's earlier career and relations with the CYL, see Yang Chong-mei, *Hu Jintao: The Chinese Communist Party's Cross-Century Successor* (Taipei: China Times Press, 1999), pp. 65–113.

5. For a discussion of Fourth- and Fifth Generation cadres with CYL affiliations, see Ting Wang, "The Rise of Late Fourth Generation Cadres," *Hong Kong Economic Journal* (a Hong Kong daily), November 7, 2001.

6. For a discussion of the career of Li Keqiang see, Willy Wo-Lap Lam, "Taming the regional 'warlords,'" www.cnn.com/Asia, July 17, 2001; Ting Wang, "The CYL's Dark Horse Li Keqiang Rumored to Be a Candidate for the Party Central Committee Secretariat," *Hong Kong Economic Journal*, November 29, 2000.

7. For a discussion of the impact of Shanghai cadres in other parts of the country, see Willy Wo-Lap Lam, "CCP Awaits Zeng's Pick of the Crop," *South China Morning Post* (a Hong Kong paper), July 5, 2000.

8. For a discussion of the views of Jiang Mianheng, see Allen T. Cheng, "Shanghai's King of IT," *Asiaweek*, February 9, 2001.

9. For a discussion of the views of Wang Huning, see "China's Emerging Neo-conservatism," www.Chinaonline.com, August 13, 2001.

10. For a discussion of Zhu's main lieutenants, see Xiao Zhengqing, *The Think Tank of Premier Zhu Rongji* (Hong Kong: Pacific Century Press, 1999), pp. 2–227.

11. For a discussion of Zhu's relationship with younger protégés, see Willy Wo-Lap Lam, *The Era of Jiang Zemin* (Singapore and New York: Prentice Hall, 1999), pp. 366–68.

12. For a discussion of the relationship between Deng Xiaoping and the "princelings," see Anthony Spaeth, "China's Privileged Princelings," *Time* (Asia edition), October 30, 1995; Terry McCarthy, "The New Guard," *Time* (Asia edition), October 15, 1999.

13. For a discussion of the career of Xi Jinping, see Xiao Chong, ed., *Prominent Fourth-generation Cadres* (Hong Kong: Xia Fei Er Press, 1998), pp. 322–31.

14. Third Generation Leftists have had difficulties recruiting *disidai* successors. The relatively few *disidai* Leftists include the vice Party secretary of Jilin Province, Lin Yanzhi, Zhejiang Party Secretary Zhang Dejiang, and economist Yang Deming. However, Zhang, 55, a graduate of Kim Il Sung University in North Korea, apparently quit the Leftist camp after he was reprimanded for failing to support Jiang's Three Represents.

15. Author's interviews with Wang Xiaodong, Yang Fan, and Han Deqiang in Beijing, August, 2001; for a sample of the views of Lu Zhoulai, Han Deqiang, Fang Ning, and Wang Xiaodong, see their collective work, "On Sino-U.S. Relations Two Years After the May 8 Incident," www.tianya.com.cn, May 15, 2001.

16. Cited in "China Reforms Its System for Selecting Cadres," New China News Agency (NCNA), June 5, 2001; see also "Senior Leaders Appointed After Open Selection," NCNA (English service), May 25, 2001.

17. Author's interviews with sources in Guangzhou, October 2001.

18. See "China Requires 180,000 Foreign Trade Professionals After WTO Accession," *Wen wei po* (a pro-Beijing Hong Kong paper), November 6, 2001.

19. Cited in "China Unveils New Policies to Attract Overseas Graduates to Return to Work for the Country," www.Chinesenewsnet.com, August 20, 2001.

20. For a discussion of the career of Liu Hong, see "The Stars of Asia," *Business Week*, June 14, 1999; "'Let There Be Light,' Says This Watchdog," *Asiaweek*, September 24, 1999.

21. For a discussion of Laura Cha's career and views, see "CSRC's Laura Cha: Securities Market Reform Needed Post-WTO Entry,"www.Chinaonline.com, November 6, 2000; Shi Yu, "China's Stock Market Being Sensibly Regulated," *Beijing Review* Web site, www.bjreview.com.cn/bjreview/EN/NationalIssues/China200114a.html.

22. Cited in Willy Wo-Lap Lam, "China Progresses with the Times," www.cnn.com/Asia, September 5, 2001.

23. See "Private Economy Expands Quickly in China," NCNA (English service), October 24, 2001; "China's Middle Class Will Swell to 200 Million People in Five Years' Time," *People's Daily* Web site, www.people.com.cn, July 20, 2001.

24. The earliest and most prominent private entrepreneur to have been inducted into senior advisory councils was former Vice President Rong Yiren, also a former vice chairman of the NPC and head of the Federation of Industry and Commerce. According to Jiang Zhenghua, Chairman of the *minzhudangpai* Farmers' and Workers' Party, 1,433 Party members have been appointed to various levels of people's congresses, while another 231 are working as cadres in government and judicial departments. Cited in "Jiang Zhenghua: The CCP 16th Congress Will Push Forward Democratic Political Construction," China News Service, November 28, 2001.

25. Cited in *Ming pao* October 27, 2001; *Wen Wei Po*, October 27, 2001.

26. See, for example, "Guangdong Arrests Officials Involved in the Corrupt Election in Heping County, He Yuan City," China News Service, August 7, 2001.

27. Cited in "Beware of People Buying Positions of People's Representatives," *Baokan wenzhai* (a Shanghai weekly), August 13, 2001.

28. For a discussion of the reform ideas of Hu Qili, see Wu Guoguang, *Political Reform Under Zhao Ziyang* (Hong Kong: Pacific Century Press, 1998), pp. 25–31.

29. For a discussion of the political views of Hu Jintao, see Ren Huiwen, "Hu Jintao Pushes Theoretical Innovations," *Hong Kong Economic Journal*, January 19, 2001.

30. For a discussion of the political views of Pan Yue, see Xia Fei, "Pan Yue's Reform Plans Blasted by the Left and Right," at the Web site www.duoweiweek.com, see www.duoweiweek.com/58/ChinaAffairs/4457.html; "Influence of New 'Neo-authoritarians'," *Far Eastern Economic Review*, May 7, 2001.

31. Cited in Jiang Zemin, *Party Construction in the New Era* (Beijing: People's Press, 1991), p. 44.

32. For a discussion of the significance and future of village elections, see Rebecca McKinnon, "China Experiments with Rural Democracy," www.cnn.com, June 25, 1998; Willy Wo-Lap Lam, "On the Wave of Political Reform," *South China Morning Post*, June 21, 2000; Frank Ching, "China's Creeping Democracy," *Far Eastern Economic Review*, March 8, 2001.

33. Author's interview with Chinese sources in Beijing, August 2001.

34. The well-known "economics first" principle, or the argument that "the party's major task is economic construction," was first raised by Deng Xiaoping in the early 1980s.

35. Jiang pointed out in a speech on July 31, 2001, that "the party must progress with the times, and that it must have innovations in theory," cited in NCNA, July 31, 2001.

36. In a speech in September 2001, Jiang pointed out that the CCP must consult the *minzhudangpai* more often to ensure the improvement of "party work style," see NCNA, September 28, 2001.

37. The idea of the *guojiahua* of the PLA, or putting the Army under the control of the government or the State instead of the Party, was raised in 1987 and 1988. However, the idea was killed by Jiang and other relatively conservative leaders. Until late 2001, articles in major army media still stressed the imperative of party control over the military. See "Suppress the Influence of Wrong Political Viewpoints and Resolutely Uphold the Party's Absolute Leadership over the Army," *Liberation Army Daily* (a Beijing army mouthpiece), June 6, 2001.

38. See, for example, "China to Abolish More Than 1,000 Executive Fiats in the Run-up to WTO Entry," in *Ming pao*, November 16, 2001; and "Government Work Will Become More Transparent and Trustworthy," *Wen wei po*, November 14, 2001; "State Council Abolishes Outdated Regulations," NCNA, October 19, 2001.

39. Cited in "Shenzhen to Implement Nine Types of Legalization," *Wen wei po*, November 5, 2001; "Shanghai to Change the Role of Government," *Wen wei po*, November 5, 2001.

40. Cited in Willy Wo-Lap Lam, "China Progresses with the Times."

41. For a discussion of the privatization of small and medium-sized SOEs, see, for example, "Medium and Small State Firms Should Be Sold," *Economic News Paper* (a Beijing paper), November 7, 2001.

42. For a discussion of the reform of state-owned enterprises, see Chen Qingtai, "Certain Questions on the Reform of Large-Scale State-Owned Enterprises in Our Country," *Qiushi* magazine (a Beijing monthly), no. 13, 2001.

43. Cited in "Federation of Industry and Commerce Lobbies for Constitutional Amendment to Protect Private Property," *Ming pao*, May 24, 2001.

44. See "Linghu An Says Yunnan Officials Must Propagate a 'Business-Friendly Concept'," China News Service, November 17, 2000; author's interview with Cao Siyuan, November 2001.

45. For a discussion of the post-September 11 relations between the United States and Central Asia, see, for example, Michael Fathers, "A Balancing Act," *Time*, October 22, 2001.

46. Cited in Willy Wo-Lap Lam, "Diplomatic Pain, Political Gain for Jiang," www.cnn.com/Asia, April 11, 2001. For an official characterization of Deng's foreign policy, see "Liu Huaqiu on China's Foreign Policy," at the Web site of the Chinese embassy in Washington, www.chinese-embassy.org/eng/2004.html.

47. For a discussion of anti-United States sentiments, see, for example, Tong Xiaoxi, "Questions Exposed by the Crisis of the Collision of Chinese and American Airplanes," at the Web site www.redflag.com, see redflagsh.myetang.com/redsee/tong.html.

48. For a discussion of the "collusion" between Party bureaucrats, capitalists and multinationals, see Wu Li, "The Situation in and out of China After May 8," at the Web site www.redflag.com, see redflagsh.myetang.com/redsee/wu58.html.

49. For a discussion of China's power projection and possible conflict with the United States, see Willy Wo-Lap Lam, "China Keeps Watch on U.S. Policy Shifts," www.cnn.com/Asia, October 3, 2001; and Charles Smith, "Rand Report Warns of Conflict with China," www.Newsmax.com, June 19, 2001.

50. For a discussion of Beijing's concept of the "anti-China containment policy," see Willy Wo-Lap Lam, "Beijing Battles U.S. 'China Threat' Theory," www.cnn.com, March 6, 2001; Zalmay Khalilzad, "Sweet and Sour: Recipe for a New China policy," at the Rand Web site, see www.rand.org/publications/randreview/issues/rr.winter.00/sweet.html.

51. For a discussion of the relationship between the late president of Taiwan, Chiang Ching-kuo, and democratic developments on the mainland, see Don Shapiro, "A Determined Island Goes Its Own Way," *Time* (Asia edition), September 27, 1999; Jasper Becker, "China's Democracy Dilemma," *South China Morning Post*, March 20, 2000.

───── 13 ─────

Remaining Relevant

The Challenges for the Party in Late-Leninist China

David Shambaugh

As the Chinese Communist Party (CCP) has passed its eightieth anniversary on July 1, 2001, and faces its Sixteenth Congress in the fall of 2002, the CCP confronts a number of difficult challenges. This chapter examines many of these challenges, discusses steps being taken by the Party to tackle them, and places them in the historical context of the evolution of communist parties. While the problems that the CCP confronts today add up to a collective challenge to Party authority, each has its own origins and consequences.

Some of the challenges facing the CCP today are intrinsic to single-party states—such as leadership succession. Some are the result of the broad processes associated with socioeconomic modernization—such as sharpened social stratification, rising corruption, and growing pressures for an enfranchised civil society. Some are of the Party's own making—such as widespread alienation and cynicism in society about politics in general and the Party's leadership in particular (both of which have contributed to the legitimacy and identity crises the CCP faces today). Some are the result of the declining efficacy of the coercive tools of an authoritarian or (formerly) totalitarian state—such as rising crime, dissent, and intellectual diversity. Some are the product of the growth of a market economy—such as the Party's inability to monopolize the distribution of goods and services (hence breaking "neo-traditional" networks of those formerly dependent on such resources). Some—such as corruption—are the result of insufficient rule of law, political checks and balances, and commercial transparency. Some are the product of organizational changes undertaken within the Party—such as the introduction of new recruitment criteria and the difficulties experienced in "Party [branch] building" (*dang* [zhibu] *jian*) at the local level. While many of these phenomena have indigenous origins, no doubt many problems confronted by the CCP are also stimulated by China's "opening to the outside world" and the attendant manifestations of globalization and interdependence that buffet the country on a daily and increasing basis.

All of these phenomena, and others, are apparent in present-day China and cumulatively add up to a comprehensive set of challenges for China's Communist Party as it enters a new century and its eighty-first year of existence. Taken together, they pose the problem of the CCP "remaining relevant" in the extremely complex environment of today's China. If the Party fails to remain relevant, is it valid to wonder whether it can endure as a ruling party? If the Party's rule is severely challenged, it can still likely maintain itself in power through armed force and coercion—although even this is no longer entirely certain. But if the CCP is to remain in power without having to resort to force and coercion, it must effectively develop sufficient responses to the aforementioned challenges. To be sure, the CCP seems aware of a number of these problems and challenges (although they may not define them in the same way), and the Party and State leadership are attempting to address them. Yet one wonders if they are not doing too little too late?

In this regard, it may be instructive to conceptualize the loss of Party control in China as an incremental process, a gradual process of decay, instead of a zero-sum implosion of power as occurred in the former Soviet Union and its satellites in Eastern Europe and Mongolia. If we conceptualize it as such, then we can focus more clearly on the apparent fissures in the Party and its progressively atrophying control, rather than anticipating a sudden collapse of power. After all, earthquakes may suddenly erupt—but the geological conditions that produce them gradually emerge over time. As such, the best that analysts—whether geologists or Sinologists—can do is to examine the shifting tectonic plates and track the changing conditions that may eventually coalesce in a shattering event.

Accordingly, this chapter is a brief attempt to examine some of these variables in China today that will affect the Party's future. As these variables and considerations are multiple, I will focus on two broad categories in this chapter. First, I will offer a number of observations on elite turnover and the leadership transition that the Party will experience in the near future. Second, I will address Party transformation institutionally, that is, how the CCP is adapting to the multiple influences on it.

Questions and Considerations About Elite Change

Perhaps no issue has historically proved more difficult for communist parties (or authoritarian regimes more generally) than ensuring smooth leadership transitions and elite circulation.[1] Communist parties worldwide have wrestled with this problem since the days of Lenin. While the nomenklatura system is good at ensuring continuity and circulation of cadres down through the ranks of communist parties, it has not proved capable of ensuring smooth or efficient transitions of leadership at the top of the system—where rivalries, factionalism, stealthy maneuvering, violence, purges, and arrests have all been the norm.

The CCP has certainly had its share of such leadership upheaval since its inception in 1921. As Lowell Dittmer has observed, "Elite strife is the Achilles' Heel of the Chinese political system."[2] Recall the following incidents of elite struggle in the CCP: the disputes between Mao, Li Lisan, Wang Ming, and the "returned Bolsheviks" in 1928–30; the Ruijin Incident of 1932; the Luo Ming Affair in 1933; the purges following the Fifth Plenum of the Sixth Central Committee in 1934; the Zunyi Meeting struggle in 1935; Zhang Guotao in 1936; Wang Ming and the returned Bolsheviks again in 1937; the Gao Gang–Rao Shushi Affair in 1952–53; the Lushan Plenum and purge of Peng Dehaui in 1959; Mao's "retirement to the second line" in 1962; the "Four Clean-ups," "Socialist Education Movement," and "Learn from the PLA" campaigns of 1964–65; the purges of Peng Zhen, Liu Shaoqi, Deng Xiaoping, and many other central and provincial Party leaders in 1966–67; the Lin Biao Affair and subsequent surges in the PLA in 1971–72; the struggle of "rehabilitated cadres" during 1973–75; the purge of Deng Xiaoping in 1975; the elite maneuvering around the time of the death of Mao and subsequent arrest of the Gang of Four in 1976; the purge of the "Small Gang of Four" in 1977; the removal of Hua Guofeng in 1978–79; the Chen Yun–Deng Xiaoping rivalry throughout the 1980s; the purge of Hu Yaobang in 1987; the purge of Zhao Ziyang and his associates in 1989; the ferreting out of the "Yang family village" in the PLA in 1992–93; and the removal of Qiao Shi in 1997. There have been many different causes and consequences of the above incidents of elite struggle in the CCP,[3] and not all of them were involved with succession to the senior leader per se, but the persistence and prominence of such struggles over time highlight the difficulties the CCP has had in maintaining leadership unity and continuity.

The Retirement Norm

Given this history in the Chinese Communist Party, and the generic problem in single-party states, it is rather remarkable that the leadership succession to Jiang Zemin and the broader ascent of the "Fourth Generation" is occurring at all. That is, there used to be only two principal "exit paths" from Chinese elite politics: death or purge. Now there is a third: voluntary retirement. This is a normative convention that the Party, military, and government in China have all worked very hard to institute over the past fifteen years.[4] Over this period of time, retirement has evolved from being a norm to being an enforced regulation throughout the Party, military, and government. Only the very top of this triad has not adhered to the new convention—but with the expected retirements at the Sixteenth Party Congress, and subsequently in the military and government, the process will be complete. This will represent a remarkable accomplishment and qualitative change, as it will be the first time in the history of all communist parties that the senior elites have voluntarily relinquished their positions and institutionalized power. Instilling the retirement norm was one key element of Deng Xiaoping's broader efforts to instill greater predictability and efficiency into the functioning of the CCP (others had to do with decision-making procedures, the organization and scope of party rule, and "inner-party life").

Not only has the retirement norm now been institutionalized, but so too has an equally important convention: Retired leaders actually disengage from the policy process and do not attempt to intervene into or manipulate decision making from "behind the screen," as was commonplace in the past. This norm of enforced retirement took hold during the 1990s, particularly in the CCP and PLA, and was implemented by the very leaders that will now be retiring themselves. Thus it will be very interesting to see, and a real test to the new practice, if the senior "Third Generation" leaders actually refrain from meddling in active policy deliberations. It would not be unusual for them to be consulted from time to time, or for them to continue to read and comment on classified documents, but time will tell whether the likes of Jiang Zemin, Li Peng, Zhu Rongji, Qian Qichen, Li Lanqing, Wei Jianxing, Zhang Wannian, Chi Haotian, Fu Quanyou, and others will adhere to the norm that they themselves did so much to implement or whether they will usurp it. Even if they do not actively meddle in the policy process, their individual and collective presence could cause policy paralysis and serve to restrict initiatives by the successor Fourth Generation leadership. To be sure, the Fourth Generation leadership will be powerfully constrained by a "path dependency" inherited from their predecessors, but such meddling could seriously inhibit new departures in policy necessary to cope with the substantial number of challenges and problems outlined at the beginning of this chapter. To effectively deal with these multiple problems, bold vision and initiative are required.

Ready for Prime Time?

The "vision" question raises the issue of the socialization of the Fourth Generation elite. That is, how have their past experiences shaped the worldview and workstyle of the successor leadership? There is, of course, no answer to this question—as only time will tell what kind of leaders they are and how they tackle policy problems. Cheng Li's contribution to this volume and other writings are very suggestive of their backgrounds.[5] His extensive research indicates that the Fourth Generation are fairly well educated (most possessing collegiate or vocational education), that their training remains predominantly in engineering (although some are trained in finance and the law), that the majority have had experience in provincial-level administration, and that they are generally nonideological and are pragmatic. This may all be true, but there are a number of other factors in their backgrounds to consider.

For example, despite the slight diversification of education and training noted above, the Fourth Generation continues to be dominated by those trained in engineering. This suggests a continuation of the technocratic approach to policy. Technocrats are the opposite of ideologues. They are pragmatic problem solvers, but have a strong propensity to approach problems in a piecemeal and incremental fashion. They tend not to define issues systematically and look for comprehensive solutions. Even if they identify policy challenges as being holistic in nature, their instinct is to divide the problem into its constituent parts and deal with each individual part incrementally and progressively. Thus, like its predecessor, we can probably expect the Fourth Generation leadership to move cautiously, to tinker with policy options, to experiment a lot, and to deal with policy challenges in relative isolation from each other. This is a pragmatic, and often effective, style of policymaking. But the downside of such a leadership style is that linkages between issues, and the need to address the multifarious dimensions of a problem simultaneously, are often not grasped. This tendency could prove to be a real liability for the Fourth Generation leaders, as many of the policy problems they will confront in today's China are extremely complex and contain multiple dimensions and linkages to both China's domestic and international environments. This is the reality of the twin processes of modernization and globalization. Most issues are interconnected. Consequently, they require a comprehensive and systematic analysis and understanding of the dimensions of a given policy problem, but they also require variegated and integrated policy responses to tackle the problem at multiple levels. Technocrats tend not to think or manage in such a way. Moreover, technocrats are not trained in several aspects of the social sciences—sociology, political science, economics, anthropology, and international relations—and hence are intellectually poorly equipped to recognize policy linkages between and across these spheres. This handicap could come back to haunt the Fourth Generation.

A second, related handicap of the Fourth Generation is the relatively insulated lives they have led. They are not well traveled, very few (if any) speak foreign languages, virtually none were educated abroad, and they have had only limited and superficial exposure to foreign countries in recent years. This insularity can prove a handicap in two regards. First, many of the domestic issues China faces today and increasingly in the future have international dimensions—aspects that will not be easily recognized by those with minimal exposure to the outside world. Second, China is increasingly engaged in world affairs in a number of ways, with a number of countries and international institutions, across a variety of functional areas—the Fourth Generation will likely find it difficult to proactively lead this involvement. The likely consequence of the second factor is that the Fourth Generation leadership will likely delegate management of these issues to the ministries and bureaucracies concerned.

A third element of their socialization concerns their higher education. On the one hand, a larger percentage of this generation of leaders has experienced university or technical vocational education. This is good news. A strikingly large number are graduates of Qinghua University (in various fields of engineering). Herein lies an interesting difference—namely that the Fourth Generation was not trained in the former Soviet Union (as was the case with many in the Third Generation). Not only did they not physically experience the Soviet Union during the 1950s, but they also did not directly experience Soviet education. Moreover, they were not directly exposed either to the Stalin era or the de-Stalinization period. Having graduated from Chinese institutions between 1960 and 1965, this is the first generation to have experienced the Sino-Soviet Split. The effect of this experience is unclear, but it does distinguish them from their predecessors—who displayed a demonstrable empathy for the Soviet Union and Russian culture. It is difficult to prove, but I have always assumed a correlation between the extensive time spent by the Third Generation leadership in the former Soviet Union and their consistent desires to improve Sino-Russian relations during the 1990s. It will be interesting to see if a generation that came of age only knowing enmity for their northern neighbor will have an impact on future relations.

A fourth socializing variable of importance is the fact that this is the Cultural Revolution generation. Many had their educations interrupted, some joined Red Guards, others witnessed their parents and relatives persecuted, while most were dispatched to the countryside for substantial periods of time. It is very difficult to predict how these experiences have affected the Fourth Generation, but I would anticipate that they:

- have a deeper appreciation of the backwardness and conditions in the countryside (which may make them favor policies intended to allocate and redistribute resources to the interior and poorer areas of the country, including the policy to develop the West);

- have a deep and ingrained sense of the importance of social and political stability;
- are suspicious of ideology and mass movements;
- may have an appreciation of the need for institutionalized constraints on power; and
- may grasp the need for genuine reform of the Party.

These conjectures may or may not be valid assumptions—and, in any event, it remains to be seen how these proclivities would translate into policy. Yet one should not assume that the Fourth Generation leadership will start afresh when they ascend the political stage at the Sixteenth Party Congress—they bring with them distinct experiences and socialization that will undoubtedly affect they ways in which they approach and tackle policy problems.

In Uncharted Territory: Can the Party Adapt to the Revolution of Rising Expectations?

There is no shortage of theorizing about the evolution of communist parties. Prior to the collapse of communist parties in Eastern Europe and the former Soviet Union, and throughout the prolonged period of the Cold War, the study of "comparative communism" was a bona fide subfield within comparative politics and comparative sociology.[6] The demise of most communist party-states in the former Soviet bloc produced a veritable cottage industry of such scholarship.[7] Some of this literature attempted to apply the "lessons" of Soviet bloc states' collapse to China.[8] If this literature has a central thread, it is that there is no singular path to "extinction" for communist party-states.[9] While there are commonalities apparent in the Soviet and East European cases (e.g., the rise of civil society, alienation in society, loss of Party control over the military and security services, leaders' uncertainty and wavering over regime responses, charismatic counter-elites such as Havel and Walesa, etc.), there was no singular "path dependency" that brought these regimes down. Each had its own unique features and imploded through a different combination of variables.

For the Chinese Communist Party (at least) two operative questions arise from the collapse of these other communist party-states: If there is a continuum along which communist party-states pass prior to their failure, where does China lie today? What lessons did the CCP draw from these failed states and what steps has the Party subsequently taken to prevent their repetition in China? These are large questions that cannot be adequately addressed in such a short essay,[10] but I wish to raise a number of issues for consideration below.

China and Stage Theories of Communist Evolution

Various stage theories have been posited about the phases through which communist party-states pass. Many descriptions of the characteristics and substance of these stages are similar, although the terminology used is often different. Most theorists of comparative communism agreed that ruling communist parties pass from an initial stage that emphasized ideology and social transformation (often employing classic "totalitarian" methods of terror and propaganda) to a second stage of guided economic development that emphasized technical rationality and efficiency (which applied "softer" "authoritarian" methods that utilized bureaucratic management). The German political scientist Richard Lowenthal identified this transition as that from "utopia to development."[11] In another article, he describes it simply as the "post-totalitarian" transition in which the Party "matures" by responding to pressures from "below" instead of imposing change from "above."[12] Chalmers Johnson observed that the shift from the first to second stage represented a movement from a "mobilization" to a "post-mobilization" regime.[13] Samuel Huntington and Zbigniew Brzezinski used different terms to describe essentially the same phenomena, but each posited more lengthy spectrums of systemic change that took account of the increasing diversity and demands that occur in society as a result of the economic growth generated by the previous stage. Huntington identified a three-stage model of "transformation" (of political system), "consolidation" (of regime control), and "adaptation" (of ruling party to pressures generated by society).[14] Brzezinski, writing with great prescience in 1989 on the eve of the uprisings in Eastern Europe and the Soviet Union, posited a four-stage model of evolution from "communist totalitarianism" to "communist authoritarianism" to "post-communist authoritarianism" to "post-communist pluralism."[15]

Where does China fit on these continua? Surprisingly few China specialists have attempted to systematically apply these comparative perspectives and address themselves to macro-level political change in the People's Republic of China. Most studies of Chinese politics today focus on increasingly smaller units of analysis and fail to generate broader views or predictions about China's or the CCP's future. There are, however, some studies that have attempted to look at the big picture.

Some studies, such as Gordon Chang's sensationally titled study, *The Coming Collapse of China*, posit cataclysmic change. Chang argues that the signs of the CCP's "disintegration" are everywhere and it is just a matter of time before the Party is overthrown (Chang seems to envision a revolutionary-type overthrow of the regime rather than a gradual demise). Chang summarizes his prognosis as follows:

The Communist Party has struggled to keep up with change over the last two decades, but now it is beginning to fail as it often cannot provide the basic needs of its people. Corruption and malfeasance erode the party's support from small hamlet to great city. Central government leaders do not know what to do as the institutions built over five decades become feeble. Social order in their nation is dissolving. The Chinese are making a break for the future, and the disaffected are beginning to find their voice. The cadres still suppress, but that won't work in the long run. The people are in motion now, and it's just a matter of time before they get what they want.[16]

Other China analysts are more circumspect about the evidence of the erosion of regime control and potential for its collapse and systemic political change in China. A collaborative study that I edited concluded that while there *are* signs of unprecedented social instability and political problems in China today, the regime is not necessarily in danger of disintegration or collapse.[17] The contributors to this study concluded at the time (1999) that China was in a state of "stable unrest" that could continue indefinitely. Much of the unrest and discontent in society was oriented against specific grievances in specific locales at specific points in time, and was not more broadly aimed at the central party-state itself. Moreover, such outbreaks of social unrest that have appeared across China are disconnected from each other, that is, there is little "connecting tissue" between these "nodes" or pockets of unrest. While the contributors to this study did agree that the party-state was being challenged on many fronts in unprecedented ways, and many of the factors that had been present in the former Soviet Union and Eastern Europe *are* present in China today, it was equally noted that a number of important factors exist in China that were absent in these other former communist states that has served, and can continue to serve, to buffer the CCP: a growing economy and increasing levels of wealth, extensive trade and investment ties to the outside world, a generally cohesive multiethnic society, a stable political leadership that has coped well with succession issues, and strong regime control over the military and internal security services.

Other studies emphasize the economic differences between China and former communist states, and argue that China is more likely to continue down the path of East Asian developmental states—both economically and politically—than to follow the path of the Soviet/East European model.[18] Others argue that the Leninist institutions in China, while not as dominant as in the past, remain strong.[19] This is true not just of the Party and government institutions, but particularly of the military and internal security services. This is important, as the military and security services serve as a key "firewall" between state and society. When the militaries and internal security forces of the Soviet and East European regimes proved unwilling and unable to use force to maintain the ruling communist parties in power, they quickly collapsed. While no amount of force or cohesive security units is ultimately sufficient to save an illegitimate and discredited party-state from collapse, they are important factors in sustaining regimes in power.

One study of the Chinese Communist Party that places the CCP in a comparative context is the work of Bruce Dickson.[20] Dickson's superb and insightful study synthesizes much of the previous literature on authoritarian and communist party-states, but particularly attempts to apply the aforementioned typology of Samuel Huntington to the evolution of the CCP (and the Kuomintang [KMT] on Taiwan). He finds that the CCP today fits very well into Huntington's "adaptation" phase of authoritarian party evolution. Dickson concludes that a number of differences and impediments exist that distinguish the CCP from the KMT, and he argues that the former will not follow the latter down the path to democratization.

Dickson's analysis and Huntington's model lead us to the real nub of the issue: How does the Party adapt itself to the new revolution—the revolution of rising expectations? To recognize that the Party's Leninist tools of control have grown progressively more blunt over time, or that the Party is riddled with cancerous corruption from within, or that social discontent is rising across the land, are all fairly obvious to most observers and analysts. There is little doubt that the CCP of today is experiencing weakened authority and is enduring significant challenges to its legitimacy and rule. The operative questions are: how severe are these problems, what is the Party doing about them, and are the responses (attempts to adapt) proving successful?

Can the CCP Remain Relevant?

These are large and difficult questions to answer, but they are central to the principal question of this study: How can the Party remain relevant to an increasingly diverse and demanding society? One's ability to "answer" these questions depends in part on the level of analysis and variables one examines.

For example, if one focuses at the level of senior CCP leadership, it can be concluded that elite succession has been handled fairly successfully since 1989. Of course, the transition to the Fourth Generation leadership will provide a decisive answer, but in the wake of the 1987 and 1989 purges of Hu Yaobang and Zhao Ziyang, respectively, elite conflict has been kept to a minimum and elite turnover has, by and large, been predictable and smooth (the ouster of Qiao Shi and the Yang brothers being exceptions).

If one examines the Party's macro-level relations with the other two legs of the Chinese Communist triad of power—the government and the military—the CCP does not seem to be in danger. Separation of Party and government (*dang-zheng fenkai*) has effectively been accomplished in institutional terms (although the "interlocking directorate" still exists among top leaders) and the Party has largely disengaged from intervening in economic decision making down to the enterprise level. Despite some significant changes in civil-military relations, the PLA still remains essentially a Party-army and the CCP can still count on the loyalty of the PLA (and other internal security forces).[21]

If one takes a different level of analysis—Party membership and organization—the picture is more mixed. It is certainly true that the Party faces a major problem with corruption, cronyism, and nepotism—although, as the work of Lu Xiaobo illustrates, these have been perennial and longstanding problems in the CCP.[22] Part of the corruption problem owes to an economy of relative scarcity and the Party's "neo-traditional" methods of garnering and distributing prized resources to its members and their families.[23] Part of the problem relates to the predatory tendency of rent seeking by local cadres who no longer have a monopoly of key resources. Whatever the source of the problem, the Party recognizes corruption to be a threat of the gravest nature—a matter of "life and death" according to Jiang Zemin—and it is dealing with it in increasingly direct and harsh terms. Similarly, if one examines Party committees at the local level, it is evident that Party officials are increasingly entrepreneurial and perform a range of non-Leninist roles; as a consequence, Party committees (particularly in the countryside) have atrophied badly.[24] Various campaigns in recent years to improve Party building (*dang jian*) at the local level have proved largely ineffective.

From these perspectives, it is easy to conclude that the CCP has become a hollow shell. Yet, if one examines Party membership and recruitment, as Bruce Dickson's chapter in this volume does, there is evidence of the Party adapting to new circumstances. Long before Jiang Zemin's speech in July 2001 (on the occasion of the eightieth anniversary of the CCP) made it official, the Party had embarked on a drive to recruit the "advanced classes" of Chinese society—entrepreneurs and technocrats—while ferreting out those less educated and less competent. Similarly, if one looks at the capacity of key Party organs, such as the Propaganda and Organization Departments, a mixed picture also emerges. The Propaganda Department no longer has anywhere near the control and influence it enjoyed in the past (as is quite evident in Anne Stevenson-Yang's chapter), yet it remains capable of significant censorship and media manipulation. The Organization Department continues to control the nomenklatura appointments throughout the nation, and seems to have strengthened its overall influence inside the Party apparat (*dangwu xitong*) under the directorship of Zeng Qinghong.

Thus, if one examines the Party as an organization, there is mixed evidence of decay and adaptation. Yet, if one looks at a third level of the Party's role—vis-à-vis society—there is reason to conclude that there is far more decay than adaptation. This can be seen on a number of levels.

First, as Huntington's typology predicts and Carol Hamrin's contribution to this volume emphasizes, China—and the Communist Party—have entered into a qualitatively new phase of development. This phase is characterized by the revolution of rising expectations and rising public demands for an improved quality of life. The citizenry's increased demands for improved welfare, health care, education, environment, social order, public infrastructure, communications, and so forth, all are rising. This is to be expected, as it follows a more generic pattern evident in other newly industrialized countries. Once the citizenry reaches a threshold where essential material needs are satisfied and lifestyles have diversified and improved to the point that they have today in much of China, people begin to expect improvement in these other areas of life (including spiritual). With these demands come different but *raised* expectations on the regime to address and meet these new demands. Not only do citizens expect the demands to be addressed, but they require adequate channels to articulate the demands in the first place.

In both respects, responsive government is required. It is apparent that the party-state (at all levels) is attempting to meet the increased demands for improved quality of life, and is doing fairly well overall in this regard. But it is equally evident that the Party is not adequately addressing the need to create better channels of interest articulation. This is because the Party leadership has a zero-sum view of political power and a neuralgic reaction to the enfranchisement of civil society. This is one of the principal "lessons" that the Party leadership seems to have drawn from the uprisings in Eastern Europe in 1989, that is, enfranchising labor unions, autonomous churches, and other civic organizations is a slippery slope to enfranchising a political opposition. Instead, the CCP has concluded that a mixture of suppression and co-optation of such social groups is needed. As I have argued elsewhere, such a strategy may work in the short term but is not ultimately sustainable.[25]

The Vision Thing

The other related problem confronting the Party and its popular and political legitimacy is its lack of vision, or at least an original vision, for the direction in which it seeks to lead the nation. A Marxist-Leninist future certainly seems out of the question, as this theology has been diluted beyond recognition in contemporary China. Yet no comprehensive alternative vision has been substituted and offered by the Party. Jiang Zemin's "Three Represents" theory certainly does not stir the nation. Nor do the Party's calls to build a "socialist spiritual civilization" or "socialism with Chinese characteristics." Quite simply, the Chinese Communist Party lacks, and has not articulated, a convincing vision of where it seeks to lead the nation. It is in desperate need of a systematic and convincing rationale to justify itself and its continued rule. It certainly has not articulated an *original* vision in the aftermath of Marxism-Leninism. Aside from the propagandistic clichés noted above, what the Party seems to advocate today is really no different from the core themes that all Chinese rulers since the Self-Strengtheners of the 1870s have advocated: attaining wealth and power; enhancing nationalism and international dignity; preserving unity and preventing chaos. In these respects, Jiang Zemin is no different than Deng, Mao, Chiang Kai-shek, Yuan Shikai, and Li Hongzhang. While not original, these core purposes do resonate deeply in China and do lend the current Party leadership considerable legitimacy and continuity with the past.

Is this traditional vision sufficient, however, for the CCP to remain relevant in today's China? Time will tell, but this observer has doubts. Responding to the revolution of rising expectations is manageable, as it essentially requires a responsive and *reactive* party-state. In this regard, if managed carefully, the CCP can adapt and respond effectively to the rising demands placed upon it by society. There is no guarantee that it will be able to do so, as it requires altering its zero-sum thinking about civil society, among other things. But to offer a convincing vision for the future of the nation is entirely different, as it entails a *proactive* party-state that has a sound sense of its own institutional identity. Leadership presupposes such a vision. To lead is to be proactive and convincing in message and direction. At the present time, the Chinese Communist Party lacks such leadership, and is becoming increasingly isolated from the society it pretends to rule. It has become a transactional instead of a transformational party. The central challenge for the Fourth Generation leadership is not only how to remain relevant to society as a ruling party, but how to inspire and lead the nation in new directions.

Notes

1. There are many studies on the subject of succession in communist party-states. See, for example, Valerie Bunce, *Do Leaders Make a Difference? Executive Succession and Public Policy Under Capitalism and Socialism* (Princeton: Princeton University Press, 1981); and Raymond Taras, ed., *Leadership Change in Communist States* (Boston: Allen and Unwin 1989).

2. Lowell Dittmer, "Patterns of Elite Strife and Succession in Chinese Politics," *China Quarterly* (September 1990): 405–30.

3. For a discussion of these see Dittmer, ibid.

4. See Melanie Manion, *Retirement of Revolutionaries in China: Public Policies, Social Norms, Public Interests* (Princeton: Princeton University Press, 1993).

5. Cheng Li, *China's Leaders: The New Generation* (Lanham, MD: Rowman and Littlefield, 2001).

6. The American Council of Learned Societies even established a Committee on Comparative Communist Studies.

7. See Gilbert Rozman, ed., *Dismantling Communism: Common Causes and Regional Variations* (Washington, DC and Baltimore, MD: Woodrow Wilson Center Press and Johns Hopkins University Press, 1992); Daniel Chirot, ed., *The Crisis of Leninism and the Decline of the Left: The Revolutions of 1989* (Seattle: University of Washington Press); Gale Stokes, *The Walls Come Tumbling Down: The Collapse of Communism in Eastern Europe* (Oxford: Oxford University Press, 1993); Bartlomiej Kaminski, *The Collapse of State Socialism* (Princeton: Princeton University Press, 1991); Robert Strayer, *Why Did the Soviet Union Collapse?* (Armonk, NY: M.E. Sharpe, 1998); Leslie Holmes, *Post-Communism* (Cambridge, UK: Polity Press, 1997); Timothy Garton Ash, *The Magic Lantern: The Revolution of '89 Witnessed in Warsaw, Budapest, Berlin, and Prague* (New York: Random House, 1993).

8. See Edwin Winkler, ed., *Transitions from Communism in China: Institutional and Comparative Analyses* (Boulder: Lynne Reinner, 1999); Barrett L. McCormick and Jonathan Unger, ed., *China After Socialism: In the Footsteps of Eastern Euorpe or East Asia?* (Armonk, NY: M.E. Sharpe, 1996); Edward Friedman and Barrett L. McCormick, ed., *What If China Doesn't Democratize?* (Armonk, NY: M.E. Sharpe, 2000).

9. See Kenneth Jowitt, *New World Disorder: The Leninist Extinction* (Berkeley: University of California Press, 1992).

10. I have embarked on a longer book-length project on the subject.

11. Richard Lowenthal, "Development vs. Utopia in Communist Policy," in *Change in Communist Systems*, ed. Chalmers Johnson (Stanford: Stanford University Press, 1970), pp. 33–116.

12. Richard Lowenthal, "The Ruling Party in a Mature Society," in *Social Consequences of Modernization in Communist Societies*, ed. Mark G. Field (Baltimore: Johns Hopkins University Press, 1976), pp. 81–120.

13. Chalmers Johnson, "Comparing Communist Nations," in Johnson, ed., *Change in Communist Systems*, pp. 1–32.

14. Samuel P. Huntington, "Social and Institutional Dynamics of One-Party Systems," in *Authoritarian Politics in Modern Society: The Dynamics of Established One-Party Systems*, ed. Huntington and Clement H. Moore (New York: Basic Books, 1970), pp. 23–40.

15. Zbigniew Brzezinski, *The Grand Failure: The Birth and Death of Communism in the Twentieth Century* (New York: Charles Scribner's Sons, 1989), p. 255.

16. Gordon G. Chang, *The Coming Collapse of China* (New York: Random House, 2001), pp. 284–85.

17. David Shambaugh, ed., *Is China Unstable?* (Armonk, NY: M.E. Sharpe, 2001).

18. See, for example, McCormick and Unger, ed., *China After Socialism*.

19. See, for example, Winckler, ed., *Transition from Communism in China*.

20. Bruce Dickson, *Democratization in China and Taiwan: The Adaptability of Leninist Parties* (Oxford: Clarendon Press, 1997).

21. For elaboration see David Shambaugh, *Modernizing China's Military: Progress, Problems, and Prospects* (Berkeley: University of California Press, forthcoming).

22. Xiaobo Lu, *Cadres and Corruption: The Organizational Involution of the Chinese Communist Party* (Stanford: Stanford University Press, 2000).

23. See Andrew Walder, *Communist Neo-Traditionalism: Work and Authority in Chinese Industry* (Berkeley: University of California Press, 1986).

24. The work of my former Ph.D. students Jane Duckett and Ignatius Wibowo are particularly germane on these points.

25. See David Shambaugh, "The Post-Mao State," in *The Modern Chinese State*, ed. Shambaugh (Cambridge: Cambridge University Press, 2000), especially pp. 186–87.

The Editors and Contributors

The Editors

David M. Finkelstein is the Director of *Project Asia*, The CNA Corporation's center for Asian security studies. A long-time student of Chinese affairs, he received his Ph.D. in Chinese history from Princeton University and studied Mandarin at Nankai University in Tianjin. He is widely published on PRC and Asian security issues. Among his numerous publications are, *China's National Military Strategy* (1999), *Engaging DoD: Chinese Perspectives on Military Relations with the United States* (1999), *China's New Concept of Security: Reading Between the Lines* (1999), "Commentary on Doctrine" (from James Mulvenon and Andrew N.D. Yang, eds. *Seeking Truth From Facts*, Santa Monica, CA, RAND, 2001, pp. 119–31), "*Sunzi Bingfa Yu MaoZedongde Zhanyi Yuanze*" (Sun Zi and Mao Zedong's Campaign Principles") (from *Xin Shiji de Zhongguo Bing Xue—Di Wujie Sunzi Bingfa Guoji Yantaohui Lunwenji* [Chinese Military Studies for a New Century—Conference Volume for the Fifth International Symposium on Sun Zi Bingfa], Junshi Kexue Chubenshe 2001, pp. 60–68) and *China Reconsiders Its National Security: The Great Peace and Development Debate of 1999* (2000). He is also a co-editor of the historical volume *Chinese Warfighting: The PLA Experience Since 1949* (M.E. Sharpe: Forthcoming). Finkelstein's 1993 historical monograph, *From Abandonment to Salvation: Washington's Taiwan Dilemma, 1949–50* (1997) was hailed in *Presidential Studies Quarterly* as "blazing a new trail" and "will take an important place in the literature of U.S.-China relations in the mid-20th Century." A retired U.S. Army Officer, Finkelstein is a graduate of the United States Military Academy, held various China-related positions in the

Pentagon, and served on the faculty of the History Department at West Point where he taught courses on the history of China and Chinese military history.

Maryanne Kivlehan is an Asia Security Analyst at the CNA Corporation's "Project Asia." A specialist in Chinese politics, foreign policy, and China's new generation of leaders, she also recently published an in-depth study of the political, legal, economic, environmental, and security dimensions of the South China Sea entitled *The South China Sea, a Regional Survey*, and co-authored a study entitled *Institutional Reforms of the Chinese People's Liberation Army: Overview and Challenges*. She holds an MA in Security Policy Studies from the Elliott School of Foreign Affairs at the George Washington University, and is a graduate of the Hopkins-Nanjing Center for Chinese and American Studies, as well Capital Normal University in Beijing, where she studied Mandarin. Before joining the CNA Corporation, she worked for an international nonprofit organization directing projects on Chinese, Mongolian, and Russian affairs. She also spent time in Bosnia working with the Organization for Security and Cooperation in Europe (OSCE) in support of the 1997 municipal elections.

The Contributors

Zhiyue Bo, a specialist on China's provincial leaders, is assistant professor and chair of the department of international studies at St. John Fisher College in Rochester, New York. He received a Bachelor of Law and Master of Law in International Politics from Peking University and a Ph.D. in political science from the University of Chicago. He is widely published in the areas of Chinese local governance and provincial leadership in China. His most recent book *Chinese Provincial Leaders: Economic Performance and Political Mobility Since 1949* (Armonk, NY: M.E. Sharpe, 2002), is based on a complete and detailed dataset of Chinese provincial leaders from 1949 to 1998.

Michael S. Chase is an associate international policy analyst at the RAND Corporation in Washington, DC. He previously worked for RAND as a graduate associate and as a professional consultant. He holds an MA in international affairs from Johns Hopkins University School of Advanced International Studies (SAIS) and a BA in politics from Brandeis University. From 2000 to 2001, he studied Chinese at the Hopkins-Nanjing Center in Nanjing, China.

Bruce J. Dickson is associate professor of political science and international affairs at George Washington University. His research and teaching focus is the domestic politics of China and Taiwan, particularly the role of political parties in promoting and adapting to political, economic, and social change. He is the author of *Red Capitalists in China: The Party, Private Entrepreneurs,* *and Prospects for Political Change* (forthcoming 2003), *Democratization in China and Taiwan: The Adaptability of Leninist Parties* (1997), and articles in *Asian Survey, China Quarterly, Comparative Political Studies, Comparative Politics, National Interest, Political Science Quarterly, Journal of Contemporary China* and several edited volumes. He is also associate editor of the journal *Problems of Post-Communism*. He received his Ph.D. in political science from the University of Michigan.

Joseph Fewsmith is professor of International Relations at Boston University and director of the East Asian Interdisciplinary Studies Program. He is the author of *Party, State and Local Elite in Republican China: Merchant Organizations and Politics in Shanghai, 1890–1930* (1985), *The Dilemmas of Reform in China: Political Conflict and Economic Debate* (Armonk, NY: M.E. Sharpe, 1994), *Elite Politics in Contemporary China* (Armonk, NY: M.E. Sharpe, 2001), and *China Since Tiananmen: The Politics of Transition* (2001). He has written extensively on contemporary politics in China, with articles appearing in such journals as *Asian Survey, Current History, Journal of Contemporary China, Problems of Communism, Modern China, China Journal, China Quarterly,* and *Comparative Studies in Society and History.*

Carol Lee Hamrin is an expert on contemporary Chinese social and political change, as well as United States–China relations. Her current research interests include the development of the nonprofit, nongovernmental sector in China; cultural change, human rights, and religious policy; and indigenous resources for conflict management. A Chinese affairs consultant, she is also a Research Professor at George Mason University in Fairfax, Virginia, where she is working with the Center for Asia Pacific Economic Cooperation (CAPEC) and the Institute for Conflict Analysis and Resolution (ICAR). Dr. Hamrin was a senior China research specialist at the Department of State for twenty-five years, and has taught at the Johns Hopkins University School of Advanced International Studies. Her recent publications include: "The Impact of Taiwan's New Political Order on the Aging PRC Political Order," in *Taiwan's New Order and Cross-Strait Relations* (conference volume, Federal Research Division, Library of Congress, June 2000); and *Decision-Making in Deng's China: Perspective from Insiders*, coedited with Suisheng Zhao (Armonk, NY: M.E. Sharpe, 1995). Forthcoming publications include: "China's Society Makes a Comeback," *ChinaSource Journal* 4:2 (Fall 2002); "China's Social Capital Deficit: Source of Instability," with Zheng Wang; "The Domestic Factors in China's Policy-Making Toward Taiwan," with Zheng Wang; *All Politics Is Domestic: Policy-Making in Washington, Beijing and Taipei* (conference volume, the Atlantic-Pacific Interrelationships Program of the Atlantic Council); "Advancing Religious Freedom in a Global Era: Prospects and Prescriptions," in Jason

Kindopp and Carol Lee Hamrin, ed., "The Church and State in China" (conference volume, The Brookings Institution Press).

Taeho Kim is a senior China analyst and former director of research cooperation at the Korea Institute for Defense Analyses (KIDA), Seoul, Korea, as well as a nonresident research associate of the Mershon Center, Ohio State University, Columbus, Ohio. A long-time student of Chinese foreign and security policy, Dr. Kim holds MAs from Pennsylvania State University and Johns Hopkins University and a Ph.D. from Ohio State University. Dr. Kim's main research interests are Sino-Russian military cooperation, China's arms acquisitions, Asian nations' threat perceptions of the People's Republic of China, and China's bilateral relationships with other Northeast Asian states. He is a coeditor of the *Korean Journal of Defense Analysis* and is the author and coauthor of several books, policy reports, and monographs. His most recent English publications include: "South Korea and a Rising China: Perceptions, Policies, and Prospects," in *The China Threat: Perceptions, Myths and Reality*, ed. Ian James Storey and Herbert Yee, (London: Curzon, 2002); "A Testing Ground for China's Power, Prosperity, and Preferences: China's Post-Cold War Relations with the Korean Peninsula," *Pacifica Review* (February 2001); and "Sino-ROK Relations and the Future of East Asian Security: A Developing Continental Balance" in *The Security Environment in the Asia-Pacific*, ed. Hung-mao Tien and Tun-jen Cheng (Armonk, NY: M.E. Sharpe, 2000).

Willy Wo-Lap Lam is a senior China analyst with CNN's Asia-Pacific Office in Hong Kong. A journalist, author, and researcher with more than twenty-five years of experience, Lam has published extensively on areas including the Chinese Communist Party, economic and political reform, the People's Liberation Army, foreign policy, China-Taiwan and China–Hong Kong relations. A Beijing correspondent from 1986 to 1989, Lam is a former associate editor and China editor of the *South China Morning Post*, Hong Kong's leading newspaper. Lam also writes on Chinese affairs for a number of international publications and Web sites. Lam is a graduate of the University of Hong Kong and the University of Minnesota. He is the author of four books on Chinese affairs, including *China after Deng Xiaoping* (1995) and *The Era of Jiang Zemin* (1999).

Cheng Li is a Fellow of the Woodrow Wilson International Center for Scholars, Washington, DC, and professor of the Department of Government at Hamilton College, Clinton, New York. Born in Shanghai, Li came to the United States in 1985 and later obtained an MA in Asian studies at the University of California at Berkeley and a Ph.D. in political science at Princeton University.

From 1993 to 1995, Dr. Li worked in China as a fellow of the U.S.-based Institute of Current World Affairs, observing grassroots changes in his native country. He has served as a commentator for the Hoover Institution's quarterly journal, *China Leadership Monitor*, Stanford University, and an adviser for the School of International Relations and Public Affairs, Fudan University, Shanghai. He is a member of the Institute of Current World Affairs in Hanover, New Hampshire. Dr. Li recently published one of the first detailed analyses of China's new generation of leaders: *China's Leaders: The New Generation* (2001). Other publications recent include: "China in 2000: A Year of Strategic Rethinking," *Asian Survey* 41, no. 1 (January/February 2001); "Jiang Zemin's Successors: The Rise of the 4th Generation of Leaders in the PRC," *China Quarterly*, no. 161 (March 2000); and "Promises and Pitfalls of Reform: New Thinking in Post-Deng China," in *China Briefing: A Century of Transformation*, ed. Tyrene White (Armonk, NY: M.E. Sharpe, 2000). Dr. Li is currently working on two book manuscripts: *Chinese Technocrats* and *Urban Subcultures in Shanghai*.

James C. Mulvenon, an associate political scientist at the RAND Corporation in Washington, DC, is a specialist on the Chinese military. His current research focuses on Chinese strategic weapons doctrines (information warfare and nuclear warfare), theater ballistic missile defenses (TBMD) in Asia, Chinese military commercial divestiture, and the military and civilian implications of the information revolution in China. He has recently completed a book on the Chinese military's business empire, entitled *Soldiers of Fortune* (Armonk, NY: M.E. Sharpe, 2001). Dr. Mulvenon received his Ph.D. in political science from the University of California, Los Angeles.

David Shambaugh is professor of political science and international affairs and director of the China Policy Program in the Elliott School of International Affairs at the George Washington University, and nonresident senior fellow in the foreign policy studies program at the Brookings Institution. During 2002–2003 he is a Fellow at the Woodrow Wilson International Center for Scholars. Before joining the faculty at George Washington, he taught for eight years at the University of London, School of Oriental and African Studies. He also served as director of the Asia program at the Woodrow Wilson International Center for Scholars, editor of *China Quarterly*, an analyst in the Department of State Bureau of Intelligence and Research, and on the National Security Council. He has previously authored or edited twelve volumes; his newest studies are *Modernizing China's Military* (2002) and *Making China Policy* (2001). He has also published articles in *Foreign Affairs, International Security, Survival, China Quarterly, China Journal, Washington Quarterly, World Policy Journal, Washington Post, New York Times, Far Eastern Economic*

Review, Asian Wall Street Journal, International Herald Tribune, and other periodicals. Professor Shambaugh received his Ph.D. in political science from the University of Michigan, an MA in international affairs from Johns Hopkins University of International Studies (SAIS), and a BA in East Asian studies from the Elliott School of International Affairs at George Washington University.

Anne Stevenson-Yang is president of Clarity Data Systems, a software company in Beijing, as well as vice president of business development for Metromedia China Corporation, its corporate parent. Before joining Metromedia, she founded and ran 66cities.com, which is a Chinese contract publisher of a magazine and a series of books as well as two Web sites. She came to China in 1993 as China director of the U.S.-China Business Council. Previously, she worked as an editor and journalist in Washington, DC, and New York.

Murray Scot Tanner is Professor of Political Science at Western Michigan University. He has published widely on Chinese politics, in particular leadership politics and succession, the dilemmas of legal reform, policing, internal security and political stability. His articles have appeared in such journals as *Comparative Politics, China Quarterly, China Journal, Problems of Post-Communism, Current History,* and others. He is also the author of *The Politics of Lawmaking in Post-Mao China: Institutions, Processes, and Democratic Prospects* (1998).

Guoguang Wu, associate professor in government and public administration at the Chinese University of Hong Kong, is a leading analyst on Chinese domestic politics. He received his bachelor's degree at Peking University and his doctorate in political science from Princeton University. In the mid- and late 1980s, Wu was a senior editorial writer for the Chinese newspaper *People's Daily.* He also served as a policy adviser to the Chinese leadership with responsibilities that included advising Chinese Prime Minister Zhao Ziyang on political reform and preparing the political report of the CCP Central Committee to the Thirteenth National Party Congress. Professor Wu is the author of many books and articles on Chinese politics, including *Zhao Ziyang and Political Reform* (1997), *China after Deng* (with Wang Zhaojun, 1993), *On Central-Local Relations* (with Zheng Yongnian, 1995), *Jiang Zemin's Challenges* (with Wang Shaoguang et al., 1996), *Liberalization, Institutionalization, and Democratization* (1997), and *Toward the 15th Party Congress: The Power Game in China* (1997). He is also the editor of several volumes, including *The State, the Market, and Society* (1994), and a contributor to journals including *The China Quarterly.*

INDEX

52; as part of Third Generation, 16, 21–22; and party building , 210; and political stability, 57–58; political ties of, 26, 48, 51–52, 74–75, 177–78; reforms of, 162, 172–73, 251; relationships with advisors, 156–57; Southern Tour, 48–49, 156; and succession, 4, 7, 9, 45, 71–72; theoretical contributions of, 12, 85, 87; and think tanks, 153, 159; and training cadres, 72, 109–10

Deng Xiaoping Theory, 179
Development Research Institute of the State Council, 156
Ding Guangen, 126, 223, 238
Ding Sheng, 71
distribution companies, 227–28
Doje Cering, 102
Du Daozheng, 232
Du Ying, 158

economic development, 5, 84–85, 136, 261
economic disparities, regional, 5, 18
economic reform, 157, 187, 204, 214, 252, 262–64
Economic Research Center, 158–60
editors, removal of, 231, 233, 238
education, foreign, 256–57
elections, village, 260, 262, 265
embassy in Belgrade, bombing of: Hu Jintao's speech following, 8, 26–27, 45, 62; and nationalism, 264–65; and new LSGs, 134; press accounts of, 232, 239; public protest following, 58; and Sino-U.S. relations, 41, 50
energy needs, 264
enterprises, private, 170
entrepreneurs: and the CCP, 13–14, 167, 181, 187, 188–89, 200; and *mishus*, 148; in the "non-critical realm," 190; in political office, 200–201; political participation by, 197–201; recruitment of, 12,

187–88; rise of, 257–58. *See also* red capitalists
environmental concerns, 42
ethnic tensions, 42
exams, open, 256
expertise: governmental, 157–58; need for, 11, 157; privatization of, 159–60

factional politics, 30–31, 111
factions, taboo against, 87
FALSG, 126–28. *See* Foreign Affairs Leading Small Group
Falungong movement, 209, 212
Fang Ning, 255–56
Fang Xinghai, 257
Fazhan daobao (newspaper), 258
Federation of Industry and Commerce, 263
Fifteenth Party Congress, 39, 40
Fifth Generation, 4, 6, 15–17; recruitment of, 256
Fifth Generation *(diwudai)*, 251; training of, 251
Financial and Economic Leading Small Group, 126, 128–29, 263
First Generation, 21
force, to maintain power, 280
Foreign Affairs Leading Small Group (FALSG), 126–28
foreign policy, 264–65
Four Modernizations, 72, 154
Four Requirements, 72, 73
Fourth Generation *(disidai)*: attitudes of, 276–77; challenge of, 283; character of, 5–6, 17; experiences of, 21–26, 273–74, 275–77; handicaps of, 275–76; and leadership change, 4, 9–10, 16, 135; leadership of, 6–9, 23–25; and LSGs, 135; and the military, 41; and *mishus*, 148; prospects of, 251, 274–75
Fu Quanyou, 53

Gang of Princelings, 16, 28, 88, 111, 254–55
Gao Changli, 54